D1554165

Triumph at Midnight of the Century

A CRITICAL BIOGRAPHY OF ARTURO BAREA

The Cañada Blanch / Sussex Academic Studies on Contemporary Spain

General Editor: Professor Paul Preston, London School of Economics

Published

Cristina Palomares, *The Quest for Survival after Franco: Moderate Francoism and the Slow Journey to the Polls, 1964–1977.*

Michael Eaude, *Triumph at Midnight in the Century: A Critical Biography of Arturo Barea*

Soledad Fox, *Constancia de la Mora in War and Exile: International Voice for the Spanish Republic.*

Isabelle Rohr, *The Spanish Right and the Jews, 1898–1945: Antisemitism and Opportunism.*

Gareth Stockey, *Gibraltar: "A Dagger in the Spine of Spain?"*

Richard Wigg, *Churchill and Spain: The Survival of the Franco Regime, 1940–1945* (paperback edition).

Published by the Cañada Blanch Centre for Contemporary Spanish Studies in conjunction with Routledge / Taylor & Francis

1 Francisco J. Romero Salvadó, *Spain 1914–1918: Between War and Revolution.*
2 David Wingeate Pike, *Spaniards in the Holocaust: Mauthausen, the Horror on the Danube.*
3 Herbert Rutledge Southworth, *Conspiracy and the Spanish Civil War: The Brainwashing of Francisco Franco.*
4 Angel Smith (editor), *Red Barcelona: Social Protest and Labour Mobilization in the Twentieth Century.*
5 Angela Jackson, *British Women and the Spanish Civil War.*
6 Kathleen Richmond, *Women and Spanish Fascism: The Women's Section of the Falange, 1934–1959.*

7 Chris Ealham, *Class, Culture and Conflict in Barcelona, 1898–1937.*
8 Julián Casanova, *Anarchism, the Republic and Civil War in Spain 1931–1939.*
9 Montserrat Guibernau, *Catalan Nationalism: Francoism, Transition and Democracy.*
10 Richard Baxell, *British Volunteers in the Spanish Civil War: The British Battalion in the International Brigades, 1936–1939.*
11 Hilari Raguer, *The Catholic Church and the Spanish Civil War.*
12 Richard Wigg, *Churchill and Spain: The Survival of the Franco Regime, 1940–45.*
13 Nicholas Coni, *Medicine and the Spanish Civil War.*
14 Diego Muro, *Ethnicity and Violence: The Case of Radical Basque Nationalism.*
15 Francisco J. Romero Salvadó, *Spain's Revolutionary Crisis, 1917–1923.*

Triumph at Midnight of the Century

A CRITICAL BIOGRAPHY OF ARTURO BAREA

EXPLAINING THE ROOTS OF THE SPANISH CIVIL WAR

Michael Eaude

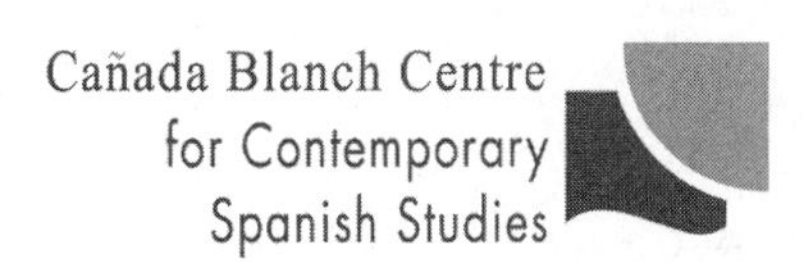

EDITORA REGIONAL
DE EXTREMADURA

SUSSEX
ACADEMIC
PRESS
BRIGHTON • PORTLAND

2 4 6 8 10 9 7 5 3 1

First published 2009 in Great Britain by
SUSSEX ACADEMIC PRESS
PO Box 139
Eastbourne BN24 9BP

and in the United States of America by
SUSSEX ACADEMIC PRESS
920 NE 58th Ave Suite 300
Portland, Oregon 97213-3786

First edition in Spanish: Michael Eaude, *Arturo Barea. Triunfo en la medianoche del siglo.* Editora Regional de Extremadura, Mérida, 2001.

British Library Cataloguing in Publication Data
A CIP catalogue record for this book is available from the British Library.

Library of Congress Cataloging-in-Publication Data
Eaude, Michael.
Triumph at midnight of the century : a critical biography of Arturo Barea : explaining the roots of the Spanish Civil War / Michael Eaude.
p. cm.
Includes bibliographical references and index.
ISBN 978-1-84519-288-4 (h/c : alk. paper)
1. Barea, Arturo, 1897–1957. 2. Barea, Arturo, 1897–1957—Criticism and interpretation. 3. Authors, Spanish—20th century—Biography.
I. Title.
PQ6603.A64Z618 2009
863′.62—dc22
[B] 2008018037

Typeset and designed by SAP, Brighton & Eastbourne.
Printed by TJ International, Padstow, Cornwall.
This book is printed on acid-free paper.

Contents

List of Illustrations

Jacket illustration: Arturo Barea "Juan de Castilla" preparing to broadcast a talk on the BBC Latin American Service in 1955. Between 1940 and 1957, Barea made over 800 weekly talks. They were anecdotic chats that started off in the war as anti-fascist propaganda and developed into explanations of British life and culture.

Illustrations are placed on pages 96 to 107.

The author and publisher gratefully acknowledge the following for permission to reproduce copyright material.

Cover photo, 17 and 18: BBC.

Cover photo, 1, 2, 6, 7, 11, 12, 13, 14, 15, 16, 17, 18, 19, 20, 22: Uli Rushby-Smith.

3, 4, 5, 9, 10, 21: Bruce and Margaret A. Weeden.

8: Leonor Rodríguez Barea.

The Cañada Blanch Centre for Contemporary Spanish Studies

In the 1960s, the most important initiative in the cultural and academic relations between Spain and the United Kingdom was launched by a Valencian fruit importer in London. The creation by Vicente Cañada Blanch of the Anglo-Spanish Cultural Foundation has subsequently benefited large numbers of Spanish and British scholars at various levels. Thanks to the generosity of Vicente Cañada Blanch, thousands of Spanish schoolchildren have been educated at the secondary school in West London that bears his name. At the same time, many British and Spanish university students have benefited from the exchange scholarships which fostered cultural and scientific exchanges between the two countries. Some of the most important historical, artistic and literary work on Spanish topics to be produced in Great Britain was initially made possible by Cañada Blanch scholarships.

Vicente Cañada Blanch was, by inclination, a conservative. When his Foundation was created, the Franco regime was still in the plenitude of its power. Nevertheless, the keynote of the Foundation's activities was always a complete open-mindedness on political issues. This was reflected in the diversity of research projects supported by the Foundation, many of which, in Francoist Spain, would have been regarded as subversive. When the Dictator died, Don Vicente was in his seventy-fifth year. In the two decades following the death of the Dictator, although apparently indestructible, Don Vicente was obliged to husband his energies. Increasingly, the work of the Foundation was carried forward by Miguel Dols whose tireless and imaginative work in London was matched in Spain by that of José María Coll Comín. They were united in the Foundation's spirit of open-minded commitment to fostering research of high quality in pursuit of better Anglo-Spanish cultural relations. Throughout the 1990s, thanks to them, the role of the Foundation grew considerably.

In 1994, in collaboration with the London School of Economics, the Foundation established the Príncipe de Asturias Chair of Contemporary Spanish History and the Cañada Blanch Centre for Contemporary Spanish Studies. It is the particular task of the Cañada Blanch Centre for Contemporary Spanish Studies to promote the understanding of twentieth-century Spain through research and teaching of contemporary Spanish history, politics, economy, sociology and culture. The Centre possesses a valuable library and archival centre for specialists in contemporary Spain. This work is carried on through the publications of the doctoral and post-doctoral researchers at the Centre itself and through the many seminars and lectures held at the London School of Economics. While the seminars are the province of the researchers, the lecture cycles have been the forum in which Spanish politicians have been able to address audiences in the United Kingdom.

Since 1998, the Cañada Blanch Centre has published a substantial number of books in collaboration with several different publishers on the subject of contemporary Spanish history and politics. A fruitful partnership with Sussex Academic Press began in 2004 with the publication of Cristina Palomares's fascinating work on the origins of the Partido Popular in Spain, *The Quest for Survival after Franco: Moderate Francoism and the Slow Journey to the Polls, 1964–1977*. This was followed in 2007 by the deeply moving biography of one of the most intriguing women of 1930s Spain, *Constancia de la Mora in War and Exile: International Voice for the Spanish Republic* by Soledad Fox and *The Spanish Right and the Jews, 1898–1945* by Isabelle Rohr, a path-breaking study of anti-Semitism in Spain. And this year, 2008, sees the publication of a revised edition of Richard Wigg's penetrating study of Churchill's relationship with General Franco and Michael Eaude's revaluation of the great Spanish writer Arturo Barea.

PAUL PRESTON
Series Editor
London School of Economics

Series Editor's Preface

One of the most important books ever written about Spain during the Civil War and the years leading up to it is *The Forging of a Rebel* by Arturo Barea. More autobiography than novel, the book's three volumes provide vivid accounts of life in Madrid in the early years of the century, of the experiences of conscripts during Spain's African wars, of growing social tension during the Second Republic and of the horrors of war in Madrid. It is all the more surprising then that while Barea's book has been widely acclaimed, the author himself remains a virtually unknown figure. That has changed somewhat in recent years because of the publication of collections of his lesser writings with commentaries by Nigel Townson. However, the major development in this regard was the publication in 2001 of the Spanish translation of an earlier version of Michael Eaude's seminal work, *Arturo Barea: Triunfo en la medianoche del siglo* (Mérida: Editora Regional de Extremadura, 2001). Barea spent the last eighteen years of his life in exile in England where he found his greatest success as a writer. It is thus a cause of celebration that Sussex Academic Press in conjunction with the Cañada Blanch Centre for Contemporary Spanish Studies is now publishing a thoroughly up-dated English edition of this important book.

Barea's own writing is an invaluable source for the texture of Spanish life in the first third of the century. His account of his childhood and adolescence in Madrid follows on from the accounts of the great novelist Benito Pérez Galdos. His recollections of his service in the Moroccan Army in the 1920s is unforgettable. Few memoirs capture so vividly the brutality and depravity of Spain's African wars. At one point he describes how his own critical faculties were overcome by the mass hysteria generated by the histrionic performance of the Head of the Spanish Foreign Legion, Lieutenant Colonel José Millán Astray: 'His voice thundered and sobbed and howled. He spat into the faces of these men all their misery, their shame, their filth, their crimes, and then he dragged them along in fanatical fury to a sense of chivalry, to a renunciation of all hope, beyond that of dying a death which would wash away the stains of their cowardice in the splendour of heroism.' This rhetoric hid a multitude of sins. The psycopaths, drunkards and outcasts of the Legion were treated brutally and, in return, given free rein to indulge their own bloodlusts. 'When it attacked, the *Tercio* knew no limits to its vengeance. When it left a village, nothing remained but fires and the corpses of men, women and children. Thus, I witnessed the villages of Beni Arós razed to the ground in the spring of 1921. Whenever a legionary was murdered on a lonely cross-country march, the throats of all the men in the neighbouring villages were cut unless the assailant came forward.'

Barea's account of his own experiences in a village in the province of Toledo during the Second Republic provide a unique insight into the intensification of social hatreds. Yet it is his writing on his time in Madrid during the Civil War that is perhaps most memorable. Despite the presence of some of the world's best newspapermen in Spain, many of whom later wrote memoirs, one of the most graphic records of the siege of the capital would come from his pen. Barea was a quietly modest man, deeply thoughtful and entirely committed to the cause of the Spanish Republic. In early September 1936, a few days after Francisco Largo Caballero had formed his government, Barea had been offered a job at the press office located in the iconic Telefónica building. Barea thought the censorship 'clumsy and futile' because it was aimed largely at the elimination of the slightest suggestion of anything other than a Republican victory. Although Franco's African Army was coming inexorably nearer to Madrid, newspaper reports were allowed only to talk of them being halted.

Work in Madrid became more nightmarish. Bombing raids and artillery pounding were constant. By the evening of 6 November, the crackle of rifle fire could be heard nearby. His boss, Luís Rubio Hidalgo, told him that the government was leaving for Valencia because the fall of the capital was inevitable. He gave Barea two months' wages and ordered him to close down the censorship apparatus, burn the remaining papers and save his own skin. Barea ignored Rubio's instructions and saved some important photographs of children killed in rebel bombing raids. He then worked as normal that night, preventing an American journalist from cabling that Madrid had already fallen.

On 7 November, with no censorship in Madrid, some correspondents, trying to get a scoop, had transmitted 'news' of the fall of the capital. In the press office, Barea was outraged by 'reports breathing a malicious glee at the idea that Franco was, as they put it, inside the town'. He was appalled that the world was thus missing what he called 'the blaze of determination and fight' of the people of Madrid: 'I had never been as completely convinced of the need for a war censorship as when I read those petty and deeply untrue reports and realized that the damage abroad had been done. It was a defeat inflicted by the man who had deserted.' Realising that there had to be some censorship machinery, Barea ignored Rubio's orders and, believing that some control over the foreign press was required as long as Madrid held out, simply kept the service going.

On the morning of 11 November, Barea was visited by Stalin's unofficial representative, the *Pravda* correspondent, Mikhail Koltsov, who was initially incandescent with rage that, after the flight of Rubio Hidalgo and before Barea had managed to set up alternative arrangements, some damaging despatches had got out. Once Koltsov had calmed down and heard Barea's story, he spirited him to the Ministry of War where he secured permission from the newly appointed Junta de Defensa for the press office to carry on in Madrid under the auspices of the General War Commissariat.

Arturo Barea's deep commitment to the Republican cause eventually would see his health undermined by overwork, worry and growing phobia about the incessant bombing raids. He had to juggle the competing instructions of the War Commissariat in Madrid and Rubio Hidalgo in Valencia. Catching a few hours of sleep on a camp bed in his office, Barea kept himself going on coffee, brandy and cigarettes. The toll that the work took on him can be discerned in the description of Barea left by the English journalist Sefton Delmer as 'a cadaverous Spaniard with deep furrows of bitterness around his mouth, dug deeper by the shadows from his candle. He looked the very embodiment of Spanishness, tense and suspicious, clenched ready to take national umbrage.' Barea's job became easier only when he was joined, on a volunteer basis, by Ilsa Kulcsar, a thirty-four year-old Austrian Socialist. She was short, plump and altogether unprepossessing. 'She was over thirty and no beauty', yet as they talked night after night, he would soon fall in love with her. Theirs was to be one of several, and indeed one of the most enduring, love affairs that flowered in the midst of the war.

One of the incidental pleasures of Michael Eaude's marvellously readable book is its account of the life of Ilsa Kulcsar. Born in Vienna in 1902, on the same day as, but five years after, Arturo Barea, Ilsa Kulcsar had studied economics and sociology. She joined the Communist Party before passing over to the Austrian Socialist Party in the mid-1920s. She had been involved in the Austrian resistance after the failed Vienna uprising of February 1934 and subsequently had fled with her husband to Czechoslovakia. She had come to Spain with credentials from some Czech and Norwegian left-wing papers, without a salary. Her linguistic skills – she had French, German, Magyar, English and other languages – secured her a job in the press office where she persuaded Barea that the censorship should be more flexible. Her argument was that the conventional triumphalism imposed by the military mentality made the Republic's defeats and economic hardship inexplicable and its victories trivial. She easily convinced him that the truth about the government's difficulties could produce reporting that would eventually be to the benefit of the Republican cause.

On their own initiative, Arturo and Ilsa relaxed the censorship and thereby established good relations with the correspondents. They helped them to get hotel rooms and petrol vouchers and often asked for their help in return. The efforts of Arturo and Ilsa were a great success. However, on visiting Valencia in December 1936, Barea realised how much resentment there was among those who had left the capital for those who had stayed. Indeed, Ilsa was briefly arrested because her friendship with the Austrian Socialist leader Otto Bauer had led to her being denounced as a Trotskyist. When she was released, they finally admitted that their future lay together.

Barea's work in the censorship brought him into frequent contact with General Vladimir Gorev, the senior figure in Madrid of Russian military intelligence. As both military attaché and thus the principal Russian advisor to General José Miaja, the head of the Junta de Madrid, Gorev took a burning interest in the articles of the foreign correspondents. Every morning he would pour over the previous night's censored dispatches, sometimes disagreeing with Arturo Barea and Ilsa Kulcsar, sometimes explaining why certain military issues required censorship. He was fascinated by the way in which many correspondents had evolved from open animosity to the Republic to more objective reporting. He was inclined to attribute this to the greater freedom given to reporters by Arturo and Ilsa.

Despite good relations both with Gorev and the majority of the foreign correspondents, the tensions between Valencia and Madrid continued. Finally, the combination of divorcing his wife in order to be with Ilsa and the strain of his work and the running struggle with Rubio took their toll. Barea was going through some kind of nervous breakdown and Ilsa was still dogged by accusations that she was a Trotskyist.

In April 1937, Arturo and Ilsa were visited in Madrid by the great American novelist, John Dos Passos, who helped them with their work one evening and later remembered 'a cadaverous Spaniard and a plump little pleasant-voiced Austrian woman'. Dos Passos wrote sympathetically of the two censors: 'Only yesterday the Austrian woman came back to find that a shell fragment had set her room on fire and burned up all her shoes, and the censor had seen a woman made mincemeat of beside him when he stepped out to get a bite of lunch. It's not surprising that the censor is a nervous man; he looks underslept and underfed.'

Eventually, Barea was advised by Rubio's increasingly important assistant, and eventual successor, Constancia de la Mora to take a holiday. Barea was shunted into radio censorship and occasional broadcasting until eventually, his health broken, he and Ilsa would leave for England in 1938. Barea's health never recovered and a colleague, the head of the United Press Office, Lester Ziffren, had a similar experience. After Webb Miller, also of United Press, saw the carnage left after the massacre perpetrated when the rebels entered Toledo, according to his friend Jay Allen, he left Spain 'with a walking nervous breakdown'. As Michael Eaude's perceptive biography of this fascinating and sensitive man demonstrates, it would take a long time in England before Barea recovered.

Acknowledgments

I would like to thank the following Institutions which allowed me to consult material or generously sent me information and/or photocopies:

Manuscripts Division, Department of Rare Books and Special Collections, Princeton University Library (correspondence between Emir Rodríguez Monegal and Arturo/Ilsa Barea).

Written Archives Centre, BBC, Caversham (seven files of radio talk transcripts and letters on Arturo Barea and one on Ilsa Barea: Coll. C0652).

Hoover Institution Archives, Stanford University (Letters between Burnett Bolloten and Arturo/Ilsa Barea: Burnett Bolloten Collection, box 5, folder 10).

Ministerio de Asuntos Exteriores, Archivo, Madrid (Reports from Spanish Embassies in Buenos Aires, Santiago de Chile, Montevideo and London on Ilsa and Arturo Barea).

The New York Public Library (Book Review Digests for Arturo Barea's US publications).

McFarlin Library, Department of Special Collections, University of Tulsa, Oklahoma (Correspondence between Arturo/Ilsa Barea and the Pen Club).

Don Bateman Collection, Library, University of Bristol (pamphlets and documents on Spain).

Faber and Faber Archive (Sales of Arturo Barea's books in the UK).

Times Literary Supplement Centenary Archive (articles by Ilsa and Arturo Barea; and reviews of books by Arturo Barea).

I am very grateful to the following, who knew Arturo and/or Ilsa Barea and gave up their time to talk or write to me about them:

Lesley Bennett (Eaton Hastings, 1950s), Bill Carter (Faringdon), Margaret Carter (Faringdon), Roland Gant, Martha Gellhorn (Madrid 1937), Joan Gili (Oxford), Peter Heller (BBC), Gladys Langham (Former Secretary, Faringdon Labour Party), Professor Isabel de Madariaga, Professor Ian Michael (Oxford University), Dr. Gerald Moser (Pennsylvania State University), R. Martínez Nadal (BBC), Vladimir Rubinstein MBE (BBC),

Helen Shepherd (formerly of Pennsylvania State University), Maruja Wallich (niece of Barea) and Lord Weidenfeld (BBC).

In particular, I would like to underline the invaluable help of Olive Renier (1912–2001) and Margarent Weeden (née Rink) (1912–2005), close friends in England of Arturo and Ilsa and collaborators with Ilsa Barea on the translation of Barea's trilogy. Fine writers in their own right, they were generous, kind and encouraging in their advice, information, views and support.

I would also like to thank the following, who have all assisted me, in many and differing ways, to complete this book:

Marta Altisent, Marisa Asensio, Charlie Astrue, Susana Castaño, Ian Clark (TLS), Constance Cruickshank (Faber & Faber), Dr. Andy Durgan, Anthony Eaude, Anthony Edkins (Bookseller), Elisa de Santos and other staff at the *Archivo del Ministerio de Asuntos Exteriores* (Madrid), Professor Fernández Gutiérrez (University of Tarragona), Dr. John Gilmour (my PhD supervisor at the University of Bristol), Dr. María Herrera Rodrigo (University of Barcelona), Elvira Huelbes, Sally King, Dr. Barry McLoughlin (Vienna), Regina Martínez, Manuel Pecellín (Diputación de Badajoz), Professor Paul Preston (LSE), Nicolás Rita (Madrid), Pilar Rita Rodríguez (Madrid), Leon J. Stout (Pennsylvania State University), Reverend Robert Swanborough (Faringdon), Professor Gareth Thomas, Dr. Antoni Turull (University of Bristol), John Wainwright (Taylor Institution Library, Oxford), Jeff Walden and other staff (BBC Written Archives Centre, Caversham), Bruce and Margaret A. Weeden (Australia) and Frances Wollen (Victor Gollancz).

I owe a great debt of gratitude to Leonor Rodríguez Barea (Madrid), who talked to me with sincerity and insight of her uncle, Arturo Barea.

Editions of Barea's Books Used

Valor y miedo. Barcelona: Plaza y Janés, 1986. (VM)
The Forging of a Rebel (including *The Forge, The Track* and *The Clash*). London: Granta, 2001. (FR)
La forja de un rebelde (including *La forja*, *La ruta* and *La llama*). Madrid: Debate, 2000.
Struggle for the Spanish Soul. London: Secker & Warburg, 1941.
Lorca, the Poet and his People. London: Faber & Faber, 1944. (*Lorca*)
Spain in the Post-War World. London: Fabian Publications, 1945.
The Broken Root. London: Faber & Faber, 1951.
Unamuno. Cambridge: Bowes & Bowes, 1952.
El centro de la pista. Madrid: Cid, 1960. (CP)
Palabras recobradas. Madrid: Debate, 2000. (PR)
Cuentos completos. Madrid: Debate, 2001. (CC)

Note: The letters VM, FR, *Lorca*, CP, PR and CC (in brackets above) are used in the notes as abbreviations for the respective books. I have used the English-language editions in all cases, except where they do not exist (VM, CP, PR & CC).

List of Abbreviations

BBC	British Broadcasting Corporation.
COMINTERN	Communist International.
JSU	Juventudes socialistas unificadas (United Socialist Youth).
LRB	Leonor Rodríguez Barea (Arturo Barea's niece).
PCE	Partido comunista español (Spanish Communist Party).
POUM	Partido obrero de unificación marxista (Workers' Party of Marxist Unification).
PSOE	Partido socialista obrero español (Spanish Socialist Party).
PSUC	Partit socialista unificat de Catalunya (United Socialist Party of Catalonia).
SIM	Servicio de investigación militar (Military Investigation Service).
TLS	Times Literary Supplement.
TVE	Televisión española (Spanish Television).
UGT	Unión general de trabajadores (General Union of workers).
USSR	Union of Soviet Socialist Republics.
WAC	Written Archives Centre of the BBC at Caversham.

This Book is dedicated to my parents,
Philip and Margaret Eaude

Introduction

Successful Exile – Political and Personal Aims

Fourteen years ago, the opening line of the first draft of this book lamented: "Today Arturo Barea (1897–1957) is largely unread". The baldness of this assertion has to be nuanced in 2008, thanks to Debate's 2000 and 2001 publication in Spanish of three thick volumes of Barea's work and to Granta's reissuing of the trilogy in English in 2001. Though not a household name, in the Spanish state today he is read no less than other Spanish exiled novelists who dealt with similar subject matter, such as his contemporaries Max Aub and Ramón Sender. And in Britain and the USA, he is the only Spanish novelist of his generation to be reprinted in the twenty-first century outside of university presses. Yet his critical reputation remains low. In Spain, he is less studied in universities than Sender or Aub. As Barea, in his youth a ferocious anti-academic, would also have thought, I interpret this as something of a compliment to his qualities.

When reference is made to his work in Spanish literary surveys, he is usually viewed as a spontaneous, intuitive writer, full of naïveties and rough edges; a source for how things used to be but of little lasting value. One 1990s survey maintains this approach. Andrés Trapiello, writing on *Valor y miedo*, gives Barea no credit for conscious organisation of his material:

> *It is as if the theme was imposing its tyrannical laws on literature, and not the reverse.*[1]

This view of Barea reflects the initial impact of his writing. Barea had the gift, most notably in his central work, the 800-page *The Forging of a Rebel*, of drawing vivid scenes full of movement and life. The reader's first impression is often overwhelming: a world of vitality and colour and a writer impassioned for social justice. Written in the late 1930s and early '40s, the "midnight of the century" when Europe was falling under even greater despotism than previously, Barea's books are shouts of denunciation and demands for a better life for the impoverished majority.

These first impressions are sound, but do not tell the whole story. Barea's books are constructed with much greater care and skill than he was usually given credit for. In the three-page introduction to *The Track* (the second volume of *The Forging of a Rebel*), Barea wrote:

> *I wanted to discover how and why I became what I am . . . not through a psychological analysis, but by calling up the images and sensations I had once seen and felt.*[2]

Here Barea is stating that the evocation of "images and sensations," i.e. the sensuous vividness and immediacy his writing is noted for, is a conscious purpose in his writing. Further evidence of Barea's intentions occurs at the end of *The Clash*, where he tells of his struggle in Paris during the summer of 1938 to clear his mind of political propagandism and literary abstraction, a struggle which included destroying a whole draft of *The Forge*. His well-known words bear repeating:

> *I tried to wipe the slate of my mind clean of all reasoning and to go back to my beginnings, to things which I had smelled, seen, touched, and felt.*[3]

Barea set out deliberately to write concretely and sensuously: his avoidance of more abstract commentary was a conscious decision. In this, his style of writing was consonant with his aims.

As well as Barea's personal objective, that almost standard purpose of autobiographers of restoring their mental health through an investigation of the source of present ills in the past, his other clearly stated aim was a "general objective". Barea wanted "to expose some of the roots" of the Spanish Civil War and to be vocal on behalf of what "are usually called the common people".[4] They were the people he came from and he was aggressively proud of his working-class heritage: with good reason, for they were the people who nurtured him as a child and the class who defended Madrid against fascism.

The quotes in the preceding paragraph reveal the political component of Barea's purpose. Barea desires to speak on behalf of the silenced masses. More, he wants his books to be weapons which those silenced masses can take up to understand their world and so change it. He was not a political writer in the sense of offering a coherent political solution to Spain's problems; that is, anyway, not the province of the novelist. He is a political writer in the sense that he is an interpreter, not just an observer. He looks back into the reasons why the Civil War occurred. In this he is firmly in the tradition of Unamuno and the "Generation of 1898" – and consciously so – in their search for what was wrong with Spain.

This book does not primarily investigate Barea's position in Spanish thought and literature, nor is it a comparative literary study. Rather, it seeks to evaluate his books as literary investigations into Spanish society and political evaluations of it, and focuses on his *vivencia* (lived experience) and how he transformed this into gold in his books. Nevertheless, his political aims as an interpreter of Spanish life clearly place him alongside other novelists of the Civil War, his compatriots such as Aub, Sender, Joan Sales and Gironella as well as foreigners like Serge, Malraux, Orwell and Hemingway, in their attempts to understand the issues and roots of that war.

Barea's personal and political aims intertwined. He started writing, not in peace and leisure, but during a personal breakdown in the middle of a brutal war. Writing both saved him from going mad and gave him the sense that, despite his uselessness (on leaving Spain before the war was over) as a political activist, he could still contribute to the working-class movement.

One of Barea's great strengths was that he knew, not just on behalf of whom, but to whom he was writing: the millions of Spaniards of his generation and social origins. Because of the defeat of the Republic and four decades of censorship, he was to be hardly read by this audience. Yet his clarity about who his potential public was – something many of his exiled Spanish contemporaries lacked or lost – helped him to rise above resentment and despair at defeat and exile and achieve his best writing.

Barea's golden years of literary production were from 1937 to 1944. In this period he wrote *Valor y miedo*, the three volumes of *The Forging of a Rebel*, *Lorca, the poet and his people* and *Struggle for the Spanish Soul*, as well as several short stories and his ground-breaking critical article "Not Spain, but Hemingway".

He was over 40 when his first book was published. Thus he came to letters late. His life was flipped over in the middle, like a pancake. He changed job, country, language, friends and wife. The chapters to follow examine this context to Barea's books alongside the writing. Through archive research and interviews, I found information about both his life in Spain and, in particular, his exile after 1939 in England, where he gave over 800 talks for the BBC Latin American service. This material enriches understanding of his work.[5]

Despite his forced exile, as a political refugee from the Franco dictatorship, in a country where he never properly wrote or spoke the language, Arturo Barea lived in England the happiest and most fruitful part of his life. His second wife Ilsa, a Viennese of broad culture and revolutionary politics, gave him a more sophisticated intellectual outlook and the support of a passionate relationship of equals. He mellowed: the fiery anti-intellectual young man from the slums of Madrid became a fine literary critic as well as novelist. But just as in his stories and novels, so in his criticism, Barea never lost sight of the realities of Spanish working-class life. He wrote on several occasions that Spaniards have two hungers: for food and for knowledge. And in all his writing his eyes were focused on explaining the unjust system which kept the peasantry and working-class he came from ignorant and starved; and not on explaining it to intellectuals, but with a language and approach designed to explain it to the working-class themselves.

The investigation into Spanish reality, with which writers such as Ganivet and Unamuno charged the youth after 1898, runs through all Barea wrote: stories, critical articles, broadcasts and novels. It provides Barea's *oeuvre* with its basic unity of purpose. Although he started to write, in *Valor y miedo*, under the influence of the ideas of Stalinist social realism, he developed, both intellectually and in practice, a critique of the cruder type of realism. He rejected what he felt was the "surface realism" of an earlier writer about Madrid, Pío Baroja. He identified more with Ramón Sender, the outstanding Spanish novelist of Barea's generation, in trying to penetrate beneath the surface of how things appeared, to reach a deeper "psychological realism". Sender recognised a kindred spirit and paid Barea one of his high-sounding compliments:

> *Here is a soul with vision, and perhaps a sensitive witness, faithful to the spirit of the Spanish people in the midst of the confusion that surrounds us.*[6]

Barea's vision is greatly aided by his objectivity, a quality which at first glance seems anomalous in an autobiographical – and, thus, subjective – novelist. But Barea's is not the objectivity of the detached commentator. He shared with many *engagé* writers of the 1930s the view that real objectivity was only possible through partisanship. Proclaimed "objectivity" was often, in the view of such as Martha Gellhorn, Sender or the revolutionary Victor Serge, a cover for repeating the ideas of the *status quo*, of the ruling class. Barea is partisan in the cause of the oppressed:

> *[They are] the millions who shared the same experiences and disappointments [as me, but who] do not usually write.*[7]

Despite this partisanship, the badge of honour of these writers was that they told the truth. Barea had the ability – it is too rare, but should be essential in a partisan – to record what he actually saw, without allowing what he saw to be falsified by what he believed. Thus he observed brutality without averting his eye; he recorded negative aspects of working-class behaviour without trying to prettify; he saw many faults in his own behaviour without either yielding to the temptation to conceal them or revelling in the confession of his sins.

This objectivity in looking at himself as well as his sincerity (infrequent qualities in a censor, Barea's job during the Civil War) enabled Barea to provide a unique first-hand record of Spain in the first 40 years of the twentieth century. He used himself and his own reactions as a touchstone for the experiences of his generation. His honesty can only be faulted in his political attitude to Stalinism and occasional boasting, but never in his observation of concrete detail and events.

Barea does not rate among the greatest writers. He is limited by one of his strengths: his inability to write well about what he himself had not experienced. He does not have the breadth of invention or imagination of Max Aub or Sender. He is limited too by a lack of political overview in explaining the "midnight of the century" through which he lived: a defect which sets him below Serge or Orwell.

There are other factors that made him, till recently, a neglected writer. His grammatical and linguistic errors were an obstacle to many critics, though not I suspect to common readers in Spain. These are exaggerated by the poor editing of the Buenos Aires 1951 first edition of *The Forging of a Rebel* in Spanish, repeated in all subsequent editions until, in the most recent from *Debate*, corrections have removed the most glaring grammatical errors. He is also hard to fit into the categories and generations critics are fond of. He was an individualist, who went his way separate from political or artistic schools. He also had the misfortune to die relatively young, before he could have an impact on the post-Franco generations. Most importantly, however, Barea is too direct, crude and brutal: not qualities valued in a more ironic age, which has wished till recently to draw a veil over the conflicts of the Civil War.

Barea invented a form in Spanish letters, the autobiographical novel. An outstanding historian of the Civil War, Burnett Bolloten, considered *The Forging of a Rebel* "a magnificent book . . . It contains most valuable historical data".[8] The best political English writer of his generation, George Orwell, thought *The Forge* "excellent".[9] And the most successful post-war Spanish-language writer, Gabriel García Márquez, considered the trilogy to be the best book written by a Spaniard in Castilian since the Civil War.[10]

This study aims to give substance to these words of high praise by examining the seven golden years of Barea's creativity, born in the Civil War and brought to fruition in English exile, alongside the anguished ferment of his first forty years and the milder decline of his last thirteen. Barea found sudden, unexpected success in his first years of exile, when absence from Spain sharpened his aims and intensified his memory of the past.

1

Arturo Barea

His Life up to 1939

The known facts of Arturo Barea Ogazón's early life are mainly those gleaned from *The Forging of a Rebel*. The author was born in Badajoz, close to the Portuguese border, at 8.20 p.m. on September 20, 1897.[1] His father Miguel died there, aged under 40, shortly after Arturo's birth. In the memorable phrase of Arturo's crude and honest paternal grand-mother Inés:

> *When your mother became a widow, all God did for her was to leave her alone in the hotel with two duros in her pocket and your father stiff and cold in his bed.*[2]

The unfortunate Miguel had nearly died 14 years earlier, for he had been involved in the Republican uprising of 1883: "Your father was one of the sergeants of the Villacampa rising, and it was a miracle he wasn't executed".[3]

Barea's father had remained connected to the army as a recruiting agent. As such he travelled, often accompanied by his family. Within a few weeks of Arturo's birth, his bereaved mother Leonor, the new baby and her three other children had returned from Badajoz to Madrid, where Leonor's brother José offered them some sort of protection.[4]

Torn in two

The impoverished widow was advised to hand her children over to charitable institutions, but refused. This loyal act of a hard-working and self-sacrificing woman, already 38 years old when Arturo was born, provides motive enough for Arturo's lifelong adoration of her. He was to dedicate to her his greatest triumph, the trilogy ("to my mother, the Señora Leonor"). His mother's unstated needs and his desire to provide a decent old age for her were decisive factors in Arturo's early turn away from a life as a writer or circus *artiste*, to search for more moneyed paths.

In Madrid, Leonor earned her living by washing soldiers' clothes in the

Manzanares River in the company of other washerwomen and by working as a servant in the house of her brother José. She lived with her children in an attic above stables in the Calle de las Urosas, one of the many garrets in the old slum district of El Avapiés or "Lavapiés," as it came to be known in Arturo's lifetime. This was Arturo's *barrio*:

> *There I learned all I know, the good and the bad, to pray to God and to curse Him, to hate and to love, to see life crude and bare as it is, and to feel an infinite longing to scale the next step upwards and to help all others to scale it.*[5]

Arturo's eldest brother Vicente (given the name of José in the trilogy) was sent to live with his mother's eldest brother, Juan, owner of a drapery store in Córdoba, at the age of eleven.[6] From an early age the only sister, Concha, helped Leonor with her domestic and laundry work. Miguel (Rafael in the trilogy) also had to start work as early as he could.[7]

Arturo's destiny was different. He was taken into his Uncle José's more middle-class home and there began to be instilled with the idea that he would gain an education and one day be the heir of the childless José and his wife Baldomera. The child nurtured the desire to be an engineer.[8] This division in Barea's life, starting before his earliest memory, created the conditions for the duality of his vision as a writer. The child inhabited both the poor and the comfortable worlds, but he was fully at home in neither: a crucial factor in his development. It taught him to look at people, even his own family, from a certain distance.

The young Arturo spent most of the week at his aunt's and uncle's, and weekends in the cockroach-infested garret with his mother, sister and brother. Until 1910 he attended one of the *Escuelas pías*, San Fernando, in the Calle Sombrerete.[9]

In the long summer holidays, like so many Madrid children before and since, he would be taken or sent to the *pueblo* – the village – or, in Arturo's case, three *pueblos*. The most lyrical passages of the entire trilogy (Chapters 3–6 of *The Forge*) describe the summer of 1907, which Arturo spent in the three *pueblos* where he had family: Brunete (on his father's side), Méntrida (on his mother's) and Navalcarnero, where his father's mother, Inés, lived. This experience of two or three months in the country was repeated all the summers of his childhood up to 1910.

On these summer visits the young Arturo was wrapped in the practical everyday love and life of big, varied, working families. He was no longer the affection-starved orphan obliged to act properly in his aunt's strict house, nor the child clinging rather pathetically to his mother's skirts in the garret during the rare moments she was not working. He could throw off respectable, tight-fitting clothes along with restrictive customs. He could forget that he was the prize in the middle of a tug-of-war between his mother and aunt.

And in the country, Arturo's desire to be an engineer was founded at his Uncle Luis's forge:

> *In one hand he would hold the great tongs which gripped the end of a red-hot horse-shoe, and in the other a little hammer, with which he . . . struck the hot iron when he wanted to shape it. That was always a marvelous thing to me.*[10]

The transformation of metal from one shape to another fascinated the boy. The marvellous in this process combined in his mind with the generous personality of Luis, who "wanted to bring good luck to the whole world".[11]

The sudden death of Barea's Uncle José in 1911 changed Barea's circumstances drastically, dashing his hopes to become an engineer. At first, under the influence of her confessor, his aunt Baldomera wanted to place the boy in a Jesuit school and herself retire to a convent. The splendid intervention of his atheist grandmother Inés frustrated the Jesuits' desire to seize the boy.

Because of arguments over José's inheritance, relations between Arturo's aunt and her many poor relatives deteriorated: she even quarrelled with Arturo's mild mother. Despondent and irritable at the adults' selfish squabbling (evidence for some critics of Barea's rancour and resentment), the 13 year-old had to leave school and go to work.

Strictly speaking, he did not <u>have</u> to leave school. But his pride at not becoming a charity boy, as his priest-teachers had suggested, meant that he took a job in a costume jewellery shop, *La Mina de Oro*, in the calle Carmen – a place that was no goldmine even for the proprietor.[12] Arturo slept in the shop and on top of his food earned 10 pesetas a month. He didn't last long. In outraged reaction to a curse and a cuff from the owner Don Arsenio, he knocked Don Arsenio's gramophone to the ground. Thus he showed his quick temper when his pride was touched and lost the first of several jobs.[13]

Arturo returned to school to study accountancy. But he had grown. His aunt, forced to adapt, could no longer treat him like a child. In the summer of 1911 he sat entrance exams in simple accountancy and letter-writing for Banking.[14] And on August 1, 1911, two months before his fourteenth birthday, he became an employee of the Crédit Lyonnais, unpaid for the first year. He was no longer able to spend the summer running through the fields of Méntrida.

As he was growing into adolescence, Barea took on what was to be the shape of his body all his life, until he filled out in his last decade: quite tall for a Spaniard of his time, lean and gaunt. When he was 25, he commented: " . . . my face had hardly changed since I was sixteen".[15]

On first starting work in the bank, he became so thin that his mother sent him to a doctor, who scared Arturo with the opinion that he was in danger of developing tuberculosis. To build up his chest and muscles, he joined the *Club Atlético Español* (Spanish Athletics Club), which was rather less grand than its name: "[The club] . . . was housed in an alley in the most wretched brothel quarter, where it vegetated in a gloomy cellar".[16] And after typhus, he came back from Morocco, "very thin . . . just bones", in the words of his mother.[17]

Alive and fighting

In the bank, Arturo rapidly learnt the ropes, but soon became disillusioned with his prospects. His experiences there, along with his haughty refusal to accept injustice against himself and his extension of this refusal to include others of his class, led him to join the UGT.[18] The UGT (General Union of Workers) was the union set up by the PSOE (Spanish Socialist Party). Its reputation and educational influence, through the *Casas del Pueblo* (People's Houses) set up round the country, tended to be greater than its actual industrial strength. "White-collared, black-coated" employees like bank workers were just as exploited as manual workers, but lacked the organisation to better their conditions through strike action.[19] The young Arturo, introduced by his older friend Luis Pla, was part of the first wave of white-collar employees to become unionised in Spain.

On the day the papers were announcing the start of the First World War, in August 1914, Arturo stormed out of the Crédit Lyonnais in umbrage: "I'm mad with disgust and rage and contempt! This fellow here in his frock coat . . . is a swine and the Bank is a pig sty!"[20]

The evidence for what he did during the war is scanty, as the period falls between *The Forge*, ending in 1914, and *The Track*, which begins in 1920. It appears that Barea was lucky in his precipitous exit from the Crédit Lyonnais. He found a clerical job two days later; and then work in an agency which processed applications to the Government for patents. However, he soon left the agency to become a travelling buyer for a German merchant, buying diamonds in France for re-sale in Spain and Latin America.[21] The young Barea enjoyed the money and prestige of this exotic job. For someone of his background to be staying in hotels in Paris at the age of 18, with money in his pocket, was a miracle. He wrote later:

> *This period greatly affected my psychology for various reasons . . . It caused two opposing reactions: one, the satisfaction with himself of a kid who feels he's rich; and the other, a feeling of disgust and shame towards speculation in war-time, from which I was indirectly benefiting.*[22]

As a UGT member, he was not easy in mind at making money out of the war. He desired to make money, was intelligent enough to do it, liked the things money could buy and told himself he could thus provide for his mother in her old age. But at the same time, his conscience told him he was exploiting others and abandoning his friends in Lavapiés and the bank.

In 1915 or 1916, using the 30,000 pesetas he had inherited in his uncle's will, Barea, in partnership with other members of his family, opened a small co-operative factory to manufacture toys and dolls.[23] Spain, a neutral in the First World War, was enjoying a new prosperity as it made arms and provided food and clothing for the contenders. Victor Serge, working in Barcelona in 1917, explained:

> *We were all working for the war . . . Clothes, hides, shoes, canned goods, grenades, machine parts, everything, even fruit . . . everything that our hands made, worked, manipulated, embellished was drained off by the war . . . The war raised salaries.*[24]

Barea remarked later on another aspect of Spain's war-time economy:

> *{Our factory opened} . . . at a time when the market situation favoured it, since the World War had cut off imports into Spain.*[25]

So while goods useful to the war were sucked out of the country, there were fewer imports of non-essential goods, at a time when there was more spending money. Though conditions seemed ideal for launching a small toy factory, Arturo lost his inheritance in this venture. The factory went bankrupt, mainly due to embezzlement by one of his family members and at least partly because of Arturo's capricious dissatisfaction with making conventional dolls:

> *I wanted to offer the kids new toys, something more alive than the same old dolls.*[26]

If we are to accept the time-sequence of the autobiographical meditation "El centro de la pista" ("The Centre of the Ring", the story in his book of the same name), Barea considered joining a circus in 1915 after the factory's failure. Through both the gym and the toy factory, Barea had come to know circus clowns. In his childhood, his uncle José had taken him every Thursday to the circus, where he delighted in explaining the tricks to his uncle.[27]

Even while the factory was in operation, Barea had found the circus's allure a relief for his boredom. He wrote sketches for the clowns. He attempted to give the circus a political justification:

> *I'm no use as a capitalist. I don't want to exploit the stupidity and wretchedness of other people and I don't want them to exploit me. I can't change the world, at least this is what they tell me, and the socialists say I can't belong to them after being a boss. So now, what? I have to do something completely different to show the world its true face. They'll accept from the mouth of a clown who is good at his job what they wouldn't accept from a writer.*[28]

It is interesting that Barea linked the work of a clown to that of a writer, which he had rejected as a career option after frustrating encounters with famous writers such as Pedro de Répide and Benavente in 1913.[29] Intermittently, Barea was looking for an artistic outlet: he wanted not just to change things politically, but "to show the world its true face". This is what he was to achieve with the trilogy.

It is clear too that the young Barea was too much of an individualist to work in the union ranks as a political militant: his comment that the PSOE/UGT would not permit him to be a member is unconvincing, as they would undoubtedly have accepted evidence of a commitment in practice, as indeed the UGT did after 1931. Barea shared the classic dilemma of the radical petit-bourgeois of not wanting to work for anyone else, yet not wanting to be a boss. Writing, circus-work, running a co-operative factory can be seen as attempts to escape this dilemma.

These adolescent years show the contradictory pulls and yearnings of Barea's character. He could not stand the boredom of the factory; yet he was too scrupulous to be a boss. After his shop and bank experiences, he dreaded the prospect of being an employee. Writing seemed impossible. At this period, he defines everything negatively. The circus briefly seemed a way out:

> *I was determined to escape. Otherwise, I would eventually be trapped and turn into a good little bourgeois or a good little employee, and I wanted to be alive and fighting!*[30]

Barea finally settled, at least temporarily, this angst concerning his future by deciding not to enter the circus and instead accept a good, though conventional, job in the new Motores España (Hispano-Suiza) factory in

Guadalajara. On a rather pathetic note, "El centro de la pista" ends as follows:

> *It's just a job in the office, but perhaps they'll let me work in the manufacturing department.*[31]

These renewed dreams of becoming an engineer were not to be fulfilled. He started to work at Motores España in 1918, when he was 20. Guadalajara was the political fief of Count Romanones, Prime Minister in 1915/16, and, along with King Alfonso XIII and the Catalan magnate Miquel Mateu, a major shareholder in Motores España. At Guadalajara, "a tiny, miserly town under the iron rule of its greatest land-owner, political boss and permanent deputy to the Cortes, Count Romanones", Barea first viewed at close quarters the machinations of monopoly capital, which was later to inform his reactions against Spain's occupation of Northern Morocco.[32]

It is well worth underlining the extraordinary diversity of Barea's experience before he was 20. He had been shop-worker, bank worker and trade unionist. He had actively sought to become a writer and to join a circus. He had co-owned a factory and travelled internationally for a diamond trader. Now he became secretary to Don Juan de Zaracondegui, the managing director of Motores España. Barea dealt with the enormous payroll of this car and aircraft factory. In addition, he interviewed and took on workers.[33] Chalmers-Mitchell tells us that, faced with corruption, Barea "took refuge in an increased study of the technical side".[34]

Undoubtedly the "technical side" fascinated Barea, but he also became involved in an amorous adventure and had to leave the factory rapidly.[35] He returned to a post-war capital, which he later described:

> *. . . a turbulent Madrid, hectic with the gaiety of the wartime boom which was rapidly waning, shaken by the aftermath of the first big clashes between organised workers and the new employer class, stimulated by the many short-lived periodicals which sprang up to cater for a new, avid reading public.*[36]

Corruption, slaughter and marriage

In 1920 Barea was conscripted into the Army. For his first few weeks he could stay in Madrid, in the Montaña barracks, before being sent to Morocco.[37] He arrived in Ceuta, as a sergeant, in late 1920. Because of his ability and scientific knowledge, he was assigned to office work concerning the construction of a road. He pursued his womanising, both in Tetuan brothels (while hypocritically affecting distaste for the sexual *mores* of his colleagues) and with a woman in Ceuta. He wrote occasional pieces for army magazines. And he was faced with the fact of generalised corruption, which his scruples made him seek to avoid (always, of course, according to his own account).[38]

He caught typhus in the wake of the historic Spanish defeat at Anual in 1921: the defeat which marked the beginning of the complex sequence of events which brought Primo de Rivera to power. After the battle Barea participated in the collection and burial of corpses under the burning sun. The smell, the heat, the flies, the mutilation and blood, in short the horror of this experience, stayed with him all his life.

> *I cannot tell the story of Melilla in July 1921. I was there, but I do not know where: somewhere in the midst of shots, shells, and machine-gun rattle, sweating, shouting, running, sleeping on stone and on sand, but above all ceaselessly vomiting, smelling of corpses, finding at every step another dead body . . .* [39]

When he got back to Madrid on leave, he could not eat meat. The memory of defiled corpses contributed to his 1937 nervous breakdown during the siege of Madrid. As late as 1944 in London, the sound of an air-raid siren made him retch involuntarily: the response to violent death first experienced in Morocco. Barea was lucky to survive so serious an illness, which nevertheless, by weakening his heart, contributed to his premature death. On convalescent leave in Córdoba, he rejected the urgings of his brother and cousins and refused to enter the Army full-time on officer training.[40] Once again he had rejected the more comfortable option out of unease and a refusal to be tied to a conventional career. But we have seen how he also rejected a more unconventional life as a circus clown or a writer. Indecision and restlessness mark these years.

In 1923, Arturo left Morocco and the Army. The following year, he married disastrously. Family lore has it that he was trapped into marrying Aurelia Rimaldos by a false pregnancy. Whatever the reason, his marriage failed. With Aurelia, he had four children, born in the late 1920s and early '30s.[41] In 1921 his sister Concha had also married, and more successfully, a furniture-maker, called Agustín in the trilogy, who had been a childhood friend of Arturo's and remained close. Barea got on well too with his sister during the 1920s, although he tells us he was jealous that his mother spent so much time caring for Concha's children. Their mother found a job as a caretaker in the Calle Fuencarral with a flat attached: a way of providing Concha and her many children with a home.[42] Aurelia got on with neither Concha, nor Arturo's mother, nor for that matter his brother Miguel's wife.

Her snobbery, ignorance and conventional attitudes, along with Barea's restlessness, all rapidly contributed to removing any love or affection there might have been from the marriage.[43]

On his return from Morocco, Barea got a job in a patents office. Whether this was the same office where he had worked at the start of the First World War is not known. Here he worked until the outbreak of the Civil War in 1936; although there appears to have been at least one interval, when for several months he was temporary business manager on a large Castilian estate, the *Dehesa Casablanca*, where his brother Miguel was Permanent Manager.[44]

Arturo's job in the patents office was a good one. He had an office on the Calle Alcalá, the heart of Madrid's business district, and by the start of the Civil War had a gold *cédula*, a card identifying the carrier as belonging to a high income bracket.[45] As well as supporting his own wife and children, he was able to channel money towards his sister's family:

> *There had been a hard time . . . when my mother and Concha had to accept the assistance of charitable institutions.*[46]

Just when, by the end of the 1920s, Barea could make real his childhood dream that his mother Leonor should enjoy an old age free from financial anxiety, she died at the age of 72 or 73 in 1931.[47] Leonor had told the young Arturo anecdotes of the First Republic, when as a girl she had worked in domestic service, and lived to see the dawning of the Second Republic, the cause for which Arturo's father nearly died in 1883.

Barea was only too aware of how his mother had sacrificed any hopes of her own by refusing to put him in an orphanage and accepting the humiliation of domestic service in her brother-in-law's house, so that Arturo could gain an education. His mother had died "in harness, tirelessly working", but without bitterness.[48] However, Barea could not accept her death so easily: "Unrest and uncertainty made me seek for something unchanged and secure in human relationship".[49]

Breaking ties

In 1930/31, Barea became involved with his secretary in the Patents Office, María, in a relatively stable relationship which was to last for six years. And in 1934, he separated from Aurelia for nearly a year.[50] His lifelong dissatisfaction developed into a drawn-out emotional crisis, only resolved in the generalised crisis of the Civil War.

A more positive product of the restlessness provoked by the proclamation of the Republic and by his mother's death was Barea's return to a more active political life:

> *It is significant to notice that señor Barea was not a rebel against the existing social organisation from failure to succeed. But his past experiences and an unhappy marriage had disabused him of life, and until 1931 he withdrew entirely to his work.*[51]

It was under the influence of Carlos Rubiera, a Socialist deputy for Madrid and later secretary of the Madrid Socialist Federation (*Agrupación Socialista de Madrid*), that Barea started to work again in the UGT, organising clerical workers:

> *His {Barea's} political convictions led him into a more and more advanced form of socialism, and his work in organising black-coated labour was in acute and bitter conflict with his professional occupation, which was in daily contact with international heavy industry.*[52]

As *The Clash* covers the period from 1935 to 1938, this summary will not repeat in detail what is contained in this third volume of the trilogy. In short, Barea took part in the assault on the Montaña barracks (where he himself had been a soldier 16 years before) at the outbreak of the military rebellion on July 18, 1936. He then offered his services to the *Casa del Pueblo* and, due to his military experience in Morocco, was assigned to train soldiers. In September 1936, through contacts in the PCE (Spanish Communist Party) and because of his supposed knowledge of French and English, he went to work for the Foreign Press Bureau in the *Telefónica*. There he met Ilse Kulcsar, with whom he was to spend the rest of his life.[53] During the Government evacuation of Madrid in November 1936, Barea stayed in the city, now at the head of the Foreign Press Censorship. From June 1937 he began to broadcast, a job he retained when, three months later, he was sacked as press censor. In November 1937 he and Ilsa left Madrid. Barea was suffering a nervous breakdown, brought on by the pressures of his job, political tensions he could not resolve and the horrors of the city's bombardment. Realising the impossibility of resuming his job, he and Ilsa went to the Rock of Ifach, near Altea, then to Barcelona and left Spain, never to return, in February 1938.

Throughout this period of intense struggle and anxiety, all the conflicts of Barea's life were speeded up, thrown into a melting-pot and, for better or worse, resolved: sexual, family, political and work conflicts. The political and sexual problems are discussed in Chapter VI: family and work is dealt with here.

By 1935, Arturo Barea was in a rut. The opening of *The Clash* finds him attempting to start afresh with Aurelia by moving to the village of Novés, but unable to break from María. The elections convened for February 1936 galvanised him. As an outsider in Novés, he could play an organising role which the village's peasants and landless labourers themselves could not. He took the initiative in setting up an election meeting for the Popular Front. In March 1936, after the Popular Front's election victory, Arturo moved his family back to Madrid from Novés. Arturo liked the big flat he found in Ave María street:

> *I liked it because it was near the center and my place of work. But it had another attraction for me. It was one of the quarters that led to El Avapiés, the quarter which had dominated my boyhood.*[54]

But Aurelia felt miserable. She did not like the fact that the other neighbours were all workers. She felt she and Arturo belonged to a higher social class, as indeed in economic terms they did.[55] But her wishes were overridden by Arturo.

The elections at Novés had helped him realise that he was not just an armchair socialist. Moving to Ave María street was a reassertion of his Madrid working-class background. As the skein towards war unwound itself in the country as a whole, so Arturo began to unpick his contradictions and take sides. Ultimately, his marriage responsibilities to a woman he did not like and to their four children were nothing beside his own desires to base himself again in the Madrid he knew and to spend his time discussing politics with old and new friends in the local bars.

> *I suppose what I wanted was to get back to my own roots.*[56]

Barea's acceptance of work in the Press Censorship in mid-September 1936 was to be inextricably linked with his desire to get away from the "chilly emptiness" of his and Aurelia's home.[57] Before his first night at work, he felt "elated and light-headed . . . I had explained to myself and to the two women, one after the other, [María and Aurelia] that I would have to work during the night and sleep during the day".[58]

In those terrifying days, Barea abandoned his wife and children alone in the flat. One day, after a night of sleeplessness because of the shelling, Aurelia went to the *Telefónica* to find her husband.

I told her that she would have to take the children away from Madrid. She said that I only wanted to get rid of her; and, seriously as I felt about the removal of the children from the multiple dangers of the town, I knew that she was not quite wrong.[59]

Aurelia and the children were evacuated to Valencia in a convoy of Foreign Ministry families some weeks later.[60] In mid-1937, when Barea was on leave in Valencia, he asked Aurelia for a divorce. His sister Concha, aware of the poverty Aurelia could be facing, advised her not to sign the divorce papers. Aurelia, "the fool," in Concha's words, signed, stating: "I'm a modern woman".[61] The following year, Barea married Ilsa. After leaving Valencia in November 1937, he never saw Aurelia again.[62]

Unity and purpose

After this sad tale of lack of love, I want to comment briefly on Barea's work during the war, work that did make him feel good. The patents office was closed in August 1936. From September 1936 until September 1937, Barea worked as Head of the Foreign Press Censorship; and from July to October 1937 he broadcast propaganda talks on the radio almost daily. The job in the censorship brought huge pressure: for the first few months he worked 16 hours a day and slept in the office. Moreover, the office in the *Telefónica* building – at that time, the tallest building in the city and on top of a hill – was in the direct line of fire of the fascist troops dug in just two or three kilometres away. Both Ilsa and Arturo expected to be killed.[63]

Martha Gellhorn remembered that Barea, always wearing a beret, appeared quiet and dreamy in manner, "a silent, mousy, depressed-looking man, round-shouldered and bowed, thin, pale and ill".[64] Somewhat more generously, John dos Passos wrote that Barea "[was] cadaverous . . . looks underslept and underfed . . . chained to the galley benches of war".[65] The journalist Sefton Delmer, who later gave Barea his typewriter and helped him place his first article in England, provided a vivid account of his visit to the *Telefónica* on 16 November, 1936:

Inside . . . all was darkness, and assault guards. At last we found the censors . . . They were sitting at a table with flickering candles lighting their faces. Sandbags covered the windows. The chief [Barea] was a cadaverous Spaniard with deep furrows of bitterness around his mouth, dug deeper by the shadows from his candle. He looked the very embodiment of Spanishness, tense and suspicious, clenched ready to take national umbrage.[66]

A factor explaining part of these negative portraits, apart from the constant tension in which he lived, was that Ilsa and Arturo did not participate in the rounds of drinking in each others' bedrooms in the Hotel Florida, where the majority of foreign journalists stayed, or at Chicote or Gaylord's, full of Russian advisers and "generals".[67] Arturo preferred to drink in Serafín's bar during the brief snatches of time away from the *Telefónica*. There he could chat with people he had known for much of his life; later, find material for his radio broadcasts; and also, no doubt, enjoy the role of the man with an important job. Barea's job brought him into frequent conflict with the foreign correspondents, another factor making it difficult for him to fall into easy socialising with them. Gellhorn commented: "We were a jokey bunch. They [Ilsa and Arturo] didn't eat with us".[68] Doubtless, Arturo found less to joke about.

Barea's lifelong contradictions about what he should do and be were overcome during this first period of censorship work. When he was younger, he had darted different ways, torn between his impulse to fight injustice and his desire to make money for himself and his family. When a child of ten in his Uncle Luis's forge, he had enjoyed briefly the sense he was no longer a child split between two worlds. In 1936 Madrid, he again briefly attained the same sense of unity and purpose. He was a volunteer in a vital job, who between November 7 and 12 took absolutely vital decisions with courage and initiative, both to prevent the press censorship's collapse and to keep open Madrid's contact with the world. The job both required all his intellectual abilities and at the same time was on behalf of and alongside the working-class with whom he identified.

This feeling of having overcome his contradictions was short-lived. Yet Barea was never to return to routine work. He emerged from the Civil War doing what he had wanted, but had not dared nor been able to do as an adolescent: the crisis of the War made him a writer.

After being sacked from the censorship, then from the radio, Barea left Madrid in November 1937, going *via* Alicante to Barcelona, where he finished *Valor y miedo* and found a publisher for it. Here too he met the Stalinist functionary Leopold Kulcsar ("Poldi"), Ilsa's husband, whom Barea feared and disliked for his political dogmatism. Poldi assisted them with exit visas and left the earliest testimony to Arturo and Ilsa's happiness together: "[Poldi] told us he had found them happy as sand-boys".[69]

The unfortunate Poldi died suddenly on January 28, 1938, from a kidney disease, exacerbated by the tensions of his irregular life, with irregular food, black coffee and too many late nights interrogating POUM members.[70] His death allowed Ilsa and Arturo to marry. They left Spain for the last time on February 22, 1938, the day Barea's exit visa expired.[71] For a miserable year of physical hardship they lived in Paris in the flea-pit *Hôtel de l'Albambre* (known to them as the *Hotel del hambre* – Hunger Hotel) in Montparnasse, hand-to-mouth on the occasional article or commercial or technical translation, while the European War drew closer.[72] However, whereas Ilsa spent many weeks ill, Arturo's general health improved. He was away from the bombardments and stress of Madrid. And from Barcelona came copies of his first book, *Valor y miedo*, which gave him the confidence to continue to write. During that tough summer of 1938, through his struggles to start *The Forge*, Barea revolutionised his approach to writing.[73]

They obtained entrance papers for England and in March 1939 left the atmosphere of demoralisation, racism and approaching war. They were lucky to get out; and pleased to be going to England. "Not to Latin-America, for our war was fought in Europe," wrote Barea. "But away from this stench of decay".[74] They wished still to remain politically close. They had not given up the struggle against fascism.

11

Valor y Miedo

Propaganda and Passive Herosim

The precise reasons why *Valor y miedo* was even published remain unclear. On the Republican side during the Spanish Civil War, only twelve books of fiction dealing with the war were published.[1] Potential writers were busy fighting; the Government and parties were mainly engaged in disseminating propaganda, not encouraging fiction. Normal publishing business was disrupted.

Valor y miedo was accepted in Barcelona in February 1938, just before Barea left Spain, and came out in a small edition later that year, probably in October.[2] There is little doubt that the publishing house was associated with the PCE or PSUC: both because of its typical Popular Front name (*Publicaciones Antifascistas de Cataluña*) and because it came out at a late stage in the war, when the left of the PSOE that Barea supported, the POUM or the anarchists were, respectively, without influence, illegal and confused.

This circumstance focuses the interesting question of the political views contained in *Valor y miedo*. At the time of acceptance, Barea was about to leave the country after being squeezed out of his job in Madrid by PCE-backed interests. Moreover, his new wife Ilsa had been subject to a smear campaign that she was a Trotskyist, which in this place and at this period in history was the prelude to imprisonment or even execution. Barea, therefore, in the weeks before leaving Barcelona for France, was in a delicate situation.[3] Despite all this, *Valor y miedo* was accepted by publishers sponsored by the PCE/PSUC in the month he left Spain! Why?

It is likely that Ilsa's husband Poldi (Leopold Kulcsar) assisted in the book's acceptance. Kulcsar was an Austrian Communist Party official employed in Barcelona in the witch-hunt of the POUM.[4] Kulcsar – known as "Wagner" – knew that Ilsa was not a Trotskyist;[5] possibly (and this was Barea's stated view) his personal loyalty to Ilsa, despite her leaving him, led him to support publication.[6]

Personal considerations apart, Kulcsar would have understood another factor: that the book's publication could well have the effect of stemming possible future criticisms of the PCE by Barea. Without both Ilsa's and

Arturo's public silence concerning their exclusion from power, it is unlikely that either would have acquired an exit visa.[7]

Whatever the specific reasons for publication, the general reason is clear. *Valor y miedo* is a powerful piece of propaganda for the Republican side and faithfully reflects the ideology of the Popular Front Government in 1938. As it happened, it was a book of little luck, swallowed by the Republican defeat. Few copies were printed, and these at the relatively high cost of 12 pesetas. Not many people read it.[8]

At first glance, it is strange that the book was never later translated into English, nor apparently to any other language. Barea was popular enough in the 1940s to have found an English publisher for the stories. That he did not do so is perhaps part of his overall lack of interest in the fate of his own work.[9] A more plausible reason, however, is that shortly after these stories' publication Barea rejected their type of social realism.

Proud as he was of his first book, he went through a fundamental change of approach to his writing in the summer of 1938, when he was gestating *The Forging of a Rebel*:

> *In those noisy summer evenings when I was alone among strangers, I realized that I did not want to write articles and propaganda stories, but to shape and express my vision of the life of my own people, and that, in order to clarify this vision, I had first to understand my own life and mind.*[10]

As all he had previously written was *Valor y miedo*, it is clear he was referring to this book. Barea himself saw the stories as no more than *propaganda stories* and for that reason never sought to have them reprinted or translated.

Warding off Madness: Genesis of *Valor y Miedo*

In another sense, though, *Valor y miedo* did reach the mass audience which Barea coveted: many of the pieces had started life as broadcasts on the radio. These broadcasts arose out of the circumstances of Barea's nervous breakdown in 1937, which was precipitated by three successive blows during two days. First, Ilsa's room had been burnt out by a shell: she'd escaped by luck. Second, Barea tells us, with one of his descriptions of such literal vividness it provokes disgust:

> *A lump of gray mass, the size of a child's fist, was flattened out against the glass pane and kept on twitching. Small, quivering drops of gray matter were spattered round it. A fine thread of watery blood was trickling down the pane, away from*

the gray-white lump with the tiny red veins, in which the torn nerves were still lashing out.

I felt nothing but stupor . . . A scrap of human brain.[11]

Barea was at that very moment on the surreal mission of escorting a delegation of English women, including Ellen Wilkinson and the Duchess of Atholl, to see the Head of Madrid's Defence Council, the rough-and-ready General Miaja, and had to carry on as if nothing had happened.

The third shock occurred the very next day, when Barea saw three people killed in the street, including a proud, young woman that he and Ilsa had been admiring for her grace and stride. He suffered a nervous collapse. For several weeks, he was feverish and retching, unable to concentrate or sleep. He felt listless and depressed.[12] He tells us how he finally reacted:

A particle of palpitating gray matter had set off a hidden train of thoughts and emotions in me . . . I wanted to cry out to them {the men and women of Madrid} and to the world. If I was to stay on fighting against my nerves and my mind, relentlessly aware of myself and the others, I had to do something more in this war than merely supervise the censorship of increasingly indifferent newspaper dispatches.

So I continued to write, and I began to speak on the radio.[13]

Thus the inertia brought on by his breakdown was overcome. He tells how he had to fight for permission to broadcast, both from Miaja and the *Comité Obrero* (Workers' Committee) of the Ministry of Propaganda;[14] a victory which also signalled a general change of policy on the type of radio censorship employed.[15] His first talk was on the fall of Bilbao as "An Unknown Voice of Madrid", his radio name for the following months. He told the truth of the defeat, for to conceal what was known in the rest of the world would not protect Republican morale, but rather make the Republic look ridiculous.

In a eulogy to Barea, broadcast five days after his death, Emir Rodríguez Monegal eloquently pinpointed what Barea's Madrid broadcasts came to mean:

{Arturo Barea} talked to bring to the besieged, fighters and civilians who protected with their rifles the walls of their houses, or to women who continued with the arduous task of living among the ruins, a message of hope and a message of struggle. This voice that reached everyone because (unlike other already famous voices of Spanish writers) he knew how to talk to the people with "this rough style unadorned with linguistic flourishes" in which the people themselves talk.

In this hour of Madrid, this hour marked by the clock of history, Barea became the voice of the resistance and at the same time discovered his true vocation as an artist.[16]

Barea's radio broadcasts and his first writing – the stories which became *Valor y miedo* – had the same genesis. They were both produced in his struggle to overcome his nervous collapse. And he found the cure in telling true stories of working-class resistance to the working-class. The genesis of his writing was popular and collective. Political motivation was inseparable from the start of his literature.

A work of propaganda

Among the few critics who have commented on *Valor y Miedo*, there is a reluctance to call the contents "stories". María Herrera, co-author of the only substantial commentary on the book, calls them "stories or war-scenes".[17] And Jaume Pont refers to them as *estampas* (sketches).[18] They are, indeed, not nearly so substantial as Barea's later stories collected in *El centro de la pista*.[19]

However, this apparent deficiency is not so serious if we hold in mind the book's purpose, pointed out by Barea himself. *Valor y miedo* is a work of political propaganda in fictionalised form. In that respect, it is very similar to works of "socialist realist" writers of the period, such as the Romanian Panait Istrati, widely published in Spain during the 1930s, or the Soviet writers who glorified the achievements of the working-class in patriotic tones.[20] John dos Passos' writing of the 1930s, where he intersperses documentary factual description with fiction, in order to portray working-class struggle, is not dissimilar: the "camera eye" technique employed to effect by dos Passos is used in *Valor y miedo*.[21]

Before looking at the literary strengths and weaknesses of *Valor y miedo*, I want to examine how the book reflected the prevailing ideology of Republican Spain in 1937–1938. For, unlike dos Passos' work and unlike anything Barea wrote later, his first book goes beyond social realism to express a "socialist realist" ideology. It is heavily influenced by the set of ideas developed by the Soviet leadership in the mid-1930s to justify and explain their foreign policy, ideas which imbued the Spanish Popular Front Government. Here is not the place to explore the pros and cons of Soviet influence in Spain, but it is relevant to note certain key themes of PCE/USSR propaganda reflected in *Valor y miedo*.[22]

First and foremost is the idea of patriotism which is integral to many of the sketches, especially the first and last, thus enclosing the entire book in a veneer of Spanish nationalism:

> *He fell on the enemy trench with the knife opened. With the long-bladed knife, with which perhaps a majo {Madrid 'cockney'} in 1808 disembowelled the horses of Napoleon's Mamelukes. With the knife that, just as it did a century before, disembowelled Moors and more Moors that filled the trench.*[23]

In this brutal extract from "La tierra," Barea glorifies Spanish tradition and history, linking the defence of Madrid against the fascists to the struggle against Napoleon. In doing so, though, he doesn't exalt the *juntas populares* (popular councils) of 1808, which would be extremely relevant to a revolutionary war; but rather uses language which evokes the alien nature of the opponents, *mamelucos* and *moros*. The imagery is crude and disgusting, placing the disembowelling of horses alongside the disembowelling of Arabs.

Barea's implicit argument is the PCE's: true patriotism resided in the "people" not in the fascists. The nationalist idea of a popular defence of the fatherland (*patria*) against external forces flows directly from the Comintern theory of "Socialism in one country," which by the 1930s had replaced Lenin's call for international revolution. It is no accident that the same theme comes to the fore again in *Valor y miedo*'s final sketch:

> *Don Quijote and Sancho face the Casa de Campo; face the Paseo de San Vicente up whose slope one day in November 1936 the Moors and the German tanks came.*[24]

The statue of Cervantes' heroes is used to epitomise the resistance of Madrid. Here again Barea is not expressing the ideology of class struggle, but of a national struggle of the Spanish people against foreign interlopers. And it involves a particularly reactionary emotive language: "disembowelled Moors and more Moors . . . " (*destripó moros y más moros*).

The second theme reflecting Stalinist ideology in *Valor y miedo* is encapsulated in this frequent use of the term *moros*. Although a typically popular way of speaking of Moroccans in particular and Arabs in general, it is a racist term. In using *moros* reiteratedly, Barea was quite happy to repeat general Republican propaganda playing on popular fears.[25] The *moros* were portrayed as rapists and castrators from Africa, once evicted from Spain, then colonised by Spain, and now in historic irony brought back by Franco to break the Republic.

Moro is a term Barea would have used from his childhood and often occurs in *The Track*, his book set in Morocco. During the war, though, his easy use of so pejorative a term reflected a political choice and usage. Barea is attempting to mobilise his readers, not on a socialist or anti-imperialist basis, but by appealing to a sense of fatherland (*patria*) based on popular prejudice.

The third aspect of Stalinist ideology identifiable in *Valor y miedo* is that of a certain type of popular heroism, which can be found in nearly every sketch. One of the clearest examples is in "Servicio de Noche" (Night Service), the story of Lolita who risked her life to get the news out from the *Telefónica* during an air raid. Another is in "Héroes", in which, when the bombing starts, the young woman Julia invites people into her house with the words:

> *Afraid, of course I am. But I think I have a duty . . . Come in, come in, this is made of stone, guaranteed against Mussolini.*[26]

Without exception, Barea's heroes and heroines are working-class. But their undoubted heroism is of a particular sort: a long-suffering, resigned sort of endurance. Julia above says: "I have a duty". Paco in "La mosca" (The Fly) says he understands nothing: "[Paco has] one set idea: to kill fascists".[27]

In these examples, Barea portrays the working-class protagonists as passive and patient: doing her duty (Julia), stubbornly fighting (Paco) or humorously powerless (Ángel in the picaresque story of the same name). The strongest image of this passivity of the working-class in besieged Madrid occurs in the agonisingly poignant "Juguetes" (Toys), where the idiot child continues to sell his trinkets in the Puerta del Sol, oblivious to the falling shells, and has to be led away by the narrator: "The idiot is looking joyfully at the ticket, oblivious of the goods he's lost and the shells bursting".[28]

This vision is in strong contrast to the evocation of Revolution he gives in *The Clash* and in later comments in England, where he sees Madrid's working-class as protagonists and subjects of their history, not as passive objects:

> *. . . the night of the outbreak of Franco's rebellion, I witnessed one of the most stirring things I have ever seen: I saw and felt the force of spontaneous mass solidarity. Tens of thousands of Spaniards – of workers – that night left their homes, filled with the one and only idea: to help defeat the fascists.*[29]

Even so, a nuance is needed: in *Valor y Miedo*, not all the protagonists of the sketches are totally passive. In *Héroes* both Julia and her father take action. The soldier in *Carabanchel* who invents the stratagem of putting bed-frames over trenches so that shells bounce off the springs responds to the shelling with ingenuity. But the very slightness of what the heroes of these two sketches can achieve emphasises their lack of influence. They do not seize their destinies. They are victims of circumstance, they have the passive resignation of victims.

The soldier in "Carabanchel" is victimised by the dead donkey, rats and flies; the peasants of "Bombas en la huerta" (Bombs in the Market Gardens) have to watch helplessly the destruction of their irrigation system; in "Las botas" (The Boots) the soldier is tortured by his boots; Serafín in "Los chichones" (The Bumps) is tormented by his leaping up and banging his head whenever he hears a shell.

This mood of resigned suffering has a lot to do with Barea's own cast of mind. He was often sceptical about the efficacy of political action and frequently pessimistic. We have seen above that he composed these sketches partly as therapy to stave off a nervous breakdown. Some critics, notably John Devlin and José Ortega, argue that this mood of Barea's demonstrates his religious sensibility.[30] The powerful sketch "Refugio" (Refuge), which shows a priest arguing against the propertied classes, is some evidence in *Valor y miedo* of this religious sensibility for those who wish to find it.[31]

However, Barea's characters' passive and resigned heroism is more an example of his political aims than of a pessimistic cast of mind or any supposed religious feeling. This resigned heroism is the core of the book's propaganda effect. And it dovetails precisely with the PCE's and Comintern's spreading of a view of the Spanish people (and in particular the besieged inhabitants of Madrid) as unfortunate and heroic victims of fascist attack. The working class were not to be seen as subjects of their own history, but as dependent on the PCE and Comintern to defend them.

This view contradicted the reality of working-class self-organisation, which exploded in July and November 1936. In *Valor y miedo*, Barea does not show these revolutionary mass mobilisations, which were on both occasions key to victory. Nor does he show the workers engaging in political discussion or in collective action to decide their fates. As such, *Valor y miedo* reflects and contributes to a certain distortion of what was really happening. And so, quite contrary to Barea's express aim, some parts of the book suggest a stoic defeatism.

In *The Clash*, as argued in Chapter VI, later articles and *Lorca*, Barea was to portray this period differently, more truthfully I would venture. *Valor y miedo*, written in the heat of the war, shows Barea's mental subservience at the time to the Stalinist framework.[32] On the whole, the stories work as excellent pieces of this type of propaganda, which Leopold Kulcsar, the publishers, the Popular Front Government and Barea himself all wished to promote.

Courage and Fear

Valor y miedo, of course, should not be reduced solely to these social and political dimensions. The book's central theme is summarised in the title: "Courage and Fear". Jaume Pont explained:

> *'Courage' and 'Fear' comprise the psychological framework of Barea's stories. This and nothing else . . . make up his personal history: death as a daily and everyday spectacle, as a physical predator and as mental food for the collective unconscious.*[33]

And Barea wrote of his broadcasts:

> *I believe that all the stories I wrote and broadcast at the end of a day in the bleak, echoing Ministry, were stories of ordinary people living in that mixture of fear and courage which filled the streets of Madrid, and its trenches. All their fears were mine, and their courage warmed me. I had to pass it on.*[34]

Only six of the twenty sketches of *Valor y miedo* are actually situated at the Front. Thirteen more are placed in various parts of Madrid, usually defined by name. Thus the subject is the fear and courage of those who were closely involved in the war but were not regular soldiers. This was, as Robert Capa said, "a war of no non-combatants". Barea's idea of war was decidedly anti-heroic: he could recall the repulsive and demented courage of Millán Astray haranguing starving conscripts in Morocco.[35] Barea's heroes and heroines are the working class and the refugee peasantry who had flooded into Madrid. No general appears in these stories; and even the captain who appears in two is addressed in the familiar "tu" by his soldiers.

All these people's courage is improvised, arising from normal fear on being confronted with an extreme situation: all the more extreme because the shelling, the people blown apart, the houses crashing down, are not happening on a separate battle-field, but in the streets and places where they are living their lives.

The narrator, Arturo Barea, is one of these people. It is his own fear and reactions which he examines in many of the sketches. Ortega suggests that:

> *Two themes predominate in* Valor y Miedo*: a. the faith of the people of Madrid*

in the ideals they were defending; b. Barea's fear of bombardments, a form of destruction that obsesses and terrifies him.[36]

Barea expresses these feelings in the sketch "Piso trece" (Flat Thirteen):

I've picked up the rangefinder again and am looking. I'm stuck to the rangefinder's eyes, prolongation of my own, fascinated, incapable of moving from the place, seeing the puffs of smoke from the cannon, hearing the shell whistle moments later and hearing its explosions in the street, against the walls, on the roofs around us, hearing pillars and glass vibrating, the flat trembling, the immense room filling with noises, shouts, dust and smoke. Thinking that they are looking at me, that they are shooting at me, that the shell's coming through the air to me, that it is going to penetrate the eyepiece of the rangefinder, to follow the twisting path through the lenses and enter my brain through my eyes and explode here inside my skull.[37]

Barea cannot tear himself away from looking directly at his own possible death. Immobilised like a rabbit in a headlamp, he is unable to run down the stairs as he wants to do.

Barea describes another instance of his terror in "Esperanza" (Hope): on the terrible night of November 7, 1936, he and Ilsa waited in the *Telefónica*, unable to sleep because of the shelling. They heard the tanks' caterpillars screeching in the streets. They believed the fascists were entering the city and they would therefore be shot:

They took each other's arms unconsciously and began to talk in a low voice. They explained to each other their anguish and anxiety, plainly and with a primitive frankness, showing each other their illusions and their faith.[38]

In both these passages above, the narrator is describing the reactions and experiences of a non-combatant, having to await passively his fate. In the first quote he freezes; but in the second, human solidarity arises from the fear. In this solidarity, as in "Refugio", Barea finds hope: the "Esperanza" of the title. It was Barea's own fear, valiantly portrayed, which helped him understand and illustrate with sympathy the fear of others. In *Valor y miedo* Barea presents us with several different forms of this fear:

(A) In "Coñac" (Brandy), Don Manuel is repeatedly woken at night by the shelling.[39] Terrified, he takes to drinking brandy in secret. Turned into an alcoholic who bores militiamen on leave with tales of the Cuban War, he bears the guilt of hating his wife for her ability to sleep. "Coñac" is one of the few *estampas* that really does become a story. Its bald style and theme is reminiscent of Hemingway, though Hemingway would not have mentioned at all the real "sub-story" of fear that underlies the description of Don Manuel's night. Barea turns an anecdote into a well-rounded story with the psychological insight of how Don Manuel comes to hate his wife because of his inability either to admit his fear or to act against it.[40]

(B) In "Servicio de noche," fear is treated differently.[41] Lolita the telephone girl acts to conquer her terror. Like Barea himself, she's not a front-line soldier, but a combative non-combatant. When everyone else is taking refuge in the bomb-shelters, Lolita returns to her work:

> *The Junkers come and go, rise and fall. They seem to surround the* Telefónica *building. The windows shatter into pieces. Waves of acrid smoke slowly invade the room. The call to Paris is cut off.*
>
> *Lolita began to shout down the line to the Paris switchboard, strident shouts, with her eyes full of tears. She pressed the head-phones she wore with her hands.*
>
> *She thought the world needed to know at once what was happening in Madrid.*
>
> *She was trembling with fear.*
>
> *The connection with the International News Service was reopened.*[42]

The story ends there. Lolita has displayed courage by doing her duty, precisely when she was terrified. Unlike Don Manuel, she does not attempt to conceal her fear; and, also unlike him, the importance of the cause she believes in enables her to rise above herself. It is a moving story in the heroic tradition of Soviet socialist realism: it could have been one of Ehrenburg's dispatches to *Pravda*.

(C) In "Los chichones", as in "Las botas", Barea treats fear with rough humour.[43] What appears during the first half to be a tale condemning the bar-owner Serafín's fear is skilfully converted into a shared understanding that Serafín cannot help bumping his head whenever he wakes up in terror of the shells.

> *He's afraid when he's asleep, but when he's awake, he endures it. That's what I call a brave man.*[44]

Those who had at first laughed at Serafín's bumps end up ashamed of themselves. Fear is everywhere, the story tells us. A common recognition of its inevitability helps to deal with it. Whereas Don Manuel of "Coñac" is a coward, Serafín's acceptance of fear turns him into a hero. Barea's model of a courageous hero is thus someone like Serafín and not the "betrothed of death" of Millán Astray.[45]

(D) As a coda to this discussion of fear in *Valor y miedo*, it is relevant to comment on Barea's treatment of the same theme in the gloomy story "Mister One", published in *El centro de la pista*.[46] Barea wrote this story in April 1939, the month after the end of the Spanish Civil War and just a few weeks after his reaching refuge in England.

"Mister One" is a brief tale about Mister One, who every Saturday night silently drinks himself stupid, and Mister Two, who never drinks alcohol, but shakes and stutters after too much coffee. In the First War, Mister Two had been a conscientious objector and emigrated to South Africa. Mister One went to the war. But now the sex and love life of both of them is plagued by guilt: of desertion in the former's case and participation in bloodshed in Mister One's.

The concreteness and brutality of Barea's imagery makes the imaginative connection between sex (and peace) on the one hand and bloodshed on the other. Mister One is haunted by his killing of a German:

> *The German had breasts like a woman. The noise of the bayonet when it came out doesn't let me sleep. If I got married . . . I would hear this noise in her naked breast.*[47]

Barea is working out a syllogism in this story: he does not give the men proper names and presents their different cases in sequence. He is examining, at the end of the Spanish Civil War, the effects of war on the involuntary participant. Mister Two is a deserter; Mister One, a soldier. They become friends because both have suffered the effects of war and are unable to lead a normal life as represented by their marrying the women they love.

Barea is neutral as to whether fighting or desertion is preferable. Nor does he extend any hope that the men will resolve their problem. For Barea the fear of the person affected by war is not avoidable. In his own biography, we know that his love for Ilsa, her strength and his writing enabled him to survive his fears. Both Lolita and Serafín, as portrayed in *Valor y miedo*, find ways to do the same. In "Mister One", he envisages the despair of the millions defeated in Spain in 1939.

Some of the passages quoted here from *Valor y miedo* give some idea of the descriptive power and vividness which was the hallmark of Barea's best writing, not only in this book but throughout his career. It is important, in discussing his ideas, not to lose sight of the fact that Barea was not primarily an intellectual writer. Even in this propaganda book, he is writing about the things he had "smelled, seen, touched and felt".[48] Barea's approach to events is raw and direct, unmediated by any distancing irony.

José Ortega wrote that the language of *Valor y miedo* was "direct, even brutal at times, but always warm."[49] This directness and brutality is conveyed by a particular style, explained by María Herrera:

> *(Barea) achieves a concise and sensationalist prose, in a slow and monotonous rhythm, in which the images pass before the reader as if in a silent picture, to highly dramatic effect.*[50]

Almost any narrative passage in the book could serve as an example of this extreme detail, or concision. Here is the first paragraph of "Sol", where the cinematic and monotone effects are enhanced by the historic present:

> *At seven in the morning the sun awakes me. It begins to flood the room and is a shower of light that forces you to get out of bed. It doesn't enter my room directly; it strikes the wall on the other side of the street and forms a mirror there that reverberates violently. It is more disturbing than if it shone directly into the eyes.*[51]

On several occasions in *Valor y miedo*, the details of the descriptions create a near-phantasmagoric, mesmeric atmosphere. The detail creates, too, a brutality that goes beyond mere realism. In "Carabanchel", the longest sketch, for example, a soldier finds himself in a trench with the rotting remains of a donkey built into the muddy wall in front of him. In three pages of sustained disgust, Barea tells us of the donkey's "pimpled thin neck"; "fat and green flies"; a rat "big as a small cat, with a sinewy tail that wagged in curves like a whip end", which in his panic the soldier destroys; then the "louse . . . searching for the corner where it would swell up on blood". The louse is the final straw and the soldier . . . "ran out of the trench like a madman".[52] Described thus, the passage verges on the comic; but the power and crudity, achieved by short sentences, scenes clearly observed and the straightforwardness of presentation create an effect of horror and madness.

Barea, therefore, sometimes uses his descriptive ability not just to show, but to shock. At times, as in "Carabanchel", Barea is not merely describing the rawness of what his senses perceive. So intense are the physical descriptions that he is able to express feelings of horror, disgust and fascination.

In *The Forging of a Rebel* he was to write other scenes of gruesome death or disgust, which he had witnessed from his infancy onwards. Within Barea's social realism is an accumulation of disquiet and horror that comes from looking directly at the worst. It is no surprise that *Valor y miedo*'s composition served as therapy to emerge from a nervous breakdown brought on by the horrors of war. This strength of feeling gives the book an echo and power beyond most mundane works of socialist realism and propaganda.

Killers have no name

In *The Clash* Barea wrote of his 1937 radio broadcasts:

> *While I read my nightly talk, the entire population of the basement used to assemble in the blanketed studio. The men seemed to feel that they had a share in my broadcasts, because I spoke their language, and they were possessively critical of them.*[53]

The audience played a direct part in the composition of the broadcasts and, by extension, in the sketches of *Valor y miedo* based on those broadcasts. This audience's criticisms and advice were not discreet and Barea, given his feeling of identity with these representatives of popular Madrid, strove to satisfy their aspirations when he broadcast.

The origins of the sketches in this almost collective process influenced Barea's language. It contributed to the vividness of description we have noted, to the human warmth that Ortega refers to and also to Barea's use of popular language. Barea's dialogue and narrative are imbued with the rhythm and slang of the people of Madrid. Here's an example, from "El Sargento Ángel":

> *— Hey, you haven't taken communion today, have you? Come on then, here's a chapel.*
> *They crossed the street and went into a run-down bar.*
> *— Hey, give us some petrol to get up the hill.*
> *They drank two glasses of "rat poison" . . .* [54]

As well as slang, the sketches are full of popular turns of phrase, songs and comments. These can be found on every page. These three come on opening the pages at random:

> 1. *If she were a man, I'd give the old witch a kicking (*Si fuera hombre, la pateaba a esta tía bruja*).*
> 2. *. . . and he says to me, the arrogant bastard: – Hey, you, try on a pair, even though you've a few screws missing . . . Well, it was enough to strangle him or slag off his mother (* . . . y me dice, muy chulo: - Tú, pruébate un par, aunque a tí te faltan unos zepelines . . . Bueno, para saltarle el cuello o mentarle a la madre*).*
> 3. *He was such a good-looking old geyser! A little bit hunch-back, but . . . (*¡Era un abuelete más plantao! Era un poquillo chepa, pero . . . *)*[55]

Barea was often criticised by Spanish critics for his use of slang.[56] Fernández Gutiérrez and Herrera Rodrigo (FG & HR) point out a number of misuses of Castilian by Barea: for example, "esto" for "eso"; the "la-ismo" and the "le-ismo" (wrong use of the pronouns, la and le); omissions of "que"; wrong accenting; the elision of the "d" in the past participle; the use of an imperfect indicative rather than a past subjunctive, etc.[57] FG & HR speculate that these errors were caused by Barea's having worked in offices, where abbreviations were common, or by contamination from foreign languages. This may sometimes be so. However, the more obvious explanation is that these are not faults at all, but an integral part of Barea's attempt to articulate popular language and mood. Popular language brings the sketches to life. Barea had two potential audiences: the people of Madrid, for whom the slang made the broadcasts, and could have made the sketches if they had later read them, more familiar, more "theirs"; and the outside world, whose support for besieged Madrid Barea sought. Making the sketches "local" to Madrid by specific popular terminology helped make the propaganda of the sketches more vivid to both audiences.

Barea's practice of constantly naming places and people has a similar effect to the use of slang. We are told that "Coñac" is set in a house on the Puerta del Sol; "Los chichones" in Serafín's bar and house; "Sol" in the Gran Via; "Refugio" on "the corner of the Calle de la Cruz". Three sketches are simply named after areas of the city: "Carabanchel", "Argüelles" and "Plaza de España". His heroes and heroines are given solid, human form by being in, and belonging to, a particular place. It is Barea's way of saying: "This is true. It happened here".

The use of names also underlines the author's involvement. He tells us he has known the boy on the corner of Mayor and Correos all his life ("Juguetes"). Serafín and Paco ("Los chichones") or Sergeant Ángel ("El sargento Ángel") are all given depth by the author's involvement with them. Significantly, the enemy is never named: they are "moros" or "alemanes" (Germans). Thus the enemy is dehumanised, as in the sarcastically titled sketch "Proeza" (Prowess):

The father is called: Raimundo Malanda Ruiz.
The mother is called: Librada García del Pozo.
The ruins of the house wounded by seven bombs still conserves its number 21, Carlos Orioles street in Vallecas.
The plane was a three-engined German Junker.
The killers have no name.[58]

There is a counter-balance to the terror and fear evoked in *Valor y miedo* in the frequent humour of the characters and the ironies – crude contrasts rather than subtleties – which Barea draws out of the situations. In "Las botas", for example, Barea creates the feeling that some ill-fitting boots are going to cause a tragedy. But against expectation the soldier removes the boots in time and assists in successfully repulsing an attack. In the middle of the story, the serious dilemma, with political overtones, is posed humorously:

> *He was afraid of both: his corns and the machine-gun . . . They seemed to have drawn up a pact to martyr him . . . But finally his fear of the machine-gun was greater than his fear of corns. One was the war, and was a question of luck. The others were executioners that had made his life a misery since childhood.*[59]

A story that threatened disaster ends lightly. "Juguetes" and "Los chichones" also end more happily than Barea lets the reader hope at the stories' start. Barea uses humour to suggest that people can think and take decisions, despite their fear. As noted earlier, impotence or passivity before political events is not always the case in the smaller questions. Within "Carabanchel", the humorous use of a bed-frame to repulse shells offsets the horror of sharing a trench with a dead donkey.

The strongest example of humour as a companion of courage and antidote to war and fear is shown by Sargento Ángel at the end of the sketch of the same name. Ángel invites his friend to punch him on the jaw – a Schweikian gesture! – and then comments ruefully on the war to that same friend:

> *If only this could be sorted out by fisticuffs.*[60]

III

Moving beyond "Surface Realism"

Touching the hidden sources of things

In Paris during the summer of 1938, Barea came to this conclusion: " . . . I did not want to write articles and propaganda stories."[1] It was a bold, risky decision, taken "when I was alone among strangers", a phrase which was to define Barea's life from then on.[2] With this considered decision to put *Valor y miedo* behind him, Barea felt:

> *I was no longer afraid of going mad. My illness had been fear of destruction and fear of the rift within myself.*[3]

During the year of insecurity and poverty Barea spent in Paris, *en route* from Spain to England, he found the way to overcome his physical and mental illnesses.[4] Just as the broadcasting and writing which became *Valor y miedo* had allowed him to surmount his nervous collapse in May 1937, so now Barea found a more permanent remedy for the madness he feared:

> *I might fight my own way to clarity, and I might be able to help others in the end, if I traced my mental disease – this disease that was not only mine – back to its roots.*[5]

The search for his "roots" was to be the way out of his mental illness:

> *I began to write a book about the world of my childhood and youth. At first I wanted to . . . describe in it social conditions . . . at the beginning of the century, in the villages and slums I had known. But I caught myself putting down too many general statements and reflections which I believed but could not check, because they did not grow out of my own experience and mind.*[6]

Barea found that he was commenting and reflecting too much in his narrative: perhaps he was still thinking of making propaganda, as in *Valor y miedo*. Then, he tells us, with the force of a moment of revelation:

I tried to wipe the slate of my mind clean of all reasoning and to go back to my beginnings, to things which I had smelled, seen, touched, and felt and which had hammered me into shape by their impact.[7]

This is a crucial statement of Barea's method. He decided to try to record his childhood, without rationalising it with his later adult knowledge. He started his book again, this time using the voice of himself as a child to re-create the smells, sights and sounds of his world.

Barea told us that *The Forge* took a long time to write because "I had to dig deep into myself."[8] These are words more evocative of Proust as a master than of realists such as dos Passos or Galdós. But whereas Proust's aim was to evoke the nostalgia of an adult reminiscing and to examine the private *mores* of high society; Barea avoided nostalgia by the technique of the child's voice and was examining the common experiences of his generation.

Barea distanced himself from propaganda with this Proustian descent into sensuous memory, but not from politics. In 1956, Barea replied to a question about the origins of *The Forge* as follows:

The clash of the Spanish Civil War, leaving for France, kicked out on one side and the other, threw me into the search for why we Spaniards were like this, and searching . . . as far as possible, really right back to my birth, and I had to . . . follow from this point the reason why a Spaniard had been thrown about like this, like so many millions.[9]

His aim was dual: both personal and general. Throughout the trilogy he never strayed from this double purpose. He wrote for himself, as a way out of mental illness, as a way to understand his roots. And he also wrote in order to understand what had happened to the millions of Spaniards who had suffered the Civil War.

Thus, despite his sharp shift – represented in the scrapping of a book he had already drafted – away from "general statements and reflections" in the style of a propagandist, Barea did not lose sight of how his writing could be a weapon in the war of millions against poverty and hunger. He saw writing as a way of intervening in the struggle for socialism at a time when he could no longer be an activist himself.

The particular view of realism that Barea developed after *Valor y miedo* is clarified by reference to three of his critical essays. In his 1941 article on *For Whom the Bell Tolls*, Barea attempted to define a different view of realism from that of his one-time mentor Ernest Hemingway:

Some of the Castilian peasants Hemingway has created are real and alive . . .

> *Although all are magnificently described, in none of them has he touched the roots.*[10]

Barea goes on to question "the quality of Hemingway's creative work in this instance, and the problem of his realism as a whole". He concludes:

> *Thus the inner failure of Hemingway's novel – its failure to render the reality of the Spanish War in imaginative writing – seems to me due to the fact that he was always a spectator who wanted to be an actor, and who wanted to write as if he were an actor. Yet it is not enough to look on: to write truthfully you must live, and you must feel what you are living.*[11]

This is indeed attacking Hemingway on Hemingway's own terrain, for the American fervently held that a writer had to experience, as well as observe, his subject-matter. Barea argued that the false note in *For Whom the Bell Tolls* was due to Hemingway's not having lived and felt the lives of the Spanish working class and peasantry he was writing about. But he was also suggesting, a more general point, that Hemingway's "close observation" was insufficient, even if based on real experience.[12]

Barea developed his view of realism further in a 1946 essay, where he criticised Pío Baroja's "dry surface realism"[13] and later praised Ramón Gómez de la Serna in the following terms:

> *In Spanish prose he {Gómez de la Serna} was the first to convey, rather than to describe or explain, a sense of complexity and insecurity, of "things below the surface of things".*[14]

Barea added that the upheavals of war and revolution his generation had lived through could not be sufficiently expressed by Baroja's (or, by implication, Hemingway's) "dry surface realism". Detailed observation of the surface was necessary but insufficient. Barea found a model in the pre-war Ramón J. Sender:

> *. . . the first Spanish novelist who attempted to describe the new workers' movements from within . . . The style Sender used to describe these violent problems was . . . bizarre, harsh, full of images and lit by flashes of poetry.*[15]

Barea was never as ambitious, innovative or imaginative as Sender, but Sender's early novels showed how to add an account of working-class life "from within" to "the grim reality of things seen".[16]

It is legitimate to see in these later essays Barea's rationalisation of his own aims as he had struggled with the first versions of *The Forge* in 1938. Hemingway's "close observation" and Baroja's "surface realism" had been sufficient aesthetic tools for the propaganda sketches of *Valor y miedo*, but were now not enough.

For *The Forging of a Rebel* Barea required an approach to writing that he felt was more profound. This is in no way to suggest that Barea is a better writer than Hemingway or Baroja, but rather that he needed a realism which got under the surface of events. Hemingway's use of intense detailed surface observation to convey emotion was not something Barea could (or wanted to) imitate. Barea's widow later wrote, citing his own words:

> *. . . Arturo so much longed as a writer . . . to be "able to touch the hidden sources (las fuentes escondidas) of things".*[17]

Objective and partisan

Without exception, critics who have commented on Barea cite *The Forging of a Rebel* as his best work. And most hold the first volume, *The Forge*, superior to the others. As a consequence of the trilogy's curious publishing history, the English reaction came before the South American, which in turn preceded the Spanish. A typical comment from the time, one reflected in reviews ever since, was:

> *A unique book, every word of which rings true . . . partisanship without intellectual dishonesty or the distortion of truth.*[18]

The first Spanish-language critics were the young Mario Benedetti, who in 1951 hailed *La forja de un rebelde* as "this vivid, effective story",[19] and Emir Rodríguez Monegal, who underlined the book's "brutality and directness . . . sustained objectivity".[20]

The first criticism from within Spain was the 1952 essay by Francisco Ynduráin, entitled "Resentimiento español" (Spanish Resentment). But even the politically hostile Ynduráin acknowledged that:

> *However partisan this work is, it has a lust for truth and to find a sense in life beyond the struggle.*[21]

Another Spanish critic, Eugenio de Nora, wrote a generation after Ynduráin, when censorship for literary books was laxer:

> *There are pages of his (at least and above all, almost the whole of* La forja*) that ensure him an outstanding place as a great narrator.*[22]

For José Marra-López, Barea is "splendid and intuitive". In a generous, trail-blazing 1963 essay, Marra-López concluded:

> *He is an unforgettable writer of a couple of books. With them he poured himself out totally and marvellously . . . One has to stand amazed, once more, before* La forja *as an example of the vitality with which some Spanish works rise periodically. They are human and popular, alive in the true sense of the word . . . and this is what any writer dreams of achieving.*[23]

There is a remarkable coincidence of critical opinion. Nearly all the critics highlight both the trilogy's warmth and passion and its author's sincerity and truthfulness. Normally the quality of passion might be counterposed to that of truthfulness; as partisanship may cut against objectivity. But Barea did not hold the view that truthful objectivity is only gained from the sidelines. He plunged emotionally into his story and succeeded in retaining his objectivity.

How should we classify *The Forging of a Rebel*, a work which is the truthful story of the author's own life, yet has the ring of a novel? Nearly every novel is to a greater or lesser degree autobiographical. With Barea, however, it is not just a question of the use of autobiographical sources, but that he rigorously excludes any event he has not been involved in and writes in a non-fictional first person.

Several critics have spent time discussing whether the trilogy is fiction or autobiography. For it is neither a normal fictionalised "Portrait of the Artist as a Young Man"; nor is it a straightforward autobiography. Rodríguez Monegal pointed out:

> *. . . although his autobiography is testimony of the highest calibre, it is not only this. Reality is treated by the author through a sensitivity that selects and reacts.*[24]

In other words, there is a selection of material such as occurs in a novel. Rafael Conte put it elegantly:

> *Is this a novel or an autobiography? What does it matter? It is an exceptional narrative, outside literary time, outside any trend, any aesthetic, outside any influence.*[25]

"What does it matter?", says Conte with reason, frustrated with this pedantic debate. Though Conte is wrong to deny the importance of the historical and social background of the trilogy, he justifiably mentions the uniqueness of Barea's work. In Spanish literature, there are very few precursors in the field of the autobiographical novel, and none like the trilogy. José Ortega offered an opinion why:

> *Autobiography is not a genre that has been greatly cultivated in Spanish literature, perhaps because of the fear of Spaniards to open exposure of their intimacy, of their individuality, out of fear of losing their "precious" uniqueness.*[26]

Ortega goes on to argue that Unamuno's first novel *Paz en la Guerra* (Peace in War) was:

> *. . . a historical novel or novelised history that started off in Spanish letters the movement of humanisation through personal projection . . . Obsession and the Unamunian intimate self acquire in Barea a more social tone because of the personal vicissitudes of the author and of the closeness of the historical fact that he narrates. Both novels are useful . . . for understanding their authors' personality and the intimate life of the Spanish people.*[27]

Another critic Serrano Poncela talked of:

> *. . . Hispanic inhibition before all public opening out of the intimacies of the self, with the consequent rejection of all commitment to self-interpretation of their deepest personalities.*[28]

Whatever truth these generalisations about the Spanish character contain, they do point to the originality of Barea's trilogy, where the author was brave enough to attempt to reveal his "deepest personality". In this respect, despite Barea clearly being a social realist, the impact of modernism is not alien to his work, as was suggested above with the allusion to Proust. Barea chose not to tell things from an objective, all-seeing point of view, but rather to filter the world through a subjective consciousness. As such, he showed how the world affected his "I" and how his "I" acted on the world: he is able to transmit the particular intensity of his childhood memories. Before the revolution in the arts, represented in literature by Joyce and Proust, it is hard to imagine this psychological dimension that Barea added to social realism. His autobiographical novel would not have been possible 30 years earlier.

We should note too that after Barea's book, though not necessarily as a consequence of it, there have been far more autobiographical novels in Spanish. The shock of the Civil War jolted numerous writers into a more personal and autobiographical type of novel than before.[29]

It is important however to emphasise that *The Forging of a Rebel* is not a confessional work: neither in the sense of Unamuno "confessing" to religious and existential doubt; nor in the sense of someone like Koestler "confessing" to the reasons why he had been a Communist. Barea was interested in his own life for a clear purpose. Let Barea himself re-state the political motive of this dual aim:

> *The millions who shared the same experiences and disappointments do not usually write, but it is they who are the rank and file in wars, revolutions and 'New Orders' . . . As I was one of them, I have attempted to be vocal on their behalf, not in the form of propaganda, but simply by giving my own truth.*[30]

In the political dimension of his dual purpose, Barea sounds uncannily like his near-contemporary Victor Serge who wrote, as if in echo of the above quote:

> *He who speaks, he who writes is above all one who speaks on behalf of all those who have no voice.*[31]

Victor Serge (1891–1947) is both similar to and different from Barea in illuminating ways. They both started to write autobiographical fiction late, when they were excluded from political activity: Serge in 1929 because of internal exile in the Soviet Union, and Barea due to nervous breakdown and foreign exile. They both carried on what they conceived as a political struggle by recording their own experiences. They wrote about themselves in order to express the feelings and aspirations of silenced millions. They wrote out of solidarity with the victims of oppression.

A key difference is that the protagonist of most of Serge's books is the workers' movement itself. Serge is a participating witness of events, but as one of the mass. Barea's desire to "self-interpret his deepest personality" has no interest for Serge. Barea's protagonist is, of course, Barea: as such, his trilogy lacks the political breadth of Serge's trilogy.[32]

However, both writers believed that, in order to understand and explain the events they had lived through, they could not be detached. Detachment was a game of imposing a false order on the confusion of social conflict and revolutionary upheaval. Indeed, writers could not be objective unless they were actively involved in the events they were trying to understand.[33]

Noses pressed against the glass

Thus the conscious choice which Barea made in 1938 to write this particular blend of autobiography and fiction was a choice conditioned by his personal and political situation and the aims he set himself. However, Barea was also, like any writer, impelled by factors rooted in his own character and history.

From early childhood Barea's life was defined by his "intermediate" position in society. When he first came to consciousness, he was living between a slum attic with his mother and the middle-class apartment of his aunt and uncle. He played in the street with ragged children at the same time as he went to school on a scholarship. Later, he tended to repeat this "intermediate" position: he was a member of the UGT while directing a factory. In the army, he was a sergeant: neither officer nor illiterate private. There are numerous examples of Barea's intermediate or "between-class" status, a position in society which he adopted almost without thinking at each stage of his life, after the die was cast by the childhood contradiction of garret and comfortable flat.

It can be argued that many intellectuals from a working-class background experienced a similar trajectory, especially before the general expansion of working-class education. Among writers, D. H. Lawrence comes to mind as someone who shows alienation from his background, yet identifies with it, in a similar way to Arturo Barea. Lawrence, like Barea, was fiercely independent and antagonistic to the intelligentsia; whereas by any objective criteria of life-style, views or source of income, he was himself one of them.

Barea's background gave him the vital gift for a writer of what can be called "double vision" - not the vision of a drunk, but the ability to look at the same events from two viewpoints. The novelist Jay McInerney defined Scott Fitzgerald's double vision as:

> *. . . viewing character and scene almost simultaneously from the inside and the outside.*[34]

In an image reminiscent of the young Arturo in the Café Español,[35] McInerney wrote:

> *{Fitzgerald's} . . . narrators always seem to be a part of the festivities even as they shiver outside with their noses pressed up against the glass.*[36]

It is this "double vision" which defines Barea's unflinching eye, his ability to immerse himself and the reader in the world of the child of *The Forge* and yet at the very same time to observe that boy from the outside. To say solely that Barea lived in an "intermediate" position in society could wrongly imply that he was not involved. On the contrary, he experienced deeply both sides of the class contradictions which started in his infancy.

Barea's is an unwavering objectivity, based on knowledge gained from totally subjective immersion. Barea does not falter into either breast-beating ("Oh what a bad boy I was"), nor special pleading ("Look what a terrible time I've had"), nor rose-tinted colouring (omission of things which reflect badly on the author). Joan Gili described Barea's eye as a "camera eye".[37] Yet at the same time as the reader of *The Forge* sees events through that objective, cinematic prism, he/she is drawn inside the writer's subjective world by the child's narrative voice.

Such an imaginative gift is what gives depth and dimension to Barea's trilogy. The world the reader enters is both a real, accessible, objective, non-private world, and also the author's profoundly subjective and private reality. This double vision is what enables the circle of "passionate" and "objective" to be squared.

IV

The Child's Eye

The Forge

The Forge, "Barea's most valuable, happiest book,"[1] is divided, like the other two volumes of the trilogy, into two parts. The first part contains eight chapters,[2] all of which are named after concrete places and express the disparate influences that forge the child, Arturo. This structure highlights the multiple contradictions of Barea's childhood. Thus, the first chapter ("River and Attic") sets the context of slum poverty; the second, the middle-class world. We are taken then from the city to the country. Within the country chapters, the dry Brunete ("Wheat Lands") is contrasted with the wet fertile lands round Méntrida ("Wine Lands").

The second half of the volume is organised in a more linear manner round the crucial events of Barea's adolescence: the death of his uncle and the dashing of his hopes for a career; his beginning to work and the experiences which led to his joining the UGT; all brought together in the last chapter, "Rebel".

The child's eye

An examination of the very first two pages of the volume shows a lot about Barea's technique, style and themes. The well-known opening paragraph plunges the reader straight into the book's atmosphere:

> *The wind blew into the two hundred pairs of breeches and filled them. To me they looked like fat men without a head, swinging from the clothes-lines of the drying-yard. We boys ran along the rows of white trousers and slapped their bulging seats. Señora Encarna was furious. She chased us with the wooden beater she used to pound the dirty grease out of her washing. We took refuge in the maze of streets and squares formed by four hundred damp sheets. Sometimes she caught one of us; then the others would begin to throw mud pellets at the breeches. They left stains as though someone had dirtied his pants, and we imagined the thrashing some people would get for behaving like pigs.*[3]

These vivid images take us with cinematic directness into a child's world: the street-urchin game, speculation on soiled linen, the washer-woman with a stick. This opening is typical of how throughout the book Barea gives the reader information to understand the situation, whilst rarely explaining anything beyond the child's perception of reality.[4]

This child's-eye view can be broken down into three main functions. Most immediately, as in the first chapters of Dickens' *David Copperfield*, the child's eye and voice express the freshness of a world seen for the first time.

Secondly, the technique allows Barea to place very different worlds alongside each other, without moral value being placed on them. An example occurs on the second page, where the innocence of the child leads him to perceive the young Prince in the same terms as himself and his ragged friends:

> *{The Prince} . . . had to go for a walk in the Casa de Campo every day, between a priest and a general with white mustaches. It would have been better for him to come and play with us by the river . . . Uncle Granizo . . . told us that the general would not give his permission.*[5]

The third aspect of the child's-eye view is that it allows Barea to demonstrate with conviction an optimistic attitude to the world, hope for the future. The characters defined in the opening chapters are dirt-poor, but not miserable. This might seem a rose-tinted view of the happy poor; but Barea avoids this trap precisely by employing the immediacy and innocence of the child's voice and eye.[6]

With this immediacy, Barea achieves the extremely hard narrative challenge of portraying his characters' lives, so that the reader understands the social points the author wants to make without explicit authorial comment. One of countless examples occurs on the second page:

> *As we were children and so could not be anarchists, the police let us stay while they {the Queen and the Princes} went by. We were not afraid of the Horse Guards, because we knew their breeches too well.*[7]

The trousers are of course those of the first paragraph quoted above, and which his mother washes for a living. Barea both lets us know that anarchists are the talk of the town (how else could a child have heard of them?) and contrasts the royal family with his own life. We as adult readers gain background and information, without Barea having to lose narrative flow and power by abandoning the child's viewpoint.

After the poignant image of the prince in his carriage, "a fair-haired boy with blue eyes, who looked at us and laughed like a ninny",[8] the direct association of the child's mind is used to take us into his uncle's more prosperous world, where with maximum economy Barea signals the young Arturo's affectionate relationship with his uncle and his early interest in politics and reading:

> *I used to sit down on the floor between my uncle's legs while they talked about politics and the war of the Russians and Japanese . . . I could not stand the Russians. They had a very nasty king who was the Tsar and a police chief called Petroff . . . My uncle bought me a new number of the Adventures of Captain Petroff every Sunday. They threw a lot of bombs at him, but he never got killed.*[9]

In a final example taken from these two opening pages, the child talks of the prince:

> *. . . the priest taught him how to speak. I didn't understand that. How could he speak if he was dumb? Perhaps he could, because he was a prince; but the dumb people I knew could only talk by signs. And it was not for lack of priests.*[10]

In four lines, the child first asserts a point he has heard from adults ("the priest taught him how to speak"); but with dogged curiosity questions the point ("How could he speak if he was dumb?"); and in questioning it, tells us, as if in passing, that there is more than one dumb child in the streets (in a wealthier, less street-based world, a child wouldn't know so many people with handicaps) and a lot of priests.

In these first two pages, therefore, three quick scenes (the children playing in the washing, the prince passing by, the child at his uncle's) are sketched; and, hardly perceptibly, major themes Barea will develop have been planted in the reader's mind: children, anarchists, wealth and poverty, reading . . . These opening two pages – which could just as easily be many other pairs of pages – suggest the density and richness of the book. They also show that Arturo Barea was a much more organised and careful writer than his frequent crudities of style and harshness of subject-matter have led many critics to assert.

In the first two chapters, Barea develops the contrast between his two lives. He tells us about the representative of restriction and religious repression, Aunt Baldomera:

> *Uncle José was very good, but my aunt was a grumpy old bigot and would not leave me alone. Every evening I had to go with her to Rosary . . .*[11]

The young Arturo prefers life in the streets and his Republican mother's prayer-free *buhardilla* (garret). The narrator's optimism and energy, which carry the reader through the volume, come from the sense of freedom, so sharply contrasted with the stale, confined world of Baldomera's flat. In this extract, the young Arturo slips away from the staid family table in the Café Español:

> *... I gulped down my coffee and went off with Esperanza who had been pinching me from behind my chair because she wanted to play ... The sofas ran along the walls, and we loved to scramble on all fours through the sunk lane between their backs and the tables ... we stood up on a sofa to look at ourselves in the big mirrors.*[12]

Mario Benedetti wrote in 1951 that "The three great themes of Barea are: childhood, Spain and love."[13] The vigour of the children in Barea, the reverence, none the less strong for being conventional, towards his self-sacrificing mother and his loving evocation of Lavapiés -- for Barea, the "Spain" of his nostalgia – show the accuracy of Benedetti's view, who goes on to remark:

> *The powerful attraction of these themes is the author's awkward discomfort towards them, his journey against the current of convention, his ever more stubborn independence of criterion.*[14]

Thus, already in these first chapters, conflicts between his mother and aunt, between the streets and the café define the young Arturo's life. As was argued in Chapter III, Barea occupies an "intermediate" position in society, but this does not mean he is in a space between these two worlds. Rather, he enters fully into two irreconcilable (or only temporarily reconcilable) worlds, and this plunges him into even greater conflict.

Nor is it a simple counter-position of good and evil that Barea sets up. Benedetti goes on to talk of his "double refusal to submit" (*doble insumisión*).[15] Thus, Arturo rejects his aunt's world for the freedom of the streets and his mother's love. But he <u>also</u> rejects both the streets, realising he must get an education, and his immediate family, where his sister Concha attacks him for being a *señorito* (toff) and resents his privilege at her expense.[16]

This "double refusal to submit" is therefore a rejection of everything! The reader is taken inside the child's various worlds, the different layers and classes within society. The child's eye and voice permit Barea both to infuse the text with hope, optimism and passion for life, and at the same time lay bare the complexity and multiple contradictions in the young Arturo's life.

Torn, he enters full-bloodedly into everything and rejects everything, as he searches for his own independent criterion.

Country bliss

Like many a good novelist, Barea sets his scene, stimulating the reader's appetite, and then abruptly changes direction. After the first two chapters, the narrative of *The Forge* suddenly leaves Madrid and takes us into the older world of three nearby villages: Brunete, Méntrida and Navalcarnero. The first was to become sadly renowned for its total destruction in 1937, which gives added poignancy to Barea's elegiac descriptions. It is typical of the trilogy that themes are deepened and given resonance by association of details back and forth through the three volumes: in this case, several hundred pages later, where Barea comments:

> *There, behind that dark, flashing cloud, Brunete was being killed by clanking tanks and screaming bombs . . .* [17]

In the three country chapters of *The Forge*, especially when talking about Méntrida, Barea achieves most intensely another sort of "double vision": the people and places are there before us, new and fresh in the eyes of the child; and at the same time the chapters overflow with nostalgia for an irrecoverable world. They are undoubtedly the lyrical high-point of all Barea's writing.

> *There is such detail in the portraits and descriptions that the paragraphs begin to lengthen inevitably . . . The magical effect is almost always achieved by the language: child-like, elementary and primitive, but tremendously suggestive and stimulating.*[18]

In his 1953 essay on Cela, Barea wrote:

> *Like other Spanish writers from Miguel de Unamuno down, Cela seems incapable of finding unspoilt, genuine and strong people anywhere else than in the immutable hills and plains, least of all in Madrid.*[19]

Barea does not share the cynical tone of *The Hive* and was capable of finding "unspoilt, genuine and strong people" in the city, yet he too "escaped into a static world" of rural dignity from the "depressing ugliness" of Madrid.[20]

Along with the tone of elegiac loss, Barea is recording social history in these country chapters. He explains with careful detail how things used to be, defining the different kinds of people and meticulously naming places:

The coach leaves from the Cava Baja, from a very ancient inn called San Andrés.[21]

Thus these lyrical chapters are also the most *costumbrista* of Barea's work. The pace of the narrative slows and the paragraphs lengthen, as he enters into the minutiae of the scenes. And at one point, he departs from the child's voice, in this case successfully underlining the lost uniqueness of what the boy had known:

When I was a boy, it was surprising to see these agricultural labourers, seated at the oak table, with the Talavera jug of wine adorned with blue flowers, unwind their sashes, letting their breeches fall down; untie the knot enclosing their treasure; undo the loops of cord; and pull out with their nails the final knots before throwing onto the table the sum for the deal.[22]

The three villages are not uniform. There are contradictions between them, and even within the magical cornucopia that is Méntrida, the young Arturo suffers isolation. He is bored and again suffers the resentment of his relatives for being a *señorito*. It is a tag to which he always reacts angrily and from which he will never escape. A Spanish critic, Juan Luis Alborg, wielded these incidents against Barea:

In many episodes, there is . . . a haughty pride projected onto his family members, which does not justify at all his subsequent social rebellion. More still: which has nothing to do with it.[23]

The young Arturo is indeed a prickly child, who flares up easily at imagined or real insult. But Alborg misreads the events of *The Forge*. Barea leads us carefully through the stages of the young Arturo's development. We are shown how it is the very conditions of his life – for example, being dressed by Aunt Baldomera in a sailor suit when his friends and siblings wear rags – that cause his conflicts. It is because of these conditions, and Arturo's refusal to submit neither to taunts nor to the sailor-suit, that the child reacts. Though it is true that there is "haughty pride" in these reactions, which make him an instantly recognisable type of Spanish individualist, it is not correct to say, as Alborg does, that this haughtiness has nothing to do with his social rebelliousness. Both pride and rebelliousness stem from the conflict and contradictions described. In the other non-lyrical aspect of these chapters, Barea takes great pains to explain the origins of his uncle's wealth. He introduces Luis Bahía the money-lender: a figure who presages the usurer of Novés, Heliodoro, portrayed in the opening chapters of *The Clash* and the *cacique* of his 1947 story, *Agua bajo el puente* (see Chapter 8). Barea is too conscious a writer to be carried away by false nostalgia or his own lyrical gifts. In also showing the economical relationships in the villages, he kept firm rein on his dual purpose: to uncover, in himself and in Spanish society, the factors underlying the Civil War.

Of the two villages which Barea contrasts in most detail, the first is dry Brunete:

> *{People} . . . had nothing but an onion and bread in the morning before going to work in the fields, a gazpacho – bread, onions, and cucumber in vinegar and water with very little oil – at mid-day and a stew in the evening, made just of chick-peas and a slice of bacon.*[24]

The second is Méntrida, abundant and sensuous. Whereas in Brunete, there is the spectacle of the degrading village bull-fight; in Méntrida, the festival is relaxed. In Brunete, the adults kill bulls and the child plays by tearing wings off flies; but in Méntrida, with its abundant water, fruit and game, families lie around idyllically in the grass and couples slip away into the bushes.

In Méntrida Arturo can lose himself and submerge his ego of the spoilt Madrid child: here he is never bored. The family is all working. He fits in, both left to his own devices and accepted: he is happy. Only working flat out in the siege of Madrid 30 years later was Arturo able to lose again his sense of apartness and ego. In Méntrida the child's older relatives take on the forms of archetypal figures. His Uncle Luis, the blacksmith, eats and drinks massively and inspires Arturo with his desire to be an engineer. Luis in his forge, resonant of the book's title, is an image of work and health, which Arturo will carry forward with him. Another character, his great-grandmother Eustaquia, is 99 years old (in this summer of 1907), so spanning Spanish history back to the Napoleonic invasion.

Rich in archetypes and lyricism as the country chapters are, they nevertheless show sophistication in Barea's vision. Simple counterpoint is rarely sufficient for him. The volume is not a romantic autobiography; nor is it a documentary account of a typical childhood, with the concomitant ideology that he was defined and created by environment alone.

The movement in the book stems from Barea's showing the world coming to life through the consciousness of a small boy, influenced and defined by the passions, conflicts and character of his family. The environment is not an external documentary, but one which is formed, instant by instant, out of Arturo's perceptions. Thus Barea wields both factors, character and conditions, to explain himself. He seeks to penetrate to the roots of his consciousness and at the same time describe the social conditions that formed himself and millions more.

"In Spain you can find the happiest children in Europe, even though they are often barefoot and in rags," wrote Henry Miller, a remark doubtless coloured by Miller's *nostalgie de la boue*.[25] Yet the rowdiness and zest of children in the Madrid of *The Forge* bears Miller out. Barea has the gift of confronting the most crude and unpleasant scenes directly, yet combining his unflinching eye with humour and energy.

There is a cast of dozens in *The Forge* whom Barea treats with affection and humour: the blind musicians in the Café español, Ángel the newspaper boy, Señora Francisca, the beggars at the theatre. And in every description there is the sound of children running and shouting, throwing stones at lamps and mud at washing, sprinting with papers from door to door, fishing balls out of the sewer or fighting with gangs from the neighbouring *barrio*. Or else there is the opposite, complementary presence of a serious child watching quietly, in the Café, in the coach or on the street:

> *The gentlemen come out in their evening dress and top hat . . . the women in their . . . silk dresses . . . The beggar, with his lice-filled beard, holds the door of the carriage open with one hand and with the other bows with a rag that is his filthy cap or beret. If they stop to talk at the door of the carriage, the beggar with his head bare, without a coat, dies of cold and stamps with his espadrilles on the stones of the pavement.*[26]

You can picture the observant small boy keenly watching the social comedy. With passages like this, Barea contributes to what he himself more than once highlighted in his later criticism:

> *. . . the note of hunger . . . in Spanish reality . . . {and} in Spanish literature. It sounds, hardly softened by genteel manners, through the nineteenth-century novels of Benito Pérez Galdós; it speaks from the pages of the young Pío Baroja early in this century; it cries out from the novels of Ramón J. Sender.*[27]

In *The Forge*, the portraits of the hungry are filled with the affection and vitality of the young boy. Often the descriptions of people and situations spill over into a sort of comic, ironic commentary on appearance and reality, which is deeply rooted in Spanish life and literature. *The Forge* holds numerous examples of this picaresque influence, like the extract above about the beggars; or the story of the beggars buying meat they could not afford for themselves to try and save the life of Toby, the dead Señora Segunda's dog; or the kindly Segunda herself, living and dying in the cupboard beneath the stairs.

God

When Barea takes up the narrative after the country chapters, the young Arturo has left his infancy and begins his boyhood in School and Church. These two institutions are intimately connected, as it is a Church School which he attends. Before Barea deals head on with the religious question, he has made sure there are frequent references to the Church: as usual, he creates a context, lays trails, before tackling a question frontally. Religion was introduced right at the start with the comments about the priests educating the Prince. Arturo's most direct religious influence is Baldomera, who takes him every afternoon to mass. This leads the boy to associate the Church with being forced to come in from playing in the street: attendance at Church becomes identified with social rigidity.

The conventionally rebellious reaction of the young boy is first given depth by his forthright grandmother Inés, who tells Aunt Baldomera: "You're turning him into a ninny with all your priests and prayers".[28] Arturo is so torn by the ensuing argument that, when asked by Inés if he prefers play to prayer, he lies:

> *I did not want to make my aunt more annoyed with me, so I said that I liked going to church very much.*

At which the infuriated Inés shouts: "You're a sissy, that's what you are!"[29] This is the first of three references in forty pages where Arturo is taunted for being a "sissy" (*marica* in Spanish).[30] The proselytising atheist Inés, mother of twenty-five children (so Barea tells us!), who, as village gossip had it, wore out her dead husband, represents the opposite pole, not only religiously but also in sexual imagery, to the timid religious fanatic Baldomera. Thus the sexual question is linked to religion in the boy's mind: and heterosexuality (fertility) and atheism are united in the figure of Inés.

Inés' arguments are the conventional ones that the world is harsh and cruel; and yet the priests get fat and rich. These are views that Arturo will be able to test out for himself when in adolescence he begins to link the Church to a dominant role in a class-divided society. For the present his conflict remains unresolved: "I wanted to believe in God and the Virgin, but the things she [Inés] said were true".[31] Crucially, Inés does not stop him going to Church. The ten year-old attends for two reasons: he feels it would be sinful not to go and he finds pleasure in going alone. It is in such passages that Barea demonstrates his depth in tackling these themes, going beyond black and white alternatives. He shows the child's religious fascination for things not understood; and then his clear-sightedness, which allows him to demystify what he does see. The child Arturo notices, for example, the higher class of skulls used in the richer funerals (a macabre touch typical of Barea). He observes the cleaning-woman spitting on her cloth to clean the Virgin's eyes . . . "just as people do when children have sand in their eyes".[32] Barea expresses the child's simultaneous attraction and rejection with such physical images.

Part Two opens with the death of Arturo's uncle and a momentous clash between Baldomera and Inés over his future, when Inés intervenes against Baldomera's plump confessor, "Father Sausage" (in Inés' words), to prevent Arturo's being sent to a Jesuit school. In a magnificent scene, Inés throws the smalmy priest (also "Father Greasebag") out of Baldomera's flat:

> *"Off with you," she shouted, "back to your hole, you cockroach!"*
> *And she slammed the door so that the glass cups on the sideboard danced and tinkled like little bells.*[33]

Arturo's religious conflict is developed by these events into a clear-cut anti-religious position. The several components of Barea's mature view are well-summarised much later in the trilogy, in the opening of *The Clash*, when Barea in a long conversation with Don Lucas, the parish priest of Novés, expresses his hostility to the Church:

> *"I don't go to church because you clergy are in the Church, and we don't get on together. I was taught a faith which by its doctrine was all love, forgiveness, and charity. Frankly, with very few exceptions, the ministers of the faith I have met possess all sorts of human qualities, but just not those three divine qualities".*[34]

After explaining this personal reason, Barea goes on to tell Don Lucas: " . . . [you should] use the pulpit for teaching the Word of Christ, and not for political propaganda."[35]

This emphasis relates directly back to the church–school experiences recounted in *The Forge*, where Arturo came to understand the social role of the Church and confirm for himself Inés' opinions. John Devlin suggests that beneath Barea's hostility to the Church lies an approach which is not in itself anti-religious. Passages such as the above are cited by Devlin to show how Barea counterposes an ideal Christianity to the rotten reaction of the Church hierarchy. But Devlin's argument is reduced to this assertion:

> *There is a warmth and a value structure that is bedrock in the ideology of Catholicism or any Western religion, for that matter . . . [Arturo Barea is one of many] . . . embittered lapsed Catholics.*[36]

These views, shared by other Catholic critics, are inappropriate on two counts. There is very little bitterness in any of Barea's writing before his last novel, *The Broken Root*. And secondly, it is tautological to suggest Barea had a religious sensibility despite his well-argued hostility, based on his own experience, to the Church. Barea's charitable and pacifist feelings are derived not from Christianity, but from various figures in his childhood such as his mother and uncles, and from the Socialist tradition with which he came into contact in his teens. Inés' and Barea's views and feelings were part of a long popular anticlerical tradition in Spain. Arturo's anticlericalism was a key aspect of what made him a rebel against the established powers, of which the Church was a principal pillar.

It is at Arturo's school that he first links social hierarchy and religion. When he steps up from the school's bottom rung through ability, he finds that those who are there through birth look down on him. The teachers in this school are that varied gaggle of priests he mentioned later to Don Lucas: the vain Padre Fidel, the sadistic Vesga, the unworldly Prefecto and Arturo's protector, the kindly Basque Father Joaquín, who explains: "You don't know why I'm a priest? The parents . . . were poor".[37]

There are two other gentle, strong priests like Joaquín in Barea's writing. The anti-fascist priest in the sketch "Refugio" (see Chapter 2) explained: "On one side there were the rich accompanied by priests; on the other side, the poor abandoned by priests".[38] Barea is talking about the Civil War. But his words are equally applicable to Baldomera's confessor thirty years before; or right back to the trilogy's second page, where the priest is teaching the dumb prince. For priests of peasant origin like Joaquín, such comfortable jobs were not open.

The other "good father" in the trilogy is Leocadio Lobo, who counsels Ilsa and Arturo at the time of their sacking from the press censorship in 1937, and whom even the anarchists respect. What the priest of "Refugio" says serves for Lobo and Joaquín too:

> *I am the son of labourers from Castile. My destiny was to plough the earth . . .*

> *but I was a smart boy. The priest in the village noticed me. He took an interest in me . . . and at the age of eleven I was sent to the seminary.*[39]

Barea saw in them his own possible fate, only averted by Inés' clear-headedness and strong will in keeping him out of the Jesuits' clutches. Barea never confuses the oppressive institution of the Church with the individuals within it, many of whom are the Church's victims as well as its servants.

Work: capitalist or proletarian pen-pusher?

The other focus of the second part of *The Forge* is the world of Work. His uncle's untimely death pitches the young Arturo – still "half-man, half-child"[40] – out of his engineering studies into a world he had not expected to enter.

In school he had learnt the hard way how he and the other two scholarship boys are separate both from the poor whence they have come and from the rich, who despise them. Arturo learns the need for basic solidarity in order to defend himself. These school experiences both extend his sister's taunts of *señorito* into a wider social setting and show how his class background excludes him from really being a *señorito*.

As well as solidarity, he learnt another important lesson in behaviour. He found that at school he could gain a certain protection by offering the services of his intelligence to the rich, the real *señoritos*. It is the first instance of a pattern that will profoundly shape his life, until the pattern is forcibly broken by exile. He can sell his labour power at a high price, enabling him to be well-paid and enjoy privileged positions. But this of course weighs against solidarity with the poor: whether the other two scholarship boys or later the UGT.

Accompanied by these contradictory lessons of solidarity and selling his services, the 13 year-old Arturo is thrown into the world of work as a *chupatintas*, a pen-pusher. In the bank he meets the near-blind family man, Luis Pla, a courageous clerk respected by Barea in all three volumes of the trilogy. Pla sets out to educate the adolescent boy:

> *"Your future is here in this place. Just think of it. A year without wages – sixty boys like you – three vacancies a year, and after twelve years' work in the place ninety pesetas a month, which is what I earn now."*[41]

This extract comes from the chapter entitled *Work*, where Barea explains conditions in the bank. Subsequent chapters also have representative rather than the concrete titles of the first half: *Capitalist*, where Arturo yearns for individual wealth to change his and his family's life; and *Proletarian*, where he perceives his true condition and joins the UGT.

The first thing Arturo encounters in the bank are the cruel practical jokes of initiation into the worlds of men and work. He defends himself, both verbally and in practice, and rapidly becomes "the quickest errand-boy in the bank".[42] The young Arturo wants to rise in the great bank. He dreams of being a permanent employee, supporting his family, becoming a gentleman. But his mentor Pla seeks to disabuse him of false hope: "It's a systematic exploitation of young boys. It's very cleverly worked out."[43]

A number of incidents, many of them picaresque in their occurrence and telling, confirm Pla's view. Medina is denied promotion in the cruellest of ways: when he had been led to believe he would be promoted because of his knowledge of English. Another employee, Recalde, "was banging his fist on the table and cursing" in fury at the miserly Christmas bonus.[44] These incidents teach Arturo an important lesson: that anyone can be dismissed at the drop of a hat and that individual rebellion leads nowhere.

The clerks often work twelve hours a day, watched and controlled by their bosses:

> *When we came home our fingers were rasped by paper dust and streaked with dry ink.*[45]

Yet not all is woe: other incidents show workers' cunning in fighting back against such treatment. On one occasion a watchman pretends not to recognise a boss and detains him at gun-point for suspicious behaviour: the boss had been tip-toeing secretively in order to spy on employees. And Pla faces down the boss when he is accused of going to bars, by drawing attention to the boss's own drinking habits.

In the *Capitalist* chapter, an interlude in the description of work at the bank, Arturo inherits 30,000 pesetas. Now he dreams of moving from the slum attic, of going up in the world; but his mother is not deceived by fantasies of wealth. She is staying put. And significantly the one article of real value which Arturo gains from his inheritance is electric light, by which he can read.

In *Proletarian*, back at the bank, he has to abandon fairy-tale resolutions to his problems and confront the realities of his job. He has already seen how the bank saps everyone's courage:

> *If the learner was afraid of being thrown out into the street before his year of*

> *unpaid work was over, the men who were already paid employees were even more afraid. That fear turned them into cowards.*[46]

Courage is not only needed in war, as described by Barea in *Valor y miedo*. Pla helps the young Arturo draw together the threads of his dashed hopes, desires for betterment and outrage at injustice. Barea tells us:

> *I pondered over these things for days. Of course I knew what the Socialists were. But I was not really interested in political questions.*[47]

But he decides Pla is right and he must join a union. Pla takes him to the *Casa del Pueblo*, where 25 years later Barea would train clerks to bear arms. There Barea joins the UGT: but not before, prickly and argumentative as always, he has entered into a tremendous row with a worker who had commented on his suit of a clerk or "señorito".

The word Barea himself uses to describe his fiery reaction in the *Casa del Pueblo* is "resentment": "I let myself be carried away by a violent impulse . . . pouring out all my resentment."[48] An older or more secure person, someone not torn by internal conflict as to whether he was a worker or a gentleman, would have responded with a calmer explanation. And a less spirited person would have kept his mouth shut.

As mentioned earlier in this chapter, Alborg, writing in 1962, argued:

> *{Barea shows} . . . resentment and lack of generosity in his temperament . . . unpleasant intolerance . . . haughty pride.*[49]

Alborg echoes Ynduraín and Aranguren's 1950s comments from within Franco's Spain that Barea had a chip on his shoulder, and suggests that life was not so hard on Barea as he pretends: "[Barea was incapable of] . . . accepting with . . . irony the inevitable caravan of human stupidities".[50]

There is a central problem to this sort of criticism: it is very much *ad hominem*, fatally mixing the author's (Barea's) own life and views with his literary production. This is inevitable to some degree, given the kind of book that the trilogy is. It is also easy to drift into the opposite danger of arguing *pro hominem* out of sympathy with the author's personality.

However, within Alborg's comments is a potentially valid literary criticism: that the "*resentment*" and "*haughty pride*" have nothing to do with and are not explained by "his subsequent social rebellion".[51] Alborg argues that the self-proclaimed aim of the book, i.e. to explain the forging of a rebel, does not work; that the narrator's social rebellion is not justified by the circumstances of his childhood, but is due to character flaws; and therefore

(Alborg does not state this explicitly, but it can be justly inferred from his comments) Barea cannot properly hold himself up as a typical member of his generation.

It is certainly true that Barea shows us an often prickly child and adolescent in *The Forge*. The hero takes nothing lying down. But this is entirely characteristic of any rebel and individualist. Barea does not pretend to be a typical person. By definition, no writer, no union activist, nor any rebel is typical, for such people are tiny minorities in society. But what Barea does argue is that the conditions which produced him were typical. He states this distinction very clearly in the 1943 foreword to *The Track*:

> *I wanted to describe the shocks which had scarred my mind, because I am convinced that these shocks, in different individual forms but from the same collective causes, scarred and shaped the minds of other Spaniards too. I wanted to expose my own reactions, because I believed that the others' reactions were determined by kindred forces, and that the world they saw was the same as mine, even though seen through different lenses.*[52]

Here Barea did not claim that his own reactions, as set out in *The Forge*, justified his rebellion, nor that he shared the same experiences as his contemporaries. However he did argue that his own and his generation's reactions were "determined by kindred forces," despite their worlds being "seen through different lenses".

Arturo Barea described an unusual child, in an unusual social situation, which gave him that "double vision" to see inside and outside his experience; a character with certain innate or circumstantial qualities of "double refusal to submit", storming against all sides. He wanted to believe in God and hated the Church. He wanted to be rich and hated being a *señorito*. He wanted to be a trade unionist and bristled at how the unionists treated him.

Barea selected his material carefully to develop these themes. But he did not manipulate his own character in order to justify with hindsight his rebellion. Rather, his character and circumstances allowed him certain insights, which led him to perceive and record some of the experiences common to his generation and class.

Dissection of the volume should not lead to its quality and unity being forgotten. We should end this chapter reasserting that *The Forge* is Barea's best book. The historian Hugh Thomas caught its overall impact:

> *{In The Forge} there are brilliant, self-confident pictures of Barea's family, all, as it were, peering over the edge of the giant cauldron of Spanish working-class feelings to see what sort of mixture will result. Don Luis, the blacksmith of*

Brunete, with his breakfasts of rabbit and brandy, is a particularly compelling figure. These 200 or so pages seem to me to be among the two or three best pieces of writing ever done which are inspired by working-class life. Or can one call that world of craftsmen about to sink, or about to rise, as fate determines, really 'working-class'? I think not: indeed, the whole sweep of this section of Barea's work reminds one of the diversity of the class . . . Priests and engine drivers, lion tamers and cashiers, matadors and beggars – all live forever caught by one short sentence or anecdote, thanks to Barea's acute and selective memory.[53]

V

Anti-Imperialism in Morocco

The Track

Fig-tree and blood-covered road

The second volume of the trilogy recounts the decisive experiences which lead Barea from the uncertainties and contradictions of his childhood, described in *The Forge*, towards the Civil War. It portrays too –- always his twin private and public purposes were in mind – the impact that the Moroccan colonial war had on his generation and Spanish society. Helen Grant considered *The Track* "the most powerful and original" volume of the trilogy.[1] It is an uncommon view: most critics prefer *The Forge* and most non-Spanish readers find *The Clash* more gripping, because of its focus on the Civil War. Yet Grant is surely right when she writes of *The Track*:

> *It is the most economical and best constructed of the novels, beginning and ending with the track of a road he {Barea} helped to build across the desert, a track soon soaked with blood and which ultimately led back to other roads soaked with blood, the blood of the Civil War.*[2]

The Track was easier to structure than the other two volumes of the trilogy, as Barea's arrival in Morocco and return to Madrid provide a natural beginning and end. In addition to this chronological and geographical frame, the volume is structured through the use of two recurrent images.

The title itself, as Grant suggests, resonates with meanings. The blood-stained *road* (or track), which Barea helps to build, heads nowhere, just like Spain's occupation of Morocco. Additionally, the "track" is the historical path which runs from Morocco to the Civil War, most clearly personified in the figures of the generals Millán Astray and Franco. It is also the compressed path of Spanish history, where forms of feudal ownership and modern factory organisation co-exist, where Franco and the anarchists developed side by side.

The track is also the road of tarmac that is poured over the aspirations of the Moroccans to freedom. With direct sarcasm (delicate irony was never his forte) Barea explains:

The kabila *no longer exists except for a few smoke-blackened patches . . . Hundreds of men are breaking up and leveling the ground for a broad track which is to lead past the foot of the hill and which will be very useful for the kabila. Well, the kabila will not be able to make use of it, because it exists no longer.*[3]

In addition to the track, Barea uses another repeated image: the fig-tree, which the soldiers have to remove in order to create the road. In the volume's opening lines, he describes this tree:

. . . its roots twisted like the veins of a robust old man, its contorted branches hung with the trefoil of its fleshy leaves.[4]

Roots and trees recur in Barea's work: in *The Broken Root* he exhausts almost every variation on the image of roots (see Chapter 9). He was originally going to call the trilogy *Roots*, which would have left Alex Haley searching for a title. In *The Track*, the fig-tree is the only living thing remaining after the destruction of the *kabila* (village), but it obstructs the new road and will itself have to go. Its root, however, is stubbornly resistant to pick and steel. Barea is struck by the idea that the tree's fertile splendour and strength indicate water in the barren land. After persuading his superiors to save the tree by building the road round it, he then creates a shaded drinking-fountain at its side. This image of the hidden spring fertilising the dry land recurs in one of his best stories *Agua bajo el puente* (Water under the Bridge), a justification of the violence of the oppressed (see Chapter 8).

For Barea, the tree represents a positive good, in contrast to the track. In the opening chapter, he interleaves its story with the meticulous detailing of military corruption. Later, in Chapter 4, entitled "The Fig Tree", the narrator comforts his mother, who is terrified by fantasies of the horrors of life in Morocco (the reality is, ironically, worse than her historical fancies of Berber slaving pirates), with embellished tales of the beautiful tree and water, which provide refreshment for Moroccans and Spaniards alike.[5]

In the shade of this tree, Barea discusses the Spanish Empire with a Moroccan village chief, a conversation echoed at the end of the volume, when Barea, lying under other trees, in the El Pardo woods near Madrid, remembers an old blind Moroccan who had come down the path by the fig-tree, then lost his way. To Barea's explanation that the landscape had changed because they were building a new road, the blind man laughed theatrically and said:

"I'll always walk on the path, always, always! I don't want my sandals to slip

> *in blood, and this road is full of blood, all of it. I see it. And it will fill with blood again and yet again and a hundred times again!"*[6]

This incident is told on the last page of *The Track*. Abstracted from the volume's vivid concrete descriptions, the symbolism of the fig-tree and the road seems simplistic. The device of a mad, blind man fortuitously dropping by to deliver the author's message is crude. In the context of the volume, however, the repeated symbols, or images, take on life. The fig-tree represents Barea's yearning for peaceful co-existence between Arab and Spaniard;[7] and the blood-soaked track leading nowhere recalls the cruel reality of corruption and death. As Barea asserts:

> *For the first twenty-five years of this century Morocco was a battle-ground, a brothel, and an immense tavern.*[8]

The embryo of fascism

The tone of *The Track* is quite different from that of *The Forge*. It is not at all lyrical, which is even more striking in the Spanish, where *The Forge* is told in the historic present, unlike the rest of the trilogy. Another major difference is the increase in direct political comment. Barea's understanding at the time of writing (1940–42) of the direction of events is no longer suppressed, as it almost always was in *The Forge*. No longer is the author observing his past through a child's eyes. He was writing it at the same time as *Struggle for the Spanish Soul*, his only book of political analysis. In this book, Barea analyses the nature of Spanish imperial ambitions in 1941, and links them to the history of the occupation of Morocco, with hindsight and also with a more explicit explanation than was appropriate in *The Track*.[9]

Despite the increased political discourse in *The Track*, Barea is still careful not to deviate into abstract commentary. He consistently presents political and historical events through their impact on the daily lives of himself and other soldiers, as if major events were stones thrown into a stream whose weight is only felt as they sink slowly into the current of daily life. One clear example is the arrival of a new High Command. The effect of this political change, which will overturn the soldiers' routine, is shown through a terrible parade in the heat:

> *We had two cases of sunstroke and five of illness. The new High Commissioner had started his career well.*[10]

Nearly all the major political developments of the war are first introduced through a description of their concrete impact on the soldiers. Barea rarely explains an event's significance until he has already presented an illustrative description or anecdote. And sometimes, as in the case of Millán Astray, the reader is left to draw his/her own conclusions, without any authorial comment at all.

General Millán is introduced when the narrator attends a pre-battle parade.[11] The fascist ideology, the brutality of the leader and brutishness of the men are seen and felt. The reader is led to feel the power of reactionary fanaticism in a genuinely shocking moment, when the narrator is moved by Millán's harangue to shout along with the aroused legionaries: "When the Standard shouted in wild enthusiasm, I shouted with them".[12] The socialist, rationalist author was aroused emotionally by the demagogic Millán. Here the author's technique of describing the scene from the participant's point of view is triumphant: it makes it harder for the reader to stand aside, draws him/her too into the scene.

Despite much more political comment than in *The Forge*, Barea retains vividness, pace and characterisation both by use of the key images (the track and the fig tree) and by telling public events through the eyes of the soldiers directly affected. These are methods of fiction, rather than essay or autobiography. And Barea thus maintains, in spite of the differences, a unity of method with the first volume: he does not propagandise directly.

As befits the middle volume of a trilogy, Barea moves forward and backward in time with his political comment. He is interested in clarifying the roots of the Civil War in Morocco <u>and</u> in explaining the causes of the Moroccan War. The following analysis of three pages at the end of the first part illustrates this method.

During his convalescence after typhus, Barea returns to Madrid and there visits his brother's boss, owner of a bakery. This small capitalist explains how he has been ruined by the superior economic power of Count Romanones. Barea makes the point that the old entrenched ruling-class not only uses its power and ruthlessness against the workers, but also against modernising progressive capitalists such as his brother's boss. The boss then starts to express his own liberal views about Morocco. But Barea is not listening. The name of Romanones has set him off on a reminiscence of his time working in Guadalajara. He explains how Motores España was set up: this firm enjoyed a monopoly of supplies to the Army and "free" shares were issued to Romanones and the King. These marginalised the inventor La Cierva, enabling Motores España to bleed the State dry, whilst producing defective goods for the Moroccan War. Barea draws then his conclusion:

> *I had an important and enviable job; the prettiest girls of the small town of Guadalajara were interested in me . . .*
>
> *It seemed fun to be part of it.*
>
> *Now, four years later, I saw the other side of the story . . . Now, with the typhus of Africa still in my bones . . . I saw that the track from . . . Guadalajara had led to Africa.*[13]

Barea demonstrates accomplished skills of narration and compression of material without loss of subtlety in these three pages. He interweaves his own youthful excitement ("it seemed fun to be part of it") on starting his prestigious job at Guadalajara, with the factory's mixed effect on the people of the town; and draws out the links between the old landed aristocracy, the Monarchy, Capital and the war in Morocco. All started from the image of the frustrated modernising baker: a new Spain struggling to throw off the straitjackets of the old.

Barea also looks forward on several occasions in *The Track*. Here, in contrast to *The Forge*, Barea does exploit the benefit of hindsight, and most interestingly in the portrayal of Franco. The theme is announced directly in the chapter called *Dictator in the Making*. First, Barea tells us the story of the unhappy Sanchiz, who had joined the Legion (the *Tercio*) "so as to be killed". Sanchiz tells the narrator:

> *"The* Tercio's *rather like being in a penitentiary. The courageous brute is the master of the jail. And something of this sort has happened to that man {Franco}. He's hated, just as the convicts hate the bravest killer in their jail, and he's obeyed and respected – he imposes himself on all the others – just as the big killer imposes himself on the whole jail. You know how many officers of the Legion have been killed by a shot in the back during an attack. Now, there are many who would wish to shoot Franco in the back, but not one of them has the courage to do it. They're afraid that he might turn his head and see them just when they have taken aim at him."*[14]

It is only after this chilling introduction to the figure of Franco that Barea draws his more general political conclusions. He discusses the problems within the Army and ends the chapter with the explicit statement:

> *Among the "warrior" party was the new Chief of the Foreign Legion {Franco}. And the Legion grew quickly into a State within the State, a cancer within the army . . . from being a hero of this kind to being a rebel – and a Fascist – there is only one step.*[15]

Anti-militarist

Barea's particular type of book, half-way between autobiography and fiction, allows him to pick the best of both genres for his purposes. Techniques of fiction are used to bring to life characters such as Sanchiz; and then history and biography draw out explicit conclusions. But Barea's approach remains what he taught himself when he started to re-write *The Forge*: that the sights, sounds and smells are more effective than direct propaganda. In Morocco these sights, sounds and smells are especially brutal. The whole volume is an analysis of an army in a cruel war, the last major colonial war the Spanish Army fought, one in which generals and common soldiers alike are shown as corrupted, maddened and brutalised.

There was nothing in itself exceptional about Barea's picture of crude reality and denunciation of the war. Marra-López described the intellectual background atmosphere of the time:

> *With the disaster of 1898 still recent . . . the generation called after this date adopted a critical, revisionist approach to Spanish society, with a sincere desire to show reality as it is and at the same time reach the intimate entrails of what it meant to be Spanish.*[16]

Only to repudiate the Moroccan War, there was no need for hindsight. The war polarised Spanish society at the time and constructed a firm majority against the military dictatorship, with which Alfonso XIII had thrown in his lot.[17] Spain's most prestigious intellectuals joined forces with the working-class in their hatred of this war. Unamuno inveighed against the war and the dictatorship from his exile in Saint Jean and became, in Barea's later words, "symbol of the spiritual fight for freedom among the intellectuals of the world".[18]

A distinction needs to be made. Few of these intellectuals were anti-imperialist on the basis of principle. That is to say, they were less interested in the war's effect on the Moroccan people and Spanish working-class than in the question of the destiny of Spain as a nation. As José Marra-López so vividly describes:

> *It is certainly true that when the disaster of 1898 took place . . . this society of petrified structures and beams gnawed through by woodworm, pure appearances of outer walls, was tired, worn out, physically and spiritually ruined, despite the marvellous reserve energy that our people has always drawn on at the most unsuspected moments . . . The longing for truth and realism, for renovation and*

> *implacable criticism, which led Spanish intellectuals to adopt anti-war positions in opposition to new colonial adventures.*[19]

In Arturo Barea the opinions of Spanish intellectuals were always suspect, both in his youth and when writing the trilogy, and had little impact on him. A greater discernible influence on him was the anti-war novels, fashionable in Europe in the wake of the 1914–1918 slaughter. The most famous now is Remarque's *All Quiet on the Western Front*, but Barbusse and Rolland and many others, now forgotten but equally popular authors at the time, were translated into cheap Spanish editions in the 1920s and '30s, for a new, eager reading public.[20] It is very likely that Barea would have read many of these books. He tells us that in Morocco he read Berta von Suttner's pacifist *Lay down Arms!* (an incendiary title for a serving soldier to carry!), for this is the book that Major Tabasco found him reading and advised him to burn:

> *"Now, once put these books into the hands of poor devils who can hardly read and write, and they act as explosives."*[21]

The Track, however, is more than a pacifist novel: Barea goes politically beyond the specific rejection of the Moroccan war and further too than the pacifist rejection of war in general. Gerald Brenan wrote: "Barea was a very humane man who hated violence and cruelty"[22] and undoubtedly rejection of war and bloodshed infuses all Barea's work. He tells us in *The Clash* how he suffered in his childhood a nervous attack at the sight of a man killed in the street. In Morocco, he witnessed the aftermath of the massacre of Anual, and later the Civil War; in Paris in 1938, and England during the Second World War, bombing and his memories of it caused him nervous crises.[23] At times he had to vomit – in that sense, he was a pacifist.

However, *The Track* is not only pacifist and anti-militarist, from the point of view of the deleterious effects on Spanish society of the war. Unamuno and Ortega y Gasset polemicised against the Moroccan War because of their desire to renew Spain. Barea went further in *The Track* by showing the rights and humanity of the Moroccans. This is evident not so much in explicit statements but in some of the people he meets, such as the chieftain Sidi Yusef and the old blind man at the end; and most of all, in the imagery of the fig-tree. In this, Barea's political reach is longer than that of these intellectuals, and longer too than Sender's in *Imán*. However, Barea was not, then or later, a full-blown anti-imperialist. His retreat to national patriotic arguments in his activities and writings during the Civil War (discussed in Chapter II), arguments that he used both before and after writing *The Track*, shows his lack of political consistency. But the view we have described exists in *The Track* and adds an important dimension to the book. The Barea who followed the tradition of "the writers of 1898" of investigating the reality of Spain was capable, at concrete moments, of a sharp shift leftwards, whether towards anti-imperialism (Morocco) or social revolution (the Civil War).

It should not be forgotten that Barea wrote *The Track* at the start of the 1940s, which meant he benefited from other fictional accounts of Morocco, such as Díaz Fernández's *El blocao* (1928) and Sender's great first novel, *Imán* (1930), which both appeared much earlier than Barea's (1943). Barea took advantage of writing many years later to assimilate these two works (and others he might have read) and to reflect on the Moroccan War in the light of the Civil War that followed. Those reflections help give *The Track* greater political depth than *Imán* or *El Blocao*.[24]

The great men of Spanish literature

In the middle of *The Track*, Barea veers off on an apparent tangent, which in fact helps him to explain his independence of criterion and his rejection of intellectuals. His pride at belonging to the people combined with a vein of crude anti-intellectualism. This "tangential" chapter contrasts the brutish anti-literate atmosphere of the army and the rarefied air of literary circles in the capital, to both of which he was equally hostile. It is a further example of his "*double refusal to submit*", that is to say, rejection of the real options open to him, reminiscent of his childhood stubbornness, suggesting his constant, restless search for a way out.[25]

Barea recalled in this chapter, entitled *Face to the Sea*, how he and his friend Cabanillas (who was to become a successful journalist) had embarked on literary careers in 1913 by sending contributions to the press. The two then sought introductions to "the great men of Spanish literature".[26] The descriptions of the two young aspirants' encounters with these *maestros* are among the best of Barea's *costumbrista* passages. He first meets a hack writer: "who bore with a swagger his self-chosen title of 'The Last Bohemian' . . . incessantly sucking his pipe which, at times, he filled with cigarette stubs".[27] This cynical character advises Barea to write pornography or plays. Barea then investigates the *Ateneo*, where:

> *. . . grave gentlemen were discussing Plato's political theory or the esoteric significance of Don Quixote. I possessed neither the necessary knowledge or interest.*[28]

Barea then starts to explore the *tertulias* (discussion circles) of literary figures. The descriptions of these are perhaps where Barea did earn the epithet of those 1950s critics who accused Barea of having a chip on his shoulder.[29] His resentment and anger at lack of opportunity emerged in a malicious sketch of Benavente, who reclines on a sofa in the Café de Castilla while his talentless acolytes talk endlessly about "Benavente's superlative prose".[30]

Valle-Inclán was monarch of another café:

> *When we entered Don Ramón was on his feet, leaning over the table, his big rabbinical beard fluttering like a pennant, his tortoise-shell glasses ceaselessly turning from one face to another, to see whether anybody would dare to contradict him.*[31]

The young Barea tells us (of course!) that one day he rose to challenge Don Ramón. The accounts of these encounters acquire allegorical proportions: the "last bohemian" represents writing sold cynically as a commodity; in the *Ateneo*, we see the dead tones of abstract discourse for discourse's sake; in Benavente, smug triumph; and in Valle-Inclán, a rage against mediocrity. From Valle-Inclán, Barea received the classic advice of a *maestro* to young writers:

> *" . . . if you want to learn how to write, stay at home and study . . . don't come to this kind of gathering . . . Here you won't reap any profit except perhaps a petty job in a newspaper office and the habit of swallowing insults."*[32]

At the end of his account of thwarted literary ambitions, Barea tells us sparely: "I gave up writing."[33]

However, in 1921 in Morocco, after his typhus and the confrontation with the violent death of others, Barea wanted to write again. It would not be until after another war crisis sixteen years later that he finally succeeded in starting to write seriously (see Chapter II). He first had to follow his own sinuous path, through the practical exigencies of earning a living and the struggle to find where he belonged.

Heart of Darkness

After these political and historical comments, I want to look closer at Barea's method in this polemical onslaught against the Moroccan War. John Devlin's reaction expresses the view of most readers:

*{*The Track *is}* . . . *of a naked and often crude brutality, born of its time, a product of the violence of the epoch.*[34]

Crudeness and brutality was indeed born of the "midnight of the century" through which Barea lived. But experiencing it is not the same as writing it. Barea is exceptional among his contemporaries for this crudeness and brutality expressed on the page. It is not that his eye is cruel (rather, it is tender), but that he looks at horror unflinchingly, without blinking. His is the gaze of someone, we should remind ourselves, who needed to see clearly in order both to understand and to overcome his own fear and encroaching madness. Putting on paper these horrific events was a therapy. Importantly (and this connects with his previously-discussed gut rejection of intellectuals) his eye, and therefore his tone and style, is not ironic, not distancing in the way that most intellectuals learn to view the world. Barea's descriptions are as close to the actual event as black words on white paper can be.

Barea saw a scene as a participant, but at the same time could describe it calmly, as a witness, without partisan passion. A comparison with Sender's *Imán* may help bring out these qualities. Look at these two passages:

1. *It smells of fermented manure. There is a sudden break in the ramp and, six feet below, several corpses, which two old women are stripping with hasty skill, while a Moor, getting on in years, smokes his small pipe of kif.*[35]
2. *In the back room were five dead men. They were smeared with their own blood, face, hands, uniform, hair, and boots. The blood had made pools on the floor, stripes on the walls, blobs on the ceiling, sprawling splashes in all the corners.*[36]

The first is from Sender; the second, Barea. They are describing the same historical event. From two passages alone, one cannot extrapolate two methods, but one can indicate the tendency of Sender towards longer phrases, more intellectual language ("with hasty skill" – "con presurosa habilidad") and the striking, unusual image (the two old women, the Arab smoking). Barea accumulates detail in short phrases, straining for the literal reality of the scene. The above quote from *The Track* continues:

On every clean, white place it had painted hands with five or two or one finger, fingerless palms and shapeless thumbs. A table and a few chairs were turned into scattered kindling wood. Countless flies, droning incessantly, were sucking blood from the thumb printed on the wall and from the lips of the corpse in the left hand corner.[37]

Few war writers have known how to express horror better than Barea. He does it by a very literal description, piling on so much detail that (as indicated when discussing *Valor y miedo*) he creates a nightmare atmosphere that becomes almost surreal.

In *The Track*, the narrator was allocated to the task of burying the mutilated, rotting bodies. The passage above is part of that description, the reality denying the dream of harmony between Spaniard and Moroccan, which Barea expresses through the fig-tree and the spring. After being immersed in the stench and horror of those days, he collapsed with typhus. In a passage of *The Clash*, while talking of later horrors during the Civil War, Barea reviewed what he had seen in Morocco:

> *When I was twenty-four years old, and I saw the room in the barracks of the Civil Guard at Melilla, which looked as though the dead men leaning over the window-sills and in the corners had splashed each other with their blood as during a battle in a swimming pool in the summer, I had vomited.*[38]

Barea shows us what happened, and THEN the effect on himself (vomiting). The two are separate, whereas in *Imán,* Sender is much more subjective. Barea had said in the introduction to *The Track*:

> *I wanted to describe the shocks which had scarred my mind . . . (which) in different individual forms but from the same collective causes, scarred and shaped the minds of other Spaniards too.*[39]

The shocks are the same, but on each mind the shock may have a different impact. It was Barea's objectives that made him more particular than Sender about separating the event from its effect.

Barea's writing does not have the richness and symbolism of Sender's fiction. There is an aspect of Barea, however, that approaches Sender's imagination: when he dwells on the morbid. Chapter II has commented on the scene in "Carabanchel" of the soldier driven mad by the rotting donkey.[40] In *The Forge* Barea used images of skulls and reburial of corpses to fuel his attacks on the Church.[41] In *The Track* he often shows a macabre interest in scenes of violence or death. In the hospital, where he is recovering from typhus, he recounts with a certain zest the deaths he witnesses.[42] Most clearly, attending the pre-battle parade addressed by Millán Astray, Barea is fascinated by Millán's dominance of his soldiers not by rank but by physical violence and prowess, as when Millán screams at a soldier: "I am more than you, more of a man than you!"[43]

Barea dwells on such scenes with the fascination of a peace-loving man enthralled by a darker side to himself, his country's history and human behaviour. He could be swept along by Millán's blood-thirsty rhetoric:

> *"What are you? The Betrothed of Death. You are the gentlemen of the Legion. You have washed yourselves clean, for you have come here to die . . . Long Live Death!* Viva la Muerte!*"*[44]

Millán's fanatical rhetoric sways Barea's emotions (and he is brave to allow us to perceive this) as well as those of the criminals and fugitives that make up the Legion.

This interest in the morbid stands in strong contrast to his rational self, which understood very well the forces (Church, Army, Capital) ranged against him and how to fight them, forces which he analysed in *Struggle for the Spanish Soul*. In the following passage from this book, Barea summarised the ideology used by Franco's regime:

> *The decline of Spain began when the national consciousness was lost, and with it the spirit of universal mission . . . Politics became a lucrative business, national ambitions were forgotten, individual interests broke up the State, anarchy ran riot . . . When Spain was completely exhausted, she fought her last wars and finally, a prey to inner strife and Marxist experiments, sank into the degradation from which Franco and* Falange *have rescued her.*[45]

The morbid passages of the trilogy show that Barea could enter emotionally this sinister world of Spain's "spiritual and cultural mission".[46] And it is to his credit that he occasionally takes us there with the curiosity of a child (the skulls), the temporary fervour of a soldier (Millán's speech), or the dull, passive self-hatred after his nervous collapse in Madrid in 1937.

The Track contains a sustained analysis of the Army. Barea portrays a world of coarseness and brutality, in language, views, ethics and behaviour. And he makes us feel the reality of "this brothel and immense tavern":

> *. . . It is frighteningly easy for a man to slide back into an animal state.*[47]

The Army is the main institution examined in *The Track*, just as the Church was in *The Forge*. Barea's view is quite clear and uncontroversial: the Moroccan campaign was a rotten adventure promoted by the Army and the gang of speculators, starting with the King, that ran Spain.

Unlike *The Forge*, *The Track* is an accumulation of anecdotes. Among the tales of everyday corruption and swindles institutionalised in the colonial army, Barea highlights the plight of the common conscript, the victim of such corruption:

> *That mass of illiterate peasants commanded by irresponsible officers was the backbone of Spain's Moroccan field armies.*[48]

The narrator listens to these conscripts' stories. Some of them explain the circumstances which had dumped them in the Army. These passages of hunger and corruption in the selection of recruits echo *Imán* and anticipate the violence and poverty of Pascual Duarte's childhood. Later, Barea quoted Gerald Brenan with approval:

> *As one reads {Spanish literature} one cannot fail to be struck by the fact that from the Middle Ages to the 18th century the note of hunger runs persistently through the novels.*[49]

In his later literary criticism, Barea often comments on this theme of hunger in Spain's literature, a constant right through to the second half of the twentieth century, and on the associated question of illiteracy, which meant that so few of Spain's citizens could read those parts of its literature which addressed the question of their hunger. Barea understood in his own life these twin hungers, for food and for learning.

In *The Track*, the Army's "mass of illiterate peasants" are not only not educated; they are brutalised and slaughtered. The recruits are cannon-fodder and a breeding-ground for fascism, but there is a more positive side in their incipient hatred and rejection of the Army:

> *The general patted his shoulder.*
> *The peasant swung round like a startled beast:*
> *"Don't touch me, God damn you!"*[50]

In his wholesale denunciation of the Army at all levels, Barea is as scrupulous to distinguish between the individual and the institution, as he was when dealing with the Church in *The Forge*. Just as there were priests whom he liked and respected; so there were soldiers like Córcoles[51] or Sanchiz he liked and officers such as Tabasco whose views are right-wing but who is correct in his treatment of others. Even when he talks of the villains of the piece: Primo de Rivera, the mad Millán or cruel Franco, Barea is rigorous in avoiding Manicheism. He illustrates the attractiveness of Primo's slap-happy style.[52] He notes Franco's renowned courage and lack of personal corruption.[53]

The officers are divided by Barea into three categories: the "warriors" like Franco full of ideas of patriotic honour and trying to win the war at all cost; Government supporters who just wanted a quiet life; and those who desired the return of the good old days of full-scale corruption without risk. And for this last activity there were many opportunities which started right at the top, as the anecdote quoted of the factory in Guadalajara shows. An Army contract, whether for planes or condensed milk, was a licence to print money. And all down the line, the officers and sergeants took their cut. A large part of *The Track* is taken up with tragi-comic stories of corruption, such as the sale of horses to the enemy, or the cook giving short rations and creaming off the extra supplies. The sergeants' ingenuity is not devoted to defeating the Moroccans, but to juggling the accounts to cover for missing stores.[54]

Flaws

In highlighting *The Track*'s unity of structure, its analysis of the forces behind the Army, its polemical *tour-de-force* against that hopeless army and the vivid language of the illustrative anecdotes, flaws which prevent *The Track* attaining the stature of *The Forge* should not be ignored.

First, there is not always a happy mixture of styles and tones in the volume. John Miller, who has written the most detailed study of *The Track*, comments that it has a limited vocabulary "with brilliant moments . . . sometimes somewhat shrill".[55] One example of a passage which is somewhat shrill is the section already mentioned concerning Millán. There is plenty of evidence to confirm the exact truthfulness of Barea's portrayal of Millán. But on the page the literal description sometimes sounds shrill and forced: a literal transcription of reality does not always function in fiction.

Secondly, concrete example occasionally becomes merely an excuse for an opinion or a historical résumé. The following is an example from the chapter *Coup d'Etat*:

> *One day I met my old companion Antonio Calzada . . . He was out of work. What he told me was the old story of war prosperity and post-war crisis.*[56]

Barea then describes for a page the dire straits of office workers after the war, but of Antonio Calzada we hear no more. He remains a cipher, an example not a character.

A third weakness is the inverse side of one of Barea's main strengths: his use of interesting anecdotes to make a point. An example of inadequate use of anecdote is his description of the gypsy family in the train.[57] Schematically, this has its place in the novel: the gypsies are smugglers, another section of the Spanish society Barea is seeking to survey. But the incident comes from nowhere and goes nowhere: it is too obviously just a good story inserted into the main narrative, as would occur in a picaresque novel.

The account of the gypsies also demonstrates a fourth weakness in Barea, which became much more damaging in *The Broken Root* and in his broadcasts and articles from Britain in the 1940s. In these later years, when his creative seam was exhausted, he often lapsed into an easy stereotyping on the basis of race or origin.

A fifth flaw of *The Track* is the narrator's sentimentalism in the portrayal of his mother, a problem that does not arise in *The Forge*, as narration from the child's point of view makes the admiration acceptable. In *The Track*, she serves as a counterpoint of love and tolerance to the harshness of life in Morocco. An image of the best, most loving of mothers, she never comes to life in any literary sense. Barea's famed objectivity deserts him when he deals with his mother: she is a blurred image of goodness. This inability to treat her artistically may well have been, as José Ortega suggests, because the fatherless Barea was obsessed with his mother as the only point of stability in his chaotic world. Ortega links his mother to the image in *The Track* of the fig-tree root "as origin and conservation of things".[58]

However, the most striking (and sixth) defect in *The Track* occurs when Barea lets his anecdotes get the better of him and the book degenerates into a type of "Confessions of an army sergeant". Barea himself was a man who loved to sit in bars and tell anecdotes. He comments in the introduction to *The Track*:

> *There are stories, true stories, which I love to tell to my friends, but have not included in this book, such as "How I entered the Sacred City in Disguise together with the General," or "How I leapt naked from a bedroom into a Moorish Café." These would have been suitable tales for an anecdotal autobiography which puts the highlights on the spectacular and amusing; but to me they carried no deeper association, either personal or general, and so I left them out.*[59]

As Barea may well have been uncomfortably aware when typing this foreword after the book's completion, the accounts of his liaison with Luisa the brothel-keeper are precisely this sort of "suitable tale . . . (with) . . . no deeper association". The story of Luisa dominates Chapter 3 and is a boastful piece of yellow journalism. And when purpose is lost, the style degenerates:

> *She beat against her breast so that the ruby jumped.*
> *"Hit you? No. I would have spat in your face and left.*
> *"I would have killed you," she said after a silence. "It would have been better to beat me . . . "*[60]

This is pure melodrama. The objection is not that it is untrue. Far-fetched as it sounds, the story of Luisa may well have been true. Yet it does not fit into the volume's framework. It neither advances the account of the Army, nor of Barea's own sentimental education. And nor does its boastful tone have the necessary ring of truth. The characters "Luisa" and "the homosexual" become clichéd ciphers round the dominant figure of the hero.

By looking at this rare passage where Barea's objectivity collapses into subjective fantasy, we can better appreciate the sustained nature of his objectivity in the rest of *The Track* and the trilogy.[61] At the end we do not recall Luisa, but what he succeeded in chronicling:

> *. . . the filth of the hospital, the gory nightmare of the massacres, the technique of petty graft, the boredom of endless marches, the boredom of night life, the noise of taverns, the unquestioning comradeship of the army, the smell of the sea at dawn, and the glare of the African sun – all this made us what we are, and this I have chronicled.*[62]

VI

The Clash

The Flame of Revolution

The Clash, for an unexplained reason titled in Spanish *La llama (The Flame)*, tells the story of Barea in the Civil War. The central theme, the clash of classes, giving the volume its title, is evoked in this passage about the destruction of Brunete, one of Barea's childhood *pueblos*:

> *It seemed to me a symbol of our war: the forlorn village making history by being destroyed in a clash between those who kept all the Brunetes of my country arid, dry, dusty, and poor as they were, and the others who dreamed of transforming the dust-gray villages of Castile, of all Spain, into homesteads of free, clean, gay men.*[1]

This Civil War theme makes it for the new non-Spanish reader the most immediately attractive of Barea's books. The account, in the first quarter of the volume, of the election campaign in Novés is a brilliant portrait of one small village, which yet brings into focus the entire array of social forces moving towards Civil War. And the subsequent quick-fire descriptions of the war's opening days contain action sequences that Martin Scorsese might be proud of.

I have dealt elsewhere with some themes central to this volume. Barea's emotional reaction to the horrors of war and his mental breakdown, the immediate catalysts of his writing, are discussed in Chapter II; his writing and the nature of the trilogy as a whole, in Chapter III. This chapter tackles three main questions: Barea's political views in the crucible of Civil War; the nature of his sexual relationships; and something of the mechanics of Barea's writing, his structuring of the novel.

Like many novels about adolescence and a writer's coming-of-age, Arturo Barea's trilogy ends at the point where the writer, having been formed, or in this case "forged", embarks on writing the very novel being read. The difference is that Barea's trilogy was written twenty years later in the writer's life than the normal "Portrait of the artist as a young man". Thus, though the volume retains all the fresh spontaneity of that type of novel, it also contains the experience of a man in early middle-age who has already led a varied life.

Whereas the first two volumes deal in turn with childhood and coming-of-age, *The Clash* is the book of that early middle-age. It contains the rupture, the break that both changed the private world of the author (the war made him a writer) and cleaved a deep wound into his entire generation (no Spaniard was unchanged by this massive catastrophe). The volume also shows the crucial changes in the narrator, when briefly he finds fulfilment in his political activity and, more lastingly, resolves with Ilsa his lifelong crises of sexual relationships.

The first half of *The Clash* provides a masterly overview of the events preceding the Civil War and of its opening days. The description of the electoral organization for the Popular Front in Novés is one of the very best passages of Barea's writing. Exciting, full of action and contrast, it achieves his self-set aim for the whole trilogy of describing his own development in relation to the experience of millions of Spaniards; and of illuminating those common experiences through the prism of his own activity. Barea maintains this tension for the first ten chapters (first part) of *The Clash*, but then the vision narrows from describing the whole to only a smaller part of the war: that part seen from Barea's job in the censorship. In the words of José Marra-López:

> *Now the story focuses on his work in the censorship, telling us what he saw through his job, which means the big opportunity to become the novel of the civil war is lost.*[2]

Other critics also touch on the failure of *The Clash* to be **THE** great novel of the Spanish Civil War. Fernández Gutiérrez and Herrera Rodrigo rebut this plaint:

> *If* The Clash *fails to become, because of this limited vision, the "novel of the war", it's because its author never intended it to be so. We are talking about the third part of a trilogy . . .*[3]

As such, the trilogy continues to deal with Barea's own life and what he himself had felt, seen and heard. Where, as was inevitable in the middle of a cataclysmic war, his own view only included a fraction of the whole, then Barea's narrative is perforce more limited.

Nevertheless, the change to a more exclusively personal account does damage the coherence of the volume and of the trilogy as a whole. The second part of *The Clash* on the Madrid censorship is great first-hand material for any student of the Civil War, but represents a break in continuity with the rest of the trilogy. The problem lies in Barea's change of perspective: the narrator is no longer moving between two worlds. Thus these pages lack the dramatic and narrative tension of his intermediate position as a sergeant in the Moroccan War, when he could both see and feel what it was like to be a common soldier or a higher officer (*The Track*); or of his position as a child in a garret at week-ends and a comfortable flat during the week (*The Forge*).

Political views

By the second part of *The Clash*, Barea has become a leading official of the Republican Government's bureaucracy. He greets delegations of visiting dignitaries; he meets famous writers; he hobnobs with Generals such as Miaja, Regler or "Carlos". Barea appears conscious of this narrowing of focus and seeks to correct it by passages such as the visits with Ilsa to Serafín's tavern, the death of his adjutant or the comic interludes of Ángel's adventures and wound in the buttock. Though these are all attempts by Barea to maintain the trilogy's continuity of vision, the problem cannot be solved just by shifts back and forth from the privileged world to poorer environments. The whole narrative focus has changed because Barea is telling the story from a different perspective.

The final chapters of the novel, after his dismissal as censor, lack continuity with the rest of the trilogy to an even greater degree. Barea's personal course parted company completely with the destiny of his compatriots, as he left Spain while the Civil War was still raging. The dramatic structure which sustains the trilogy as a whole, rooted in Barea's "double vision" and his intermediate position in society, is broken. In the second half of *The Clash*, Barea is only writing interesting autobiography. Consequently, *The Clash* fails on its own terms: it is a broken-backed book. This is different from bemoaning that *The Clash* is not the "Great Novel" of the Civil War. It is a criticism in terms of Barea's own aims and in contrast with the accomplishments of the first two volumes.

Indeed for many, *The Clash*, as well as being among the earliest, is one of the very best books about the Civil War. This is to look at it through a completely different lens, as the historian Burnett Bolloten did, writing to Barea in 1950:

> *. . . Your magnificent book "The Forging of a Rebel" . . . contains most valuable historical data that exist in none of the books yet published . . . I can talk with authority, as I have devoted myself to reading . . . over 1,800 books about the Civil War and Revolution published in a dozen countries.*[4]

And the 1930s Comintern official and International Brigader, the novelist Ralph Bates, wrote: "Barea has given . . . a wholly credible account of the first year of the war".[5]

These two quotes – from vehement anti-Communist and loyal Communist, respectively – are praise indeed for Barea's accuracy and sincerity in his factual account of events of the Civil War. Though the praise is justified, and his sincerity is patent, this does not mean his views should be accepted uncritically. Barea's political views and actions need to be examined before we can accept his "wholly credible account" and "most valuable data".

In 1931, after about fourteen years away from union activity, Barea became active again in the UGT, encouraged by Carlos Rubiera, the secretary of its National Office-workers' Federation (*Federación nacional de empleados de oficina*).[6] Barea's collaboration with Rubiera, a left socialist and leader of the Madrid Socialist Group (*Agrupación Socialista Madrileña*), suggests that he sympathised with the left wing of the PSOE, led by the veteran UGT leader, Largo Caballero. Equally, though, Barea was an admirer of Caballero's rival, the leader of the PSOE centre, Indalecio Prieto – perhaps because Prieto had lived in Barea's beloved and rowdy Lavapiés when he first came to Madrid in 1918 or because Barea later considered him "the most intelligent politician in Spain".[7]

It is tempting to see Barea's sometimes precipitous reactions as signs of revolutionary views. He was on occasion a firebrand: as when he had stormed out of the bank in a temper[8] or when, twenty-three years later, by his own account he took part in the attack on the Montaña barracks.[9] Certainly, whenever his dignity or "manhood" was touched on, he reacted with passion.

Passion and extreme reactions, however, do not define political positions, which are based on consistent action. Barea was not a Marxist, although he used some of the analytical tools of Marxism in *Struggle for the Spanish Soul*. But this means little, as several terms and categories of Marxism were common parlance for all shades of the European Left in the 1930s; and the PSOE, despite being in most ways a typical moderate social-democratic party, frequently used the rhetoric of workers' power and revolution. This was because the schism in the Second International during the First World War had affected Spain, a non-combatant country, much less.

Unlike Ilsa, formed in the revolutionary movement over two decades, Barea had no theoretical basis for his political views. Nevertheless, it is startling that Barea nowhere defines with any clarity where he stood within the left, when the very subject of *The Clash* is War and Revolution, his job was to read detailed reports on the War and he spent a lot of time in the taverns of Emiliano, Serafín and others, perpetually arguing politics.[10]

In general terms, Barea was clearer than the Socialist Party leaders. He refused to work with the Government at the outbreak of the War because he saw the Left Republican dominance as signifying a willingness to negotiate with the military rebels. Like the working masses of Madrid, Barea understood:

> *This was war, civil war and a revolution. It could not finish until the country had been converted into a Fascist or into a Socialist state. I did not have to choose between the two. The choice had been taken for me by my whole life. Either a Socialist revolution would win or I would be among the vanquished.*[11]

He saw clearly that the old political game was over. He was right that "the vanquished would be shot or locked up in a prison cell",[12] the fate of Miguel/Rafael, Barea's rebellious brother and intimate friend, and his political mentor Carlos Rubiera.

Beyond this general attitude, Barea's lack of precision about his views means that his political comments during the first 15 months of the Civil War, which he spent in Madrid, can best be seen as reflecting the rapidly shifting political situations and alliances than as reliable comments on them. Nevertheless, certain features of his politics are clear. He said later:

> *. . . on that night of the 18th of July, 1936 . . . I was not only what is called an emotional socialist. I had the membership card of a party in my pocket, I belonged to my trade union. Though I played no particular rôle in either party or trade union – I knew I would not be good at it – I was an active party worker who took part in discussions and defended the point of view of my group. I tried to be disciplined and to win new members.*[13]

Barea was probably a party member during this period for the only time in his life.[14] As the individualist and "emotional socialist" he actually was, he was not a member of the PSOE before the mid-30s and almost certainly left it in 1936/7. Definitely not a party-joining man, he later never joined the Labour Party in England, though many of his friends and Ilsa were members. He preferred to act as a clown at Labour Party fêtes.

In July 1936, the rebellion of the military was halted by the outbreak of a popular revolution. Barea describes this both in *The Clash* and later in the only political speech he is known to have given in English:

> *The night of the outbreak of Franco's rebellion, I witnessed one of the most stir-*

> *ring things I have ever seen: I saw and felt the force of spontaneous mass solidarity . . . the political labels were no longer important. But all of us who were willing to fight against the attack of the fascists had also one and the same positive aim that night. We knew that we had not only to defeat Fascism, but also to carry through the revolution which would forever free our Spain from the hands of a few masters . . .* [15]

For him, as for so many rank-and-file socialists and trade unionists, unity in struggle was the key. He assumed the slogan, ubiquitous in the February 1936 Election campaign, of "*Unión de Hermanos Proletarios*", U-H-P (Union of Proletarian Brothers), the rallying shout of the 1934 Asturias uprising. And he lamented, in a *cri de coeur*:

> *Why was it that the men in the street, the common people, the workers, the farm laborers, and the miners, were always ready to get together – and not their leaders?*[16]

In February 1936, Barea showed this unity in practice, assembling a platform for the Novés election meeting, which included an Anarchist, a Socialist, a Communist and a Republican. The inclusion of the Communist might be surprising, given the small PCE's slight influence at the time, and is suggestive of Barea's sympathies towards the fledgling party. He tells us as much when he explains that he sought help in setting up the Novés meeting from Antonio, as well as Rubiera. Antonio was a clerk in the UGT and "a minor official" of the PCE.[17]

Then, in response to the military uprising of July 17, while the Government, made up predominantly of Left Republicans, hesitated, Barea was one of tens of thousands in Madrid who at first milled about in the streets, then went to the *Casa del Pueblo* to demand arms, and next day took part in the decisive mass assault on the Montaña barracks.

As a Morocco veteran, Barea soon found a role training a clerical workers' militia for the UGT, to be known as the *Pluma* (Pen) battalion. Rapidly, the unity of that February 1936 and then the revolutionary mobilisation of July 1936, which so inspired Barea and millions of others, disintegrated, as in the following weeks the different "political labels" divided forces within the anti-fascist coalition. Barea expressed his frustration with all the parties, which, he believed, in building themselves, placed their own interests above those of the cause: "Party pride seemed stronger than the feeling of common defense".[18] His main anger was reserved for indiscriminate Popular Tribunals and murders ascribed to "anarchists" in the early weeks of the war.[19]

On August 7, he started to work with the Communists in organising the black-out. By the end of August, he had finished training *La Pluma* and entered into fuller collaboration with the Communists: "The Communist Party had taken the first big step towards the formation of an army".[20] Like many others, Barea felt that the Communists were the only force seriously trying both to stop indiscriminate killing and to construct an army sufficient to defeat Franco. With the authorisation of "Carlos", commander of the Fifth Regiment, which in these early days was the spearhead of Communist military power, Barea went to Toledo to try and arrange for grenades and ammunition to be transferred to Madrid. He failed, but on his return found a message from his old friend Antonio: through PCE sponsorship, he was offered a post in the Press Department of the Foreign Ministry, censoring despatches from foreign press correspondents. He started this job during the days after Largo Caballero came to power on September 12, 1936, and held it for 12 months until after Caballero had been deposed.[21]

At this stage, there was no contradiction between Barea's left socialism and his PCE contacts. They stood together in their commitment to broad unity and the defence of Madrid. However, Largo Caballero as Prime Minister was a terrible disappointment to his myriad supporters. Instead of pushing through with the Spanish Revolution he had long advocated with the fiery rhetoric that had led some of his followers to dub him the "Spanish Lenin", he pursued in Government a right-wing Popular Front policy. Helen Graham, in her original study of the PSOE in the war, summarises:

> *Throughout its period in office (September 1936–May 1937), the socialist left allied itself with non-proletarian political forces and adopted policies which facilitated the restoration of the bourgeois Republic.*[22]

During the crisis night of November 7, 1936, when the Government left for Valencia as the fascists were entering the outskirts of Madrid, Barea stayed at his post. The press, he felt, had to be censored: i.e., lies had to be controlled and the truth had to get out to the world. It was a time when several journalists' eagerness for the city to fall led them to file stories that it already had fallen. Indignant at the Government's flight and at reporters' dishonesty, Barea sought out the *Junta de Defensa* (Defence Council) for orders. He found the old socialist Wenceslao Carrillo, who irascibly told him:

> *"How the hell should I know {where the Junta is}? Miaja's the master, and Miaja's running round the town and letting off shots".*[23]

Carrillo told Barea to go to "the Party" to find information. Significantly, Barea's allegiance had changed:

> *We did not go to the Socialist Party, which was what Wenceslao Carrillo meant. I had lost all confidence in its power of assuming responsibility and authority in a difficult situation . . . We went to the Provincial Committee of the Communist Party.*[24]

Barea's political trajectory had followed that of many Socialists, who supported the Communists, not because of their overall political strategy, but because they were disciplined and effective, and who thought that: "it seemed obvious that no post of any importance in Madrid should remain abandoned."[25]

For a month after the famous halting of the fascist advance in the outskirts of Madrid, Barea, while working flat out in the Censorship, was buffeted between the orders of his boss in the Foreign Ministry, Rubio Hidalgo, insisting from Valencia that Barea was under his control and should therefore go to Valencia; and the Madrid *Junta de Defensa* telling him to stay in Madrid. On December 6, he finally went to Valencia for three weeks to resolve the question. Ilsa later joined him; when they came back at the New Year, Álvarez del Vayo, the Foreign Minister sympathetic to the PCE, had overruled Rubio Hidalgo. Barea was now in charge of the Madrid censorship and Ilsa his deputy.

To reach Valencia, where his Communist sponsors were to help confirm his position, ironically Barea had to rely on old anarchist friends for a car and safe-conduct. Being a native of Madrid, a genuinely non-sectarian activist and not a party member had their advantages. In Valencia, Ilsa had her first of two serious brushes with the security police. She was briefly arrested on December 27 after being denounced as a Trotskyist spy by a journalist she hardly knew.[26] It was an intimation of her vulnerability. She was a former Austrian CP member, had been critical of the CP and followed an independent line.[27] However, for the first several months of 1937, both she and Arturo were to enjoy the protection of the PCE and their Moscow advisers. The Russian journalist with powerful connections, Mikhail Koltzov, Soviet general "Goliev" (Goriev) and Miaja, the Spanish General in charge of the defence of Madrid, supported them.[28]

There was not just conflict about who controlled the censorship, but a different, though linked, tension about just how to censor. The initial defensive and bureaucratic reflex of the censorship had been to blue-pencil anything negative about the Republic. When Barea started his job,

> *Our orders were strict and over-simple: we had to cut out everything that did not indicate a victory of the Republican Government.*[29]

The journalists played every trick in the book to get through their messages. Barea hated a lot of the right-wing journalists, complacently self-satisfied at the rebels' advances on Toledo and Madrid. At the same time, "I felt convinced that our news and censorship policy was clumsy and futile".[30] Under the influence of Ilsa, he came to see his job as to allow the truth to be told and to stop lies going out. The common idea of a censor, such as Franco's censors in both war and dictatorship, is that their job is to stop the truth being told, to limit information so as to deceive. Barea turned this on its head. He saw it was unrealistic to conceal the truth about something negative. It could only bring the Republic into disrepute when, from the rebel side, a piece of news was known and reported, but this was denied by the Republicans.

This conflict had its ups and downs throughout Barea's year in the censorship. Ilsa's and Arturo's independence of criteria (as well as sheer weariness and, in Arturo's case, bad health and depression) brought them into frequent conflict with the Valencia censorship and their Madrid bosses. Through Ilsa's initiative, at the end of November, Barea decided to permit reports on the Government raid on the German embassy in Madrid, which found papers to prove that German "non-intervention" was a farce: the embassy was financing and assisting the Fifth Column within Madrid. The furious Koltzov threatened them with court-martial for publicising the delicate raid: delicate because it was a clear breach of diplomatic immunity. The next day, though, Barea and Ilsa's policy of not censoring the truth was widely praised: the world had been able to read the Republican version of the raid (and not just German protests) in their morning papers. Koltzov apologised; Rubio was delighted.[31]

The censors followed up this triumph by authorising much fuller reports from the front line. The legend of the International Brigades as the saviours of Madrid was born in this initiative, "an audacious step and an immediate success".[32] It is not too exaggerated to say that the Republican Government learnt from its Madrid censors' initiatives to use propaganda to its benefit.[33]

Communists and "Trotskyists"

However, there were always to be conflicts. Arturo and Ilsa were eventually sacked from the censorship not because of these conflicts (they were only the excuse), but because of the changed political situation. After the defeat of the anarchists and POUM in the Barcelona May Days and the consequent fall of Largo Caballero on 15 May, 1937, the PCE moved to take greater control of the censorship, as part of its increasing influence in the new Government, led by Juan Negrín. Constancia de la Mora, a secret PCE member and the new head of the Censorship in Valencia, visited Madrid in August and arranged for Arturo and Ilsa to go on holiday. In Altea they received a letter from Rubio giving them paid "indefinite leave 'for the benefit of our physical and moral recovery'".[34] Their reaction to this polite dismissal-bribe was to return post-haste to Madrid to find that Arturo was still radio broadcaster/censor, by Miaja's order; but they found themselves no longer press censors or employees of the Foreign Ministry.[35]

The new Censorship was to reverse the advances made by Barea and Ilsa. De la Mora had a particularly narrow view of censorship, which essentially involved suppressing anything that opposed the PCE line, something which had led to her being sacked briefly in early Summer 1937, when she censored a Government dispatch because the PCE disagreed with it.[36]

Nowhere does Barea mention this, but his association with Caballero supporters like Rubiera would have been remembered in the period after May 1937, when the PCE and Prieto supporters within the PSOE were working hard to root out all *caballeristas* from positions of power or influence. Unlike Barea, the PCE were not at all sentimental and quite happily dispensed with Barea when he was no longer of use, despite his status as one of the heroes who had stayed at his post on November 7, 1936. Similarly, the enemies of Ilsa were able to revive their accusations of Trotskyism.

Rosario, de la Mora's new appointment as Censor, introduced Barea to the new Civil Governor, Miaja's replacement, seeking to get him confirmed in his post as radio broadcaster. But Barea behaved badly, shouting and screaming. He could not stand the well-fed Socialist Governor and his banquet. Ironically, he who twelve months before had started to work with the Communists, because they represented order against anarchist terror and discipline against fascist terror, now found himself on the side of disorder:

> *. . . I burst into a loud, incoherent, desperate harangue, with accusations against sated, reactionary bureaucrats . . . I belonged to the impossible, intractable people, and I did not belong to the hedged-in administrators.*[37]

Later in Barcelona, Barea was unhappy with his own "impossible" reactions. He reflected uncomfortably that he had been too rigid in his approach to the bureaucracy:

> *. . . after all, I had worked with it successfully in the service of patents whose benefits went to the heavy industry I hated.*[38]

Even here, he concludes the problem lay in his nerves, his taking refuge in mental illness to escape the horrors of war and the manipulations of the bureaucracy. Clearly all these factors were real, but strangely at no stage does he refer to the political tensions within the Republic. He documents how, in Barcelona in December 1937, it was "ambitious, young men of the upper middle classes who now declared themselves Communists . . . because it meant joining the strongest group".[39] However, he draws no explicit political conclusions, though his loyalty to the Communists on the one hand and to Rubiera on the other had become irreconcilable by the summer of 1937.

In October, Barea was relieved of his work giving talks as the *Voz incógnita de Madrid* (Unknown Voice of Madrid).[40] His political work on behalf of the Republic was over. He had been squeezed out by the Communist Party's desire to control the censorship. Neither in *The Clash* nor in any other book does Barea attack the Communists explicitly.[41] In this, he had more dignity than many a party renegade. But there again, he had never actually been a party member.

What is most remarkable is the lack of any real political analysis by Barea of what was happening throughout this tumultuous year. One plausible explanation lies in his lack of political training and thus of the intellectual framework to understand the different political forces (the same could be said of Hemingway and Gellhorn). However, Barea wrote extensively about politics in *Struggle for the Spanish Soul*. He chose not to criticise the PSOE or the PCE, out of a combination of loyalty and genuine dislike of political polemic.

Like many a rank-and-file UGT militant, Barea was at first impressed by the PCE's commitment and successes; he was relieved to find the PCE was prepared to stop the killings of the early months of Revolution. When he later found that the PCE's order was turning into bureaucratic control, he was too demoralised and confused to know how to act. The failure of Largo Caballero in Government must have weighed heavily, too. He followed Ilsa's advice and kept his mouth shut.[42] The less pleasant implication – because it implies more calculation – is that keeping his mouth shut was the only way he could get out of Spain.[43]

There is another aspect of Barea's lack of political debate in *The Clash* that is still more curious. Ilsa was arrested as a Trotskyist. However, Barea's only comment throughout the whole of *The Clash* about the suppression of the POUM is a throwaway one-liner: "I had sympathy neither for the P.O.U.M. nor for their persecution".[44] The remark seems disingenuous:

Barea was Head of the Foreign Press censorship in Madrid during the campaign against the POUM, its suppression in Madrid in December 1936 and the May Days of 1937. He therefore allowed through the censorship reports which he must have known – or strongly suspected – were smears or lies about the POUM. And this when old enemies of Ilsa had attempted to have her imprisoned, or worse, as a "Trotskyist spy", the code-word for being a member of the POUM, as early as December 1936. In this respect, Barea had some political responsibility for participating in the strangling of the Spanish Revolution: something which his friend Carlos Rubiera did not accept.[45]

In short, the case for Barea's "passionate sincerity"[46] cannot be sustained without confronting this blur in his presentation of his own political views. We could say that, like so many others, Barea accepted the PCE framework, not because he liked it but because he saw no alternative. He was, of course, one of many:

> *{Hemingway} had accepted the Communist discipline in Spain because it was "the soundest and sanest for the prosecution of the war".*[47]

By the time Barea saw the negative sides of Communist policy, as his exclusion from the censorship forced him to, he was too exhausted and ill to do anything about it; and besides had no alternative policy. He was a reliable witness of the Civil War, or the part he saw of it, but not a trustworthy interpreter. One critic wrote accurately:

> *Barea . . . is not much concerned with underlining the ideology of the struggle; he lets it come through the action, the characters, the scenes, the words spoken by those involved.*[48]

The inner architecture of *The Clash*

Like the other volumes of the trilogy, *The Clash* is packed full of illustrative anecdotes and concrete descriptions of people Barea met. Especially in the early chapters, these anecdotes give a mosaic picture of the different political positions and pressures of the war. Here Barea's technique is no different from that used in the other volumes. It is reminiscent too of another famous Civil War novel, André Malraux's *L'espoir*, in its rapid changes of scene and character, a similarity that underlines the aptness of this technique for describing revolutionary upheaval.

The Clash differs from *L'espoir* in that it is always told through the eyes of the narrator. Thus the point of view does not change; and the play of different political attitudes does not interfere with the sights, sounds and smells of the action, a difference which is a strength for action sequences, but a weakness in explaining the underlying forces. The other difference – and this above all makes *The Clash* a much better book than the rather dry *L'espoir* – is that Barea writes about Madrid from the inside.

The depth of reference that Barea's being an insider gives his writing sets *The Clash* not only above the famous foreign novels of the Civil War, but also above most of those written by Spaniards. Ralph Bates' article catches this strength:

> *. . . {The} imagined necessity of propaganda too often {in other writers} render{s} the account worthless. Or the writer has not understood Spanish values and thus casts his protagonists after alien images of the hero and the villain . . . In a revolution, one sees the untested ideas, the worn stock in trade of theory . . . subjected to the abrasion of necessity . . . The whole dynamism of the revolution drifts into a new course, virtually without the participant's being aware of it. And almost invariably the ideal becomes the equivocal, and the intelligent and honest man finds himself to some degree at odds with the tenor of the enormous process. It is this I find in Barea's account of the Spanish war.*[49]

Bates was seeking, ten years after the events, to justify the PCE's overall framework, whilst accepting specific criticisms of "excesses" in PCE conduct. But he catches the sense of powerlessness, of being buffeted by uncontrollable events, that is central to Barea's book.[50]

To illustrate these points, I want to look at Chapter 9 from the first part of the volume. As in similar examinations in earlier chapters of the first two pages of *The Forge* and of three pages in *The Track*, this closer look shows both the care of Barea's composition and the way in which his themes are embedded in concrete action.[51]

Entitled *Man Hunt*, Chapter 9 contains fifteen different scenes in its eighteen pages. I will mark them in this account with a letter in brackets, which will help to indicate the speed and variation of the narrative. The chapter opens with a description of Barea's office in the days following the outbreak of the Civil War (A). One of the staff had disappeared, two had gone to the front, two German employees had vanished: there was no work, but the remainder kept the office open. After this half-page sketch, which includes comments on how other workplaces were taken over by workers' committees, Barea moves to the warehouse where his brother works (B). Here Barea discusses the use and abuse of vouchers with an anecdote of two criminals posing as anarchists, who were foiled from commandeering stock. He moves on to meal vouchers, (C) the lack of cash and sales, and Government impotence before the deteriorating situation; which leads into an explanation of how fascists and criminals (D) can easily infiltrate leftist political groups in the chaos. Nevertheless, there is endless enthusiasm, though party pride is unfortunately stronger than the spirit of unity (E).

Barea moves to the story of his training *La Pluma* (F):

> *They allotted us a commandeered house with a tennis court in the aristocratic Barrio de Salamanca. Fifty volunteers started their military training on that court.*[52]

It is an image of revolutionary change: clerks training on a private tennis-court in the wealthiest quarter of Madrid. It is, too, a *madrileño's* image: the journalists and novelists from elsewhere would not have taken part in such activity or had access to such a quintessentially local reference. From questions of political unity and military organisation, Barea then shifts back to his *barrio* in order to focus on the resistance of the civilian population.

Ángel (G), one of Barea's neighbours, has acquired potatoes in the market and distributes them to the local housewives, as well as keeping some for his own use. In this poor quarter (sudden shift from light relief to starkest horror) Barea and Ángel then witness the effects of a random bomb, slaughtering housewives, children and prostitutes indifferently (H):

> *Near me was a bundle of petticoats with a leg sticking out, bent at an impossible angle over a swollen belly. My head was swimming, I vomited into the gutter.*[53]

Barea tells us the date: August 7. The terrible scene inspires political action: Barea goes to work that night with the Communists painting the black-out (I). They come under sniper-fire, search a whole building, but fail to find the sniper. Ángel suggests they go down to see the bodies shot by the Popular Tribunals. It is the small hours and Barea is exhausted. With acute psychology, Barea understands how looking at the corpses of their supposed enemies and cracking witty remarks makes people feel less powerless (J). He understands too that they do it out of fear: "I was shaken by the collective brutality and cowardice of the spectators".[54]

The scene with Sebastián, a childhood friend who had become an assassin, follows (K). With excessive harshness (for Sebastián has been pressured into joining the execution squad), Barea condemns him to his face:

> *"I've known you all my life, and I used to respect you. But now, I tell you – and you can denounce me on the spot – that I won't ever speak to you again."*[55]

Barea's rejection of Sebastián is overstated because of his own disgust at the crowds looking at the executed bodies. We are told baldly that Sebastián was never seen again in the quarter: a few days later he was killed at the front.

Barea's old friend, the reactionary Don Pedro, is arrested. Barea persuades Antonio to intervene, for Don Pedro has committed no crime except that of thinking differently (L). The corpses by the river sickened and enraged Barea. Now Don Pedro's plight forces him to take on individual responsibility and challenge a concrete injustice.

The last five pages of the chapter take place in a ransacked church, where a succession of people are judged by a revolutionary tribunal. Barea and Antonio both believe that the tribunals are transgressions of justice. Barea shows us the confused lives of people from various sectors of society up against the bloodthirsty "Little Paws" (*Manitas*), with his predisposition to believe every accusation. Barea is able to free Don Pedro (M) and show that an accused worker has been falsely accused (N). Comically the worker leaves, expressing confidence in the tribunal, little realising how close he has been to becoming a victim of a travesty of justice. The chapter ends with the Church reminding Barea of his childhood and an image of rare peace (O):

> *Late sunlight filtered through the windows in the slender lantern of the dome.*[56]

A psychological logic drives forward these rapidly sketched scenes. Each scene impinges on the narrator and leads him to act. Thus the bomb leads to his painting the black-out and coming under fire from a sniper, which in turn causes him to visit the corpses. Again, the news of Don Pedro makes him attend the tribunals and help save two men's lives. His having witnessed the corpses earlier that day reinforces his resolve at the tribunals: the sequences of cause and effect overlap and accumulate in force. Simultaneously, the exhausted narrator is a victim of whirling, apparently causeless events. During the day and night of the chapter, there is no time to sleep. In a war, uncontrollable events suddenly occur: thus, one minute you are buying potatoes, then a bomb drops and the dead and wounded must be dealt with. Throughout the first part of *The Clash*, these two processes are interwoven: the psychological cause and effect which leads the narrator to act as a thinking being; and the random and illogical nature of events, which buffet him like a toy from pillar to post.

At the same time as he shows these contradictory processes, Barea gives a multi-layered view of the concrete problems of the war. We see the corrupted revolutionaries, "Little Paws" and Sebastián; and we are shown the horrors that have corrupted them, the fascists' indiscriminate bombing. We see people trying to go about their daily lives, in offices and streets. We see clerks drawn into weapons-training; and others disappearing to the front, out of the city or to their deaths.

With each anecdote, Barea's knowledge of the city is to the fore. As in *Valor y miedo*, he names places within Madrid; characters take on depth through their relationship to these places. Often the past is referred to, contributing to a sense of a people trying to survive *in extremis* in the places where they have always lived.

As was noted in analysing the structure of *The Forge*, Barea used contrast and counter-contrast to create a complex picture of reality. Here too in *The Clash*, he uses this method. The effect in *The Forge* was to show the differing pulls and pressures on the child. In *The Clash*, the effect is to give an impression, a feel, of <u>revolutionary</u> upheaval. These contrasts work on two basic levels: <u>within</u> the scene and <u>between</u> the scenes. Thus, within the scene: clerks in spectacles are seen drilling on a private tennis-court. The effect is one of a world turned upside down: the clerks, a few weeks before, were in a bank or office and the now absent bourgeoisie were at leisure with racquets on that court. Another example of the contrasts within a scene is contained in Chapter 9's final pages, where the tribunal takes place, not in a law-court, but in an expropriated church. By contrasts between the scenes is meant how the whole chapter moves several times from the peaceful to the violent and back again: from the ordinary lives of women in the *barrio* to the dire situation of workers suspected of being "bourgeois" to the peace of an empty Church.

The overall effect is of disruption, of a society in violent upheaval and revolution. Barea's complex, realist technique (much more sophisticated than the Stalinist school of social realism imbuing *Valor y miedo*) is similar to two of his contemporaries mentioned before, who also wrote of revolution. One was Victor Serge, who never drew heroic proletarians and one-dimensional bourgeois. Serge's breadth of sympathy superficially appeared to weaken his revolutionary argument, but in fact profoundly strengthened it by including a broader reality. He did not only talk of revolutionaries, but also of policemen and non-revolutionary workers, with their wavering and doubts, their suffering and wounded feelings.

Barea would probably not have read Serge's books when he wrote *The Forging of a Rebel*, but Ramón J. Sender, the other contemporary, was well known to him. Both Serge and the early Sender of *Seven Red Sundays (Siete domingos rojos)* employed sequences of short, sharp scenes to reflect the rapid changes and multitude of characters characteristic of revolutionary turmoil.[57]

It is a measure of Barea's honesty as a narrator that he took such pains to show this vivid and accurate picture of revolutionary disruption, given that Barea's more overt political discourse during the Chapter (and *The Clash* as a whole) is the counter-revolutionary one of the PCE. I say "more overt", because this political discourse is not explicit. However, it is clear from Barea's own reactions, comments and choices of whom to work with. His lack of preaching means that the reader is presented with a complete world and so is permitted to make up his/her own mind about the events. That is not a bad definition of a good way of presenting the truth.

Sissies and señoritos

The Clash does not only deal with the resistance of the people of Madrid. It tells too of Barea's meeting, relationship and marriage to Ilse Kulcsar, who becomes the protagonist of the second part of the volume. With Ilsa, Barea resolves the sexual and emotional torments which have been a constant backdrop to the trilogy. The rest of this chapter discusses this revolution in his private life during the revolutionary defence of Madrid.

The question of sexual relations was first raised by Barea in *The Forge*, when Arturo is ten. In his summer in Méntrida, the boy finds freedom with Aunt Rogelia and Uncle Luis, who provide a sharp contrast to his religious aunt Baldomera, long-suffering uncle and self-sacrificing mother.

> *My Uncle Luis belonged to a race of men which has almost disappeared; he was a craftsman and gentleman. He was so deeply in love with his craft that to him the iron was something alive and human . . . He rose with the dawn and "killed the worm," as he said, with a glass of brandy which he himself had distilled . . . Then he went to work in the forge. At seven he had his breakfast, a stewed rabbit, or a brace of pigeons, or something on that scale, with a big bowl of salad.*[58]

At times Luis closes the forge to make love with Rogelia, whom he had married for love against the view of his family. The boy reveres this idealised figure, who lifts up the 10 year-old on one hand, lets him drink wine "like a man" and tells him, in similar terms to his grandmother Inés:

> *"You ought to stay here in the forge as my apprentice in your holidays. And no*

> *more petticoats for you. What with the old women and the priests, they'll be turning you into a sniffling sissy."*[59]

Luis represents fertile masculinity. He works, eats and makes love with Rabelaisian appetite. Alongside him, Rogelia cooks, feeds the animals, makes love and gives birth with equally hard work, happiness and fecundity.

There is, however, a more negative side to this heterosexual healthiness. Not all is rural idyll. "They'll be turning you into a sniffling sissy", Luis tells the boy. The fear of being a "sissy" ("*marica*" in the Spanish, a word more explicitly meaning *homosexual* than "sissy") is reinforced by Inés' comments. The evidence that such conditioning has worked is shown in the exaggeration of his reactions to Concha, when she repeats the taunt, and his wild lashing out at Rogelio's sexual advances.[60]

In these early sequences of the trilogy Barea explains, something rarely done in any literature, how a young boy is taught to fear any sign of homosexuality. It is linked in his mind to being a spoilt *señorito* and to religion, to the wearing of skirts like the priests. He is thus trained to feel the need to prove his heterosexuality, a trait which emerges at several stages in the trilogy. A vivid example occurs on the very last page of *The Forge*, when, after he has resigned from the bank, it is suggested that if he apologises, he can stay. Barea replies:

> *"D'you imagine I'll climb these stairs again to lick that man's bottom? And what for? So that my mother has to go washing clothes by the river? No, my dear friend, no. I'm too much of a man for that!"*[61]

This being too much of a man to go back on his dignity, even at the age of 16, this false pride and refusal to compromise (based also on the spurious argument that he had to support his mother: spurious, because this question had not prevented his working in the bank until that moment!) is of course one of the principal stereotypes of Spanish male behaviour.

Barea's particular view, therefore, of what a sexual relationship should be is founded on his view of Luis and Rogelia, both negatively and positively. It is in part a typical *machista* point of view, based on the need to prove his sexuality publicly and on fear of homosexuality. His sexual escapades – with Enriqueta in the bank, with prostitutes in his teens, with someone in the Guadálajara factory, with prostitutes and others in Morocco, later with María – are all implicitly justified by the sexual freedom he had seen in Luis and Rogelia.[62]

If this is all there was to Barea's views of the relationships between men and women, he would be a less interesting writer than he is. However, if Luis and Rogelia provide Barea with this conventional and negative view of sex, they also offer a positive model in their mutually fructifying partnership, one that cannot exist without male respect for women. Barea's ability to rise above cynical exploitation of women was confirmed by his relationship with Ilsa. With her he enjoyed a relationship of equals, based on respect, like Luis and Rogelia's. It is significant that the only two moments in the trilogy when Barea does not feel himself the victim of rending contradictions are at Luis's forge in Méntrida and 30 years later with Ilsa in the *Telefónica*.

The Clash opens with Barea disgusted at his life with his wife Aurelia and his secretary María. María was perfect to console him for the coldness of his life with Aurelia. In a typical phrase revealing his cold objective perception of his own inner turmoil, he says: "my attitude and line of action were coldly and pointedly selfish. I knew that".[63] The long-suffering María, whose desire was to settle down in marriage with Arturo, was dumped. When the patents office closed a few weeks after the start of the war, Barea and María no longer saw each other on a daily basis. He found her tiresome, interested only in clinging to him. Already he was moving on the wider stage of the war.

Barea describes, with directness and no desire to hide his own defects, one of his fateful final meetings with María:

> *. . . Ilsa took my arm. We were crossing the expanse of the Puerta del Sol, when someone plucked at my sleeve.*
> *"Can you spare me a moment?"*
> *María was standing behind me with a hag-ridden face. I asked Ilsa to wait for me, and went a few steps with María who burst out at once:*
> *"Who's this woman?"*
> *"A foreigner who's working with me in the censorship."*
> *"Don't tell me stories. She's your lover. If she isn't, why should she be glued to your arm? And in the meantime, you leave me alone, like an old rag one throws away!"*[64]

Despite Ilsa's distaste for his way of being involved with María and his own misgivings that Ilsa might lose her confidence in him, Ilsa and Arturo become lovers that night. María has indeed outlived her purpose and been thrown away like an "old rag".

Just as Barea got rid of Aurelia and his children by plunging into his work, then evacuating them to the Levante (Chapter One), so he got rid of María. It may not have been the kindest way to resolve his emotional problems: nevertheless, his unpleasantness is mitigated for the reader because it is he himself in *The Clash* who provides the basic information about his own sentimental education, many negative aspects included. Even in this most intimate of areas, Barea sought to explain the common problems of his generation. There is no prior example in Spanish letters of such courageous autobiographical writing. The result is an optimistic portrayal of the possibility of change.

He worked on all this material in the greatest intimacy with his translator Ilsa, which implies that he did in fact resolve many of his emotional conflicts and change his pattern of sexual relationships. With Ilsa he changed. And *The Clash* is the story of that change.

1 Arturo Barea as a boy, in the school uniform he detested.

2 Leonor, Barea's mother. "At the beginning of my conscious life I found my mother. Her work-worn hands dipping into the icy water of the river. Her soft fingers stroking my tousled hair".

3 Exiles. Arturo, Ilsa and Ilsa's mother, Alice von Zieglmayer, known as "Mama".

4 Arturo and Ilsa, 1940s.

5 Studio photograph of Arturo Barea.

6 Studio photograph: Ilse Pollak/Ilsa Barea.

7 Signing a Danish translation of *The Track* at Aarhus University in 1946. On his visit to Denmark, various writers campaigned for Barea to be awarded the Nobel Prize (Jacob Maarbjerg, © Politiken, Denmark).

8 Barea, Ilsa and Barea's youngest niece, Maruja. Eaton Hastings, probably early 1950s.

9 Barea thinking about writing, 1950s.

10 Signed by Barea in Spanish: "to Margaret, with love, Arturo".

11 Arturo Barea in the garden of his last home, Middle Lodge, Eaton Hastings.

12 Arturo Barea smoking, as usual. In formal clothes, unusually.

13 Acting the clown he wanted to be as a child. In England he succeeded, performing as the clown at Faringdon Labour Party fêtes.

14 Arturo at Faringdon, 1950s. Man of books.

15 Cooking: Barea's contact in England with Spanish culture.

16 Barea telling an anecdote. "He was a born story-teller . . . He enjoyed telling stories about his life, adorned with details seen, experienced and imagined, varying them according to his public and his own mood" (Ilsa Barea).

17 Speaking while everyone's paella gets cold. 1955: probably the dinner to celebrate Barea's 800th radio broadcast.

18 Recording a BBC talk: 1955.

19 Barea looking serious and tired, in his last years.

20 Unveiling a bust: South America, 1956. "He can be considered as an ultra-leftist person of completely liberal formation and as a classic example of a left-wing, non-catholic intellectual" (Ministry of Foreign Affairs report, Madrid 1956).

CONFERENCIAS ACTUALISIMAS

Centro de la Sinceridad y de la Verdad

En este prestigioso centro de algunos intelectuales y de otros que no lo son tanto, dará una conferencia

Míster Arthur Barea ("Beria")

el escritor más glorioso de todos los tiempos, sobre el tema:

"Ramiro de Maeztu y 14.000 sacerdotes, asesinados por la República Española"

+++

CENTRO VASQUISIMO

Conferencia a cargo del mismo eminentísimo literato Míster Arthur Barea ("Beria")

Sobre el humanisimo tema.

"Los 578 asesinadcs en el buque prisión "Cabo Quilates" bajo el gobierno inefable del Honorable Presidente Napoleonchu. - Conciliar: P. Uñika" — "Carrerá de guadaris Irún — Donostia — Bilbao — Santander"

+++

CENTRISIMO DAS MORRIÑAS E ALALAS

Conferencia que profesará el inclito y perínclito literato

MISTER ARTHUR BAREA ("BERIA")

Sobre el tema:

"María Pita y la Escuadra Inglesa en La Coruña". — "Influencias inglesas en la pronunciación de Chantada de Lujo".

También disertará sobre:

"Los guardias republicanos de Casares y el asesinato de Calvo Sotelo".

+++

CENTRO ASTURIANISIMO

Conferencia que explicará el genial, colosal, incomparable y único:

MISTER ARTHUR BAREA ("BERIA")

Sobre el enjundioso tema:

"La Universidad de Oviedo y la Cámara Santa destruídas por los rojos en 1934 y la ciudad de Oviedo "masacrada" por los aviones demo-comunistas en 1936".

No falten a estas conferencias si quieren gozar fama de gentes sabias. ¡Adquirirán pinta de intelectuales y de ciudadanos libres!

¡Se obsequiará con churros, fabada, angulas y vino del "Ribeiro"!

¡¡¡ A C U D A N   N O M A S !!!

21 Anti-Barea propaganda, published in South America by Franco supporters. In line 5, Barea is referred to as Mister Arthur Barea ("Beria"), underlining his English nationality and his supposed ideological affinity to Stalin's deputy, Beria.

22 Signing a book on his successful tour of South America, 1956. "Barea's visit was an unqualified success from the word go. I would not hesitate in saying that he was the most successful visitor we have had for many years" (British Embassy, Buenos Aires).

Barea in England

1939–1957

Ilsa and Arturo Barea reached England in February 1939. On the last page of *The Clash*, Barea described his anger at the blindness of the French, among whom they had lived for the previous year, who did not want to see that war was approaching. Two French sailors corrected him:

> *The two men looked gravely at me . . .*
> *"Oh no, we shall fight. The others are the ones who won't fight."*[1]

In practice, however, this class understanding of the difference between the interests of the French and English Governments, who allowed Franco's victory, and the working-class who did and would fight, did not last. These final words of *The Forging of a Rebel* were written early in 1944, but already Barea's views had slipped towards a more patriotic view of England, as his broadcasts from that time show.[2]

With the words quoted above, Barea's own account of his life ends. But a rich substitute for his own account are the many people I was able to interview or correspond with from 1989 on and who had known Barea during the last 18 years of his life, when he became a well-known writer.

In those first weeks in England, Barea's mood was low. In addition to his political bitterness at British "non-intervention" in the Civil War, he felt personally wretched:

> *I disembarked in these islands bereft of everything, with my life cut short and no perspectives for the future, no country, no home, no job . . . exhausted in body and spirit.*[3]

It was a mood not helped by his first impressions of London from the train:

> *. . . two unending rows of houses. Narrow houses, smoky from the locomotives . . . with their lines where they hung out clothes to get dry and smoked; where old drawers, empty tins piled up.*[4]

Arturo and Ilsa went to live in Puckeridge, a village in Hertfordshire. There are some letters of Barea's to Ilsa of August and September 1939 that throw a bright shaft of light into their inner life and their adaptation to England. While Barea remained in Puckeridge, Ilsa had gone to Evesham to start work at the BBC Monitoring Service. The letters show the intimacy of Barea's and Ilsa's relationship, and his attractive combination of self-awareness and directness. They show, too, Barea's nervousness, the couple's acute money problems and Barea's verve. These are the letters of someone facing up to a new life in a tough situation, not the letters of a passive neurotic. During these days, Barea went to London to meet Ilsa's parents, whom he did not know, arriving on the train five days before the outbreak of the Second World War as bewildered and distressed refugees from Austria. He was capable, despite his anxieties, of helping them settle into their new strange surroundings in the absence of their daughter.[5]

Fladbury: Success

In August 1939 *The Spectator* published Arturo's first article in England, *A Spaniard in Hertfordshire*. Barea was set on earning a living from writing. He had already completed in Paris the second draft of *The Forge*. And in the terrible month of his arrival, when the Republic finally went down to defeat, Barea wrote *Mister One*, a nihilistic tale of two impossible choices (see Chapter II). The *Spectator* piece told how he had found an unexpectedly warm and kind reception in rural England, an England he had feared would be "indifferent or hostile".[6]

In this very first article, Barea found the theme that would run through the more than 800 broadcasts he was to do for the BBC's Latin American service between 1940 and 1957: that of observing and describing English life from his vantage-point as a sympathetic outsider. Ilsa articulated this approach in a typically fluent and verbose letter written in July 1939, when she attempted to solicit work for them both from the BBC's Spanish service:

> *Our concrete proposal would be to give a series in Castilian, apart from the news bulletins, under the heading "A Spaniard discovers England." The reason is that there is in Spain an old popular conception of England . . . which is very unfortunate, especially as it makes more easy the type of anti-British propaganda one finds nowadays in Spanish newspapers and even more so in the oral propaganda centring round the question of Gibraltar. Now we do not suggest a series of political talks, but of features, taking into account the popular prejudice and simply describing in a vivid, anecdotical and personal manner the impressions of a*

Spaniard of England, especially its rural life, landscape, then of the liberal traditions, democratic traditions, and so on (non-political of course).[7]

As well as showing the basic theme of the broadcasts that would give Arturo his main source of income while in England, this letter also demonstrates the couple's political dilemma. They had changed political climate with brutal suddenness. From a situation in Madrid where it was dangerous not to support the Communist Party, they were in a position where they must not admit to the slightest sympathy for Communism if they wanted a job. They had to protest loudly they were not "political", whilst being fully aware that any broadcasts Barea might make would contain a large amount of political propaganda. And, most bizarrely, Barea had to cite his experience as the pro-communist *Voz incógnita de Madrid* to seek work with the conservative BBC. It was not to be for another 15 months, when the "phoney war" had ended, that Arturo finally gained an interview with J. A. Camacho, Head of the Latin American service, and was taken on as a broadcaster.[8]

On Ilsa's arrival in August at the BBC Monitoring Service in Evesham, Worcestershire, Margaret Rink (later, Margaret Weeden) met her for the first time. She wrote:

{Ilsa} . . . explained to me that Arturo, who was highly strung, not at all well and very concerned about the inevitability of war, was exceedingly upset at losing her companionship and help.[9]

Arturo soon followed Ilsa from Puckeridge to Fladbury, a tiny village near Evesham, where he, Ilsa, Ilsa's refugee parents and Margaret Rink shared a large, dilapidated house, "Brooklands," for the next four years.[10]

It was at Fladbury that Barea wrote the second and most of the third volume of the trilogy, his book on Lorca and several stories and articles. It was his most fertile period. In the peace of a particularly plentiful corner of rural England, where it was sometimes hard to believe a war was being waged in Europe, Barea reaped the harvest of his struggles to survive in Madrid, Barcelona and Paris. For the year until he started his broadcasts in October 1940, he had nothing to do but "potter round . . . a large and very neglected garden," cook (he shared the cooking with Ilsa's tiny mother, "Mama" to everyone), look after their chickens, rabbits, cat and dog, entertain guests – and write. Not a bad cure for shell-shock.[11]

The Bareas had a very wide circle of acquaintances – not only refugees and journalists, but distinguished writers and academics, many of them members of the

Monitoring Service, and we had a fairly frequent stream of visitors, many of them lured by Arturo's reputation as a cook![12]

Barea was the sort of cook who made huge, delicious *paellas* or chicken dishes to his own recipes, but left heaps of washing-up, which he considered beneath his dignity to touch. It was Mama who acted as kitchen skivvy, but she and Barea across the language barrier developed a close relationship. Cooking, which Barea arrived at in middle age, became important to him for an essential reason, as María Herrera expresses perceptively:

. . . a man in love with Spanish cooking, the only palpable part of his cultural identity that connects him irrationally with his memories, with the smells and tastes of his childhood, through taste and smell, the most primary senses.[13]

In several of his stories, meals appear. The luxury, the pleasure, the intimacy of a good meal offset the hunger lurking ever-present in Spanish society. For the exile, paella became his talisman dish. In the autobiographical story, "Food Nostalgic",[14] Barea tells how he and Ilsa spent all of a payment for a translation, during their time of hunger living off the boulevard Montparnasse in 1938, to buy the ingredients for a paella and cook it on a primus stove. "I had only hunger and longing,"[15] he wrote in this story and recalls meals from his childhood, aubergines fried in the country, a tortilla made by his sister, and finally the rice made by Miguel at Ifach, when he was recovering from his nervous breakdown in 1937. His neighbours and close friends at Faringdon during the 1950s, the Vine family, came to adopt paella as their family meal, so closely did they associate it with the pleasure of Ilsa and Arturo's welcoming house and meals.[16]

Many of the talented foreign intellectuals who worked with Ilsa visited for the fine food, but also for the fine conversation: Martin Esslin, Isabel de Madariaga, Leonard Shapiro, Ernst Gombrich and the young George Weidenfeld, who remembered Barea's "Inca face, finely chiselled, with deep-set eyes".[17] Barea was looking better than he had in the Civil War.

Fladbury was a multilingual, argumentative household, with lengthy meals and a "torrent of conversation" in four languages.[18] They argued about politics (Ilsa's father, Professor Pollak, was a social-democrat) and about literature: for example, whether *For Whom the Bell Tolls* should be criticised or not. Many people thought Hemingway was too good a friend of the Republic to be criticised, but Barea stuck to his view and produced his key article on Hemingway, published in *Horizon,* the most prestigious literary journal of the epoch.

Apart from these first contacts with the glittering *literati*, Barea visited the country pubs, where he felt at home chatting and drinking – he was a heavy drinker – with the locals. This was a continuation of a lifelong habit of drinking in popular bars. For his writing it was vital: it had helped him grasp the speech and opinions of workers in Madrid, which served as the basis for his novels. In England it was to be key in the success of his broadcasts. Popular pubs also filled a psychological need in Barea: to escape from middle-class and intellectual conversation and ground his thought and conversation in experience.

Barea's creative and bucolic new life during this period was not without anxieties. A friend observed that they had "hard times, with four of them living on Ilsa Barea's salary".[19] Barea, as an "alien," had problems arranging a pass to travel to London for his interview with Camacho in July 1940.[20] Margaret Weeden wrote:

> *A. was just a bundle of nerves when I first knew him. He depended enormously on tobacco . . . He had a limp, and was too nervy and jumpy to learn to drive.*[21]

Spectres of internment as an alien, or even deportation, were real. When he did start working for the Latin American service, he feared arrest when travelling at night to his broadcasts.[22] His nerves were frequently a problem: "I've had a very troubled week with my nerves."[23]

Barea suffered too intense anxiety and guilt about his family in Spain. His beloved brother Miguel (Rafael in the trilogy) was imprisoned after the fall of Madrid: he died shortly after his release, in 1941 or 1942.[24] Both his sister Concha with seven children and ex-wife Aurelia with her and Arturo's four were living in poverty. Barea's never having known his own father will have made his abandonment of his children still harder. In *The Broken Root* Barea puts into the mouth of Pedro, the son of the exile Antolin, these words which could well have applied to him:

> *. . . the man who had left them to starve on charity lentils and on slops of water and sawdust, and had never once spared them a thought!*[25]

One of their many guests at Fladbury, Sir Peter Chalmers-Mitchell, former Head of the London Zoo, both offered to translate *The Forge* and found a publisher for it.[26] Another visitor, Cyril Connolly, commissioned articles for *Horizon*. In London, Barea met Tosco Fyvel to discuss *Struggle for the Spanish Soul*. Despite the gloomy impression Barea's physical and mental state made on Fyvel, the latter perceptively remarked:

> *. . . the memory of a bitter defeat we had tried to forget is brought back to our minds {by Barea}, with understanding but no bitterness.*[27]

It was surely this lack of bitterness that allowed Barea to survive mentally and to write so clearly and powerfully during the years at Fladbury, the centre of his richest creative period. In *The Clash* there are several instances when, describing himself, he seems literally mad, shouting at people, behaving impossibly.[28] But he had the strength to get these feelings out of his system in flares of emotion, sometimes in the immediate term self-defeating, but which meant that in the long term he did not carry the seed of self-destructive rancour in his heart. Ralph Bates wrote in a 1947 review of *The Forging of a Rebel*:

> *In part, insight into his own condition has prevented Barea losing himself in rancor. Sick of a terrible neurosis . . . he consciously refused to rationalise.*[29]

During this period, Barea sat down and wrote the *circa* 40,000 words of *Struggle for the Spanish Soul* in a month. Here he did "rationalise" or reason. He poured into its nine chapters the ideas he was excluding from the sensuous trilogy. It is an exegesis of the ideology used by Franco, with references to the forging of Franco's mission in Morocco and descriptions of the "misery and tribulation" of defeated Spain in 1940, much of it gleaned from the Spanish radio. Barea analyses the forces behind Franco – Church, Army and Spain's ruling "caste" – and the myth, with its roots in the Middle Ages, of Hispanic glory and destiny employed by the regime. He places great emphasis on the Falange, logically in that he was writing both before the Falange was sidelined and in the middle of an anti-fascist war: as with his later pamphlets, his purpose was to link Franco to Hitler and Mussolini. It is a fine essay-polemic, which holds up well today.

Juan de Castilla

Unexpectedly, just as one world was opening up for him with his writing, yet another career began. Accepted by the BBC's Latin American Service, he began to broadcast in October 1940 as *Juan de Castilla*, a pseudonym adopted to protect his family within Spain from possible reprisals.[30] The radio brought Barea renown and a steady income for the last sixteen years of his life. By 1955 he was earning £12 a talk.[31]

Camacho offered him work on a freelance basis with a clear brief: to give talks on England and the English people to counter Nazi propaganda in

South America.[32] It was a chance for Barea to return to some sort of political activity against fascism. He would have preferred the Spanish Service, but they would not have him. There is no record of what the Spanish service thought of his original 1939 application,[33] but a controversy a year later made the BBC's general attitude quite clear.

This row started with Ilsa Barea, from her position as a foreign broadcasts monitor, criticising the Spanish Service as crypto-fascists for their failure to attack the Franco regime. The row broke into the press, with a letter from Arturo Barea in the *New Statesman* and an article in the *Daily Herald.*[34] The BBC, "while it was anxious to act in the national interest, was also concerned with its own credibility".[35] The BBC's dilemma was that it wished to support British Government policy of maintaining diplomatic relations with Franco, so as to prevent Spain entering the war on Hitler's side; yet, not to criticise Franco was unlikely to keep any listeners in Spain and was just not credible in an anti-fascist war.

This was a problem solved by Rafael Martínez Nadal in a particular way. Under the pseudonym of Antoñito Torres, Martínez Nadal made weekly Sunday broadcasts for the BBC Spanish service. He never attacked Franco by name.

> *{Martínez Nadal attacked} . . . the more outrageous utterances of the official Spanish press and radio, ridiculed Italian fascism and painted a picture of Hitler as the "enemy of the Catholic belief in the supreme value of the individual".*[36]

Despite the mildness of this approach, the BBC removed Martínez Nadal from the radio in December 1943 for four months at the request of Lord Templewood, the pro-Franco British Ambassador in Madrid. Templewood was being pressed by the Spanish Government, who naturally enough maintained that, far from being crypto-fascists, as Ilsa had maintained eighteen months previously, BBC Spanish Service staff were communists. The nature of the BBC's much vaunted independence was demonstrated by its notorious (both anti-democratic and factually untrue) reply: "We do not employ Reds."[37]

It is clear that neither of the ex-Republican press censors had the slightest chance of being employed by the Spanish service, for which Barea *La voz incógnita de Madrid* was more than qualified, in this atmosphere of appeasement of Franco.

The Latin American service was next best and Barea grasped his chance. His second or third broadcast, "Los seis elefantes blancos," went out in October 1940.[38] This title ("The Six White Elephants") was the name of an apocryphal pub, a composite of those he frequented at Puckeridge,

Fladbury and then Faringdon, which became the scene of many of his anecdotal talks.

> *He had a remarkable capacity for picking up items for chats in the local pub or from friends or even a few lines in a newspaper, and making them into a 15 minute talk.*[39]

The source, therefore, of much of his material was ready to hand: his time drinking and chatting with local people. His difficulties with English presented little obstacle.

The broadcasts, in Barea's words "little stories and talks" (*cuentecillos y charlas*), were usually anecdotes about English life, chats set in pubs, often revealing peoples' understated but heroic attitude to the war, or about people he met, whether gypsies, neighbours or country labourers. During the war years, many were direct commentaries on the news, including satires on the German leaders, often using information gleaned from Ilsa who was monitoring their broadcasts. At first Barea went in the middle of night to broadcast live at 3 a.m.; but as time passed and recording techniques improved, he was able to tape his talk during the day. They were 14½ minute slots, for which Barea wrote the script, during the war years sent them for censoring to his controller, and then recorded the talk.

Barea's surviving BBC scripts are of little literary value, though they are interesting social documents.[40] They are not on the whole about Spain, but there is a thematic continuity with the trilogy. He was interested in what went on beneath the surface in the minds of the millions. One of Barea's BBC controllers, H. Lyon Young, explained something of the content and style of Barea's talks:

> *Perhaps the best way of describing Barea's commentaries would be to say that they are talks on trivialities in relation to world affairs. In other words, how the ordinary man reacts to world news, and the importance often attached to insignificant events at the time of great emotional strain.*
>
> *Barea catches the mood of the moment and writes on the thoughts of ordinary men and women, rather than on their deeds . . . He always emphasizes (that hackneyed phrase) the "human angle," e.g. Molly breaks a teacup on 'V-J' Day, and ever after 'V-J' Day will be remembered by Molly's broken teacup.*[41]

Lyon Young's comments on Barea's broadcasting are also applicable to how Barea treats major political events in the trilogy. In *The Track*, for instance, the proclamations, battles, turning-points and news from the capital filter down from a blur above into the daily current of the detail of the soldiers' lives on which Barea focuses. But the difference was that by the time of the broadcasts the political purpose of revealing how ideas were formed in the minds of rank-and-file soldiers or workers had been lost. The form, the method remained the same; but by 1946 the purpose was not political, but just to tell an interesting story within a general humanistic framework.

Barea became a master of this minor literary skill of spoken, anecdotical journalism. His style was relaxed and intimate, but he was not averse to occasional rolling, grandiose phrases. Despite his defects of sentimentalism and, at times, exaggerated praise of the English – the war-time propaganda persisting after the end of the war -- he manages to be both sincere and moving.

Technically, Barea was an expert at giving padding to a piece in order to reach the requisite 14½ minutes: small tangents in the narrative, yet which also serve to give breadth to the contents. This is very much the rambling, yet controlled, style which Ilsa commented on in the introduction to *El centro de la pista*:

> *He was a born story-teller; I often pulled his leg because he fancied himself as a story-teller in a Moroccan bazaar. He enjoyed narrating anecdotes about his life, adorned with details he had seen, experienced or imagined . . . Many of the stories collected here were born from some anecdote he had told me one night before the warm coals of an English hearth.*[42]

The surviving radio scripts show that Barea was sometimes careless in his phrasing, but a spoken talk does not need to be as polished as a published piece. His frequent anglicisms or grammatical errors were consequences of the need to produce a piece every week and of his typing his scripts straight out, with little or no correction. They probably added to the sense of intimacy his listeners felt, as if he were chatting to them every Sunday evening from an English hearth-side.

Others testified to his skill and professionalism:

> *His timing was instinctive – he never made them too short or too long and usually sat down and typed them out the night before they were needed.*[43]

And in a 1944 criticism of Barea, the Head of the Latin American service underlined his ability as a broadcaster:

> *[Barea is] . . . beginning to form mannerisms and to adopt a slightly 'sing-songy' manner, which is quite different from his old style on which his*

reputation in our service was based. I think it would be worth while to give him a word of warning. His material is too good to spoil by bad delivery; this is especially so when we know that he can do his stuff very well indeed.[44]

Presumably Barea corrected this fault, for he went on to win the listeners' poll as the BBC's most popular broadcaster to Latin America several years running in the late 1940s and 1950s. Just after his sudden death, Ilsa replied to the letter of condolence from the BBC's Director of External Broadcasting in these terms:

Perhaps he {Arturo Barea} really achieved what he hoped to do: to forge a link between this country, which he loved, and people of his own language overseas.[45]

Although after the war the immediate propaganda purpose of the talks changed, Barea continued to see his role as an interpreter and defender of the *English way of life*. In 1955, he wrote:

I still like doing them {the broadcasts} because I continually discover new things about this country of which I want to speak to people of my own language as to friends. I can only hope that I have made them share some of my affectionate discoveries among "the English".[46]

Throughout his time with the BBC, Barea – or usually Ilsa on his behalf – tried, without great success, to get his short stories accepted for broadcast. Two had been rejected in August 1940 before he started broadcasting.[47] Another called *The Winner* was rejected by novelist P. H. Newby for the Third Programme in 1953 as "conventional and overlong".[48] The same controller rejected *The Scissors* as "unbearable".[49] Early in his broadcasting career, Barea called several of his broadcasts "stories": and though the distinction between an anecdotal chat and a story may be blurred, none of the broadcasts in the BBC archives can be called "stories" in any real sense. After Barea's death, Ilsa continued to try to get his stories broadcast, with one success, *Grandmother's Lesson*, accepted in November 1958. The same controller, George Macbeth, then rejected two more.

In April 1943, the Monitoring Service moved from Evesham to Caversham on the outskirts of Reading. Ilsa moved with it, from Fladbury to Rose Farm House, near Mapledurham, even today a small startlingly isolated village by the Thames, although only two miles from Caversham. Arturo followed in October and finished the trilogy at Mapledurham in early 1944.[50] Here Gerald Brenan and Gamel Woolsey came to visit them from Wiltshire, visits reciprocated by Ilsa and Arturo on two occasions.

Barea and Brenan got on well: the latter had just published the work which made him famous *The Spanish Labyrinth*, reviewed rigorously and sympathetically by Barea in *Horizon* in September 1943. Thirty years later Gerald Brenan wrote this vivid portrait of Barea:

> *{Barea} was a dark, slight man with a lean, rather worn face – not in the least the type of Spanish intellectual, but suggesting rather a mechanic. The sort of man one would run into in any Madrid café or bar . . . He talked well in a serious, straightforward way, but needed frequent glasses of beer to keep him going. He had developed a strong liking for the English country because of its peace and tranquillity: he enjoyed talking in pubs with the local people and growing vegetables in his garden, but his experience in the war and the spate of executions that had followed it had saddened him. Also he missed Spain and the society of his fellow countrymen. Otherwise he was very like his books, truthful and serious and without recriminations or hatred.*[51]

After 4 October 1943, when Barea moved from Evesham to Mapledurham, he recorded his talks in London; though for several months after June 1944 he reverted to recording in Evesham because his shell-shock – vomiting and nausea –- was set off by air-raid sirens on his visits to London. From the end of the war, the Friday recording at Bush House was re-established, a routine he maintained for the rest of his life. He formed the habit of Friday lunch at the *Majorca*, a restaurant in Brewer Street, Soho, run by Spanish anarchists.[52] And, after about 1950, he would stay over in London most Thursday nights with his niece Maruja.[53]

Political pessimism

After Ilsa's resignation from the BBC in 1945, the Bareas lived for a few months in a rented house in Surrey, then moved to Boar's Hill, Oxford. Here he met Salvador de Madariaga, professor at Oxford and ex-Minister of the Spanish Republic. The publisher Joan Gili, who became a friend of Barea's, commented: "I cannot think of two more different characters, in their background and politically".[54] Madariaga was patrician and monarchist: Barea, plebeian and Republican. But most of all, Madariaga had preferred exile to staying in Spain during the war and had sought to reconcile the two sides, a position anathema to Barea.[55]

Over these years of literary success, Barea's political views evolved. The anti-fascist propaganda of his war broadcasts extolled the courage and tolerance of the British people. In a process not too dissimilar from Orwell's,

Barea moved to the right, blurring the key distinction between British Government and British people. His liking for the workers, country labourers and gypsies who at first populate his fictional pub coincides more and more with praise for Britain as a whole. In *The Clash* Barea defended democracy from the point of view of independent working-class action, but by the middle 1940s he had come to identify it with what he perceived as the democratic institutions of the British state.[56] This political shift was based on the British Government's stern resistance to Hitler after 1940 and, later, the promise of the 1945 Labour Government. Thus, for Barea, the Spanish War, as it receded into history, became a sort of bubble of radical hopes and attitudes, with less and less practical impact on his own day-to-day opinions and practice.

Barea's over-sweet view of the virtues of the English reflected genuine gratitude for the welcome he had received in England, which led to his acquiring British nationality in 1948. Becoming a British citizen may have been due also to his speculation about a possible visit to Spain: Antolin, his *alter ego* of *The Broken Root*, acquired a British passport to cover his visit to Madrid. During the writing of this novel from 1948 to 1950, the question of a return must have been on Barea's mind.

He was careful during the 1940s not to become involved in politics, both because he worked for a staid institution, the BBC, and because he was an alien in wartime. In 1945, two pamphlets give evidence of the evolution of his formal political views. In March 1945, Barea made a curious speech at the Caxton Hall, London, which was published in a pamphlet *Freedom for Spain*. The speech/article starts by evoking the "spontaneous mass solidarity"[57] of the immediate response to the July 1936 military rebellion. Barea argues that the crowd moved with a single mind:

> *That night there existed no political shades of opinion, no ideological differences, no party discipline which might have split us.*[58]

He praises the International Brigades' sacrifice in similar terms. Then he veers sharply from this exposition of revolutionary unity to comment:

> *In the ranks of the International Brigades were men of all social classes and of all creeds . . . A faith, or . . . a religion . . . moved the volunteers in the anti-fascist fight of Spain.*[59]

It is misleading to say that the International Brigaders came from all social classes or creeds: they were overwhelmingly working-class and the majority were Communist Party members or sympathisers. However, Barea uses this wrong assertion as the basis for arguing that "the liberty of the individual human being" is what underlay their idealism. His own socialism he defines in the most general of democratic terms:

. . . a universal faith and universal militia, into whose ranks belong all those who believe in the equality of rights and the liberty of men.[60]

These vague generalities, in what was probably his last (and perhaps only) political speech in public, are a long way from the sharpness of his analysis four years previously of the ideological roots of Francoism in *Struggle for the Spanish Soul.* There are really two speeches in one: a call for international working-class solidarity, which he then seeks to pull into a nebulous "all men of goodwill" framework.

There is, though, a purpose to Barea's argument. He is seeking the broadest possible popular front for the overthrow of Franco:

It would be grim indeed – and it is impossible to tolerate that it should be so – if, after the defeat of Nazism in the military field, Fascism in any form were to survive in Spain.[61]

His speech aimed to contribute to the pressure on the Allies to overthrow Franco in the wake of the defeat of Mussolini and Hitler.

The second 1945 piece of political writing is the much longer pamphlet *SPAIN in the post-war world*, co-written with Ilsa, who doubtless contributed the political weight, and published by the Fabian Society in August. Like the Caxton Hall speech, this was written in the heady days when the Spanish Diaspora could not believe that the victorious Allies would not move against Franco. Barea catches this atmosphere in *The Broken Root*:

With all the others, Antolin had firmly believed that twenty-four hours after the German collapse the Franco regime would cease to exist . . . More people than before came to the meeting-place at the corner of Dean Street {Soho, London}, other people than the waiters and musicians . . . he wanted to explain the atmosphere of those days, their overflowing excitement, their fantastic plans.[62]

The Bareas' pamphlet argues for the restoration of the Spanish Republic. It is a stodgy text, the house style of Fabian Research pamphlets, composed in the sombre tradition of Sidney and Beatrice Webb; but in the Bareas' case the style also reflects strains in their arguments. For the Bareas argue that German capital, by canny use of the patent laws (here Arturo draws on his own experience), Spanish front-men and conscious Nazi-inspired infiltration, gained a predominant position in the Spanish economy during the 1920s and '30s. Their case is exaggerated: German capital had grown in influence, but British and French capital retained important investments in Spain. Unnecessarily the authors use this argument of German infiltration to underline their case that the Republic should be restored. They sense that the basic moral argument that Spain is ruled by a blood-drenched dictatorship that had overthrown an elected Government will not be sufficient. Their argument seeks to link the Spanish regime economically as well as politically with defeated Germany.

In 1945 all sectors of the Spanish opposition were manoeuvring for position against Franco's fall. Carrillo and Claudín were returning euphorically from Moscow to Paris to organise the "interior"; Prieto was seeking audiences with Ernest Bevin; the pretender Don Juan was throwing his two-coloured hat into the ring, seeking to appear liberal to the Allies and trustworthy to the dictator. The Bareas, the Fabian Society and Lord Faringdon were just some of many trying to prod the new Labour Government in Britain into action on the question. All this was to no avail: Stalin, Roosevelt and Churchill had already decided at Yalta in 1944 that Franco should stay. And the Labour Government was quick to fall in line behind US foreign policy in return for the Marshall millions. The moment of possibility, April/May 1945, had passed: by the time of the Bareas' pamphlet in August, the armed French *maquis*, with its tens of thousands of Spanish Republican volunteers, was already disarmed on Stalin's orders.

SPAIN in the post-war world is mechanical, making the subjectivist error of starting from its political desires rather than from objective reality. Nearly everyone shared the Bareas' conviction that Franco had to fall. But their somewhat cranky (highlighting patents laws) and conspiratorial (German infiltration) arguments do not make the pamphlet either a very creditable piece of research or an inspiring read. For Arturo Barea, as for the entire Republican Diaspora, the consolidation of Franco in power after 1945 was a "shattering disappointment".[63] From then on his political attitudes veered towards pessimism. At Labour Party annual fairs in Buscot Park, he played the clownish role of a Spanish fortune-teller.[64] He did not join the Labour Party, unlike Ilsa, who became a leading local Bevanite.[65]

On his visits to Denmark, Pennsylvania and South America, Barea remained proud to call for the downfall of Franco and identify himself as a Spanish Republican, but no longer as a Socialist. He retained no belief in the efficacy of political action. Olive Renier noted in a diary after a lunch with Barea in 1950:

> *Arturo is deeply discouraged. He says that there is no hope anywhere. In his youth*

one could still look forward, but now we have killed all faith. The state is all-powerful, the individual has no chance. He sees no point in political activity because there is nothing you can say to people on any of the important matters which is true. You can only redress little errors, and for the rest tell lies.[66]

He sounds more like Philip Marlowe, the lone moral man, than Largo Caballero. The eloquent Olive Renier commented on this pessimistic passivity:

I suspect that for Arturo the defeat of democratic Spain was the end of politics, and the above was more or less his attitude ever since he had to cross the frontier into France . . . All else was useless, save only that one must be true to oneself. He did not tell lies.[67]

The successful writer

Ilsa, Arturo and Ilsa's parents moved to Middle Lodge, Eaton Hastings, near Faringdon, South Oxfordshire on June 1 1947. A few months later, two of Arturo's nieces, first Leonor then Maruja, came from hungry Madrid to join them. This was the exile's final home. Middle Lodge was (and is) an elegant house, at that time without electricity, by one of the entrances to Lord Faringdon's Buscot estate. It is shielded from the road by a high wall and set in a wild garden merging into the estate woodland. Barea continued to write at Faringdon, but less and with less intensity. In these years he wrote *Unamuno* with Ilsa, some stories and essays, and his novel *The Broken Root*, as well as recomposing *The Forging of a Rebel* for its 1951 Buenos Aires publication, the first in Spanish.

At Faringdon, Barea got to know a new generation, Ilsa's young Labour Party colleagues, and to them appeared mellower and more relaxed than the nervous wreck described a decade earlier by Delmer, dos Passos or Fyvel. He dined too with the great and good, meeting the Cabinet Minister Susan Lawrence at Buscot House and John Betjeman *inter al.* at Faringdon House.[68] He liked to shoot pheasant, accompanied by his shaggy black dog, in Lord Faringdon's woods and enjoyed telling their many guests that he, child of the Madrid slums, had entertained a genuine "milord" on pheasant shot in the Lord's own woods and the Lord had then done the washing-up.[69] He frequented the local pubs, always looking for material (or that was the excuse) for his broadcasts and enjoying effects such as asking for *bear* instead of *beer* in the Wellington, Faringdon, on his return every Friday night from Bush House.[70]

Barea's English was good enough for him to read extensively in the language. He had been a press censor; he devoured the English classics;[71] and he reviewed books such as Brenan's *Spanish Labyrinth* for *Horizon* and others for the *TLS*. His pronunciation was always appalling, based often on Spanish rules and the fact that his first spoken English had been in country pubs.[72] Brenan says he spoke with a Worcestershire accent, confirmed by Margaret Weeden, who remarks on his pronunciation of *pub* as *poob*, thus happily conjoining Spanish pronunciation with local dialect. Several witnesses suggest he sometimes played up his bad pronunciation in order to confound his BBC-accented visitors,[73] a provocation similar to his turning up at BBC functions in the early 1940s dressed in slippers, and trousers and jacket that neither matched nor fitted.[74] Relatively poor as he was at that time, it is hard not to think Barea was making a deliberate point about the sort of person he was. In Faringdon, he nearly always wore a beret, old pullovers and a raincoat, again suggesting adoption of roles as a foreign eccentric and a loner.[75]

By the time Ilsa and he settled in Faringdon, Arturo Barea was a well-known writer. The trilogy was widely respected and successful on its post-war US publication. He was able to enjoy some of the fruits of literary fame. In 1946 he was invited to lecture in Denmark, where he had a considerable following (the trilogy had been translated to Danish by Ilsa's sister, Lotte). While there, he called for sanctions and a blockade against Spain.[76] A group of Danish intellectuals later mounted a newspaper campaign for him to be awarded the Nobel Prize. Given that he was neither Danish nor an outstanding writer, this seemed and seems curious; but it is not so surprising, given a certain Scandinavian influence on the Nobel Prizes and that the Literature Prizes are often used as political gestures. Barea was internationally the best-known Spanish writer of the time and he was an opponent of the regime. His moment passed; and the writer himself dismissed the campaign as not credible.[77]

In 1952 he went for a six-month visiting professorship to Pennsylvania State College, out in the Alleghany Mountains near Pittsburgh: not bad for someone who had left school at 13. He filled in on his Penn. State records card that he had been awarded a B.A. in 1913 – at the age of 15! On falsifying the form, he was following the advice of Ramón Sender in the USA:

> *There's no need to have academic qualifications when you have some reputation as a writer . . . I did School Certificate in Spain and History at university, but no-one here's ever asked me about it.*[78]

Barea travelled without Ilsa *via* New York, arriving in February 1952.

He taught four courses in nineteenth- and twentieth-century Spanish literature and wanted to stay on for another year. One of his students paid him this tribute 50 years later:

> *Don Arturo was a very kind and thoughtful person. His course on Lorca left me with a lifelong love of his poetry. I recall so many hours with Don Arturo reading and explaining the poetry and years later when in Granada what Barea interpreted came alive for me.*[79]

Along with other teachers, Barea was harassed by the American Legion and Amvets as a Communist. He was either not offered a renewal of contract or declined one.[80]

While in the USA he continued to record his BBC talks, travelling to New York once a month to record four at a time under the title "Commentary from America".[81] Among his impressions from the United States is one interestingly evocative of Lorca: how in the New York traffic you feel like you are "falling into a moving machine which is trying to devour you".[82]

Towards the end of his life – indeed the last time he left England – the BBC sent him on a 48-day trip to South America. The 1951 Buenos Aires publication of the trilogy had sold 10,000 copies in the first few months. It was followed by *Lorca* and *The Broken Root*, bringing him into touch with a Spanish-speaking audience for the first time. Barea's tour was his apotheosis: he was fêted on an emotional wave of sympathy and gratitude for his books and broadcasts.

He arrived in Buenos Aires by plane on 15 April, 1956, later spending four days in Córdoba and four in Mendoza, before going to Santiago de Chile and Montevideo both for a week, reaching London again *via* Rio on June 1. His time passed in a constant round of interviews, lunches and lectures. In Buenos Aires he was housed in the Writer's House (*Casa del escritor*), headquarters of the Argentine Writers' Association. The report of the British Embassy in Buenos Aires explained:

> *{Barea's} main difficulty in Argentina was to avoid being feted, celebrated and worked to death by hordes of admirers and enthusiasts . . . Barea's visit was an unqualified success from the word go. I would not hesitate in saying that he was the most successful visitor we have had for many years.*[83]

His visit also attracted the attention of the Spanish regime, its embassies and supporters, who mounted a counter-campaign, sneering at the "English writer, Arthur Beria", referring to his acquired nationality and the supposed coincidence of his name and views with those of Stalin's henchman.[84] In the Montevideo press a comical controversy blew up concerning comments Barea made about the famous aviator Ramón Franco, the first person to fly from Spain to Argentina and brother of the dictator. Barea had known Franco in the 1920s and remarked his habit of flying in the nude during the Moroccan war, which offended certain supporters of the dictator.[85]

The reports of the various embassies to Madrid were, as could be expected, not complimentary. They noted that Barea mainly tackled literary themes, but did not avoid political questions when they arose. In Santiago, where he gave lectures on Unamuno and the contemporary Spanish novel, the leftists who went to see him were apparently disappointed at his not being sufficiently leftist:

> *In line with his acquired British nationality, Barea showed off equanimity and balance that satisfied no-one.*[86]

This hostile witness underlined that Barea was not politically very forthcoming and implied that he lacked "spark": the other ambassadors thought this too. The Ministry concluded, with disdain for an inadequate enemy, that Barea was not worth the trouble of a more concerted campaign. Barea was not to know of these assessments. He was never to return to Spain, but his reception in these Spanish-speaking countries moved and pleased him. His visit led to a series of 64 articles that he wrote for *La Nación* of Buenos Aires between the end of his visit and his death 18 months later.[87]

He mattered, too, to the people he met. Rodríguez Monegal, his host in Montevideo, caught the emotion of Barea's visit:

> *. . . the multitudes that heard and surrounded him on his tour, the new friends who brought books or radio programmes to be signed, the old friends who met the man again after so many years' vicissitudes, received from him, from his voice, a message of faith in life that was not expressed in abstract words, but by detailed day-to-day description of a village, of a bird in Spring, of a tree troubled by Autumn.*[88]

The warmth of his reception in South America melted, at least temporarily, the pessimism and fatalism he had expressed to Olive Renier and in *The Broken Root*.

Last years

In his personal life too, during his last decade, Barea seemed to find contentment, or at least reconciled himself to his situation. Joan Gili wrote:

> *They complemented each other beautifully. She {Ilsa} was the brilliant intellectual, and he {Arturo} was the intuitive eye of say "I am a camera" of Christopher Isherwood.*[89]

Olive Renier considered:

> *. . . he was not a particularly amiable man, often grumpy, and quite liable to take offence. The centre of his life was Ilse; he believed totally in her integrity and her commitment.*[90]

However, Ilsa herself was neither especially well, nor happy, during these years, after the sad deaths in exile of her parents in the late 1940s and when an independent career for her failed to take off (see Appendix 3). Health problems assailed her, too. Money continued to be tight. Some observers felt that she exerted too much control over her husband: that she interfered in the lives of his nieces[91] and talked too much at meetings where he had been invited to speak.[92]

There are various and varying images of Arturo Barea in his last years; and all of them should be able to co-exist as contradictory elements in a polyvalent character. The morose grumpy man, quick to take offence; the intelligent political and literary conversationalist, holding forth in the Majorca, at Buscot House or in Pennsylvania cafés; the writer, listening intently, looking (as a little boy had looked into the *Café español* with his nose blurring the glass), questioning his nieces intensely about Madrid; the gregarious, friendly, sentimental man among men (the *persona* of his BBC talks), who liked to drink in working-class pubs and jumped into the front seat of taxis to chat with the driver; the cook who loved the house full of guests; he and Ilsa in harmony writing together at the big table under the oil lamps at Middle Lodge, the room "lined with books and heavy with cigarette smoke";[93] the "amusing and affectionate" man who talked to children;[94] the lonely exile wandering with his black dog through the woods.

Barea had survived near-fatal times in Morocco and Madrid and achieved in his writing what he had doubted was possible. He died suddenly from a heart attack while asleep in the early morning of Christmas Eve, 1957. He was cremated and his ashes scattered at Middle Lodge. Later, Olive Renier arranged for a monument to him and Ilsa in Faringdon churchyard.[95]

VIII

Hunger to Read

Criticism and Stories

This chapter discusses Barea's literary criticism and the short stories he wrote during his time in England, work either lost in small magazines or never published until 2000 and 2001, when Debate (Madrid) printed what is probably the sum total of Barea's critical articles in *Palabras recobradas* (Recovered Words) and then his *Cuentos completos* (Complete Stories). Although most of this work is unknown, it is not for that reason second-rate. Some is: there are both stories and essays of little value or interest, except for the vicarious light cast on Barea and his other work. In this category falls the rather tired book *Unamuno*, for instance (never reprinted since it came out in English and Spanish in 1952 and 1959, respectively). Many of the essays and some of the stories are among his best work: indeed *Lorca* and such stories as *The Scissors* and *El centro de la pista* were written during his most creative period of 1937–1945. He wrote well later too, when his imaginative powers were in decline, especially the introduction to *The Hive* (1952); stories like *Madrid entre ayer y hoy* or *Física aplicada*, both of which date from 1948; or two discussed in more detail below, *Agua bajo el puente* (1947) and *La lección* (1957). Unlike *The Broken Root*, these later stories were mostly throwbacks to his infancy and so recover much of the mood and intensity of Barea's best book, *The Forge*.

From poacher to gamekeeper

Barea was a good critic, mainly because he was interested in who reads books. Unlike most critics educated in University Philology or Literature Faculties, Barea did not take it for granted that people read books. As such, a continuous, vital thread through his criticism is the consideration of how people come to read books, why and what for, a thread very likely given added tautness because his own books were unread by his chosen public. The basic reason, though, was that he knew that he himself would never have developed if the Valencian novelist, Vicente Blasco Ibáñez, had not begun to print off the classics on cheap paper at the price of 35 centimes.

As a school-boy, Barea devoured these badly translated editions of Dickens, Turgenev, Balzac or Victor Hugo, sold off stalls in the streets of Madrid. It was the only way the poor gained access to books and it was the only way they could escape the Church's prescription on what they should read.[1]

Barea's articles of criticism were not hack or contract work he did for a living (though some was indeed commissioned), but are spin-offs from his other books, always reflecting his interests. As such, his articles tend to be well-worked and thought out, somewhat more durable than novelists' normal literary journalism. Chapter III discussed how his coming to terms with what realism was in other writers, his seeking of critical distance from influences such as Baroja and Hemingway, helped his own artistic attitudes and practice mature. His crucial struggle with method in Paris during 1938 was vital for his development as a writer. All his later critical writing was solidly based on his own view of what writing should be, stemming from that 1938 crisis. To put it another way: his critical writing looked at other writings through the lens of what he had discovered about his own literary needs and style. His gift of objectivity came into play here too: i.e. he did not fall into the subjectivist trap of just appreciating those who wrote like him. But his touchstone was his own particular brand of social realism, whether coming from the American tradition through dos Passos and Hemingway or the Spanish through Baroja and Sender.

Thus, Barea's first article, on Ernest Hemingway (see Chapter 3), enabled him to define the sort of realism he wished to write and had already written (*The Forge*) at that time:[2] one which broke with surface description and went "below the surface of things".[3] He convincingly attacks Hemingway's insertion of two gypsies into a Castilian peasant guerrilla band, trounces Hemingway's use of archaic English forms to give "hollow and artificial solemnity" to Spanish speech, and justifiably attacks the unconvincing portrayal of Maria. This romanticisation was later compounded by the film (which Hemingway, to his credit, disliked): Gary Cooper's asking Ingrid Bergman "Did the earth move for you?" gave us one of cinema's great comic scenes.

Barea is on shakier ground when he flatly denies that Spanish men are capable of mass rape, even in war-time: "The brutal violence of Spaniards . . . is always individual".[4] Barea's theorising on Spanish sexual conduct was developed further in *Lorca, the poet and his people*. At times, he slips from legitimate and interesting specific arguments about Spanish behaviour to stereotypes that hold little water, both in *Lorca* and here in *Not Spain, but Hemingway*.

Barea goes on to question "the quality of Hemingway's creative work in this instance, and the problem of his realism as a whole". He argues that

Hemingway is such a good writer that he can convince us that a romantic and false view of the Spanish war is realistic. He concludes:

> *The inner failure of Hemingway's novel – its failure to render the reality of the Spanish War in imaginative writing – seems to me due to the fact that he was always a spectator who wanted to be an actor, and who wanted to write as if he were an actor. Yet it is not enough to look on: to write truthfully you must live, and you must feel what you are living.*[5]

Barea argued that the false note in *For Whom the Bell Tolls* was due to Hemingway's not having lived and felt the lives of the Spanish working-class and peasantry he was writing about. Hemingway only knew the world of the bull-ring, from which Pablo and Pilar in his novel come. With this major article, published in a prestigious journal, Barea started at the top with his literary criticism. He was the first writer to attack Hemingway's best-selling novel for falsifying Spain, which caused considerable controversy at the time.

His second critical article was a long, sympathetic and perceptive review of Gerald Brenan's *The Spanish Labyrinth*.[6] Within the review, he pinpointed a defect in Brenan's great achievement: a certain overplaying of the role of the anarchists and lack of understanding of the importance of the UGT in the development of working-class and peasant organisation in Spain outside Catalonia and Andalusia, especially in Madrid. His argument here illustrates another general strand in Barea's literary criticism: he brought to bear his own trade union and political experience. This was true not only of the essays more partial to political comment such as the one on Brenan, but was also a constant theme in his literary articles and books.

It is, of course, ironic that someone so hostile to intellectuals as Barea should have become a literary critic at all. Not only did he publish in *Horizon*, but he even reached the academic pages of Liverpool University's renowned *Bulletin of Hispanic Studies*. This is merely to confirm that he was anti-elitist rather than anti-intellectual *per se*. As mentioned earlier, he reacted strongly against privilege, in literature as in society: whether it was the Generation of 1927's interest in "high art" or the pro-Stalin social realists who promoted the 1937 Valencia Writers' Congress. (Indeed some of the protagonists of these two movements were the same, such as Alberti or Bergamín.)

Barea's evolution from poacher to game-keeper shows how he himself changed: for one could hardly call Cyril Connolly and *Horizon* any less elitist or "ivory-tower" than the Spanish contemporaries he had earlier spurned. Connolly was both broad enough in his editorial policy to welcome socialist rough diamonds like Barea and perceptive enough to encourage Barea, by 1941 winning a name for himself, to contribute.[7]

As with his other writing, his criticism is almost wholly about Spain or Spanish writers, except for a few South Americans. Barea's greatest literary achievement apart from the trilogy was in this field of criticism: the book *Lorca, the Poet and his People*. In a number of articles, Barea commented on the Spanish novel as it was evolving within Spain under Franco. He noted the early development of the regime's desire to clean its fascist face: "The days when Falangists applauded Millán Astray's shout: 'Down with the intelligentsia' are long past".[8]

Then, in *New Writing in Franco Spain*, Barea explained the censorship rules.[9] A book which had been approved by the censors before publication could still be censored AFTER publication, so forcing its withdrawal from the market. This second censorship was especially damaging, as it kept publishers in continual doubt and of course lost them money. The consequent conservatism and caution of publishers during the 1940s meant that even if interesting novels were being written, they were unlikely to be published.

Barea was not only a commentator in magazines and on the radio. Limited as his opportunities were, he yet sought to intervene. In a 1947 letter, he attacked a broadcast on the Third Programme by Walter Starkie:

> *I claim that the otherwise interesting talk broadcast by Prof. Starkie suffers from limiting its scope because of underlying political considerations.*[10]

Barea based his argument on Starkie's omission of the influence of Antonio Machado and Valle-Inclán on post-war Spain, because "they do not happen to be personae gratae",[11] and his silence on Sender. Starkie also "failed to give any picture of the type of writing inside Spain".[12] Barea's letter demonstrates his main interest: what writers tell us about their society.

The note of hunger

Barea was himself particularly enthusiastic about two 1940s books which did get published within Spain and have remained famous to this day: *La familia de Pascual Duarte* (1943) by Camilo José Cela (once a censor, like Barea) and Carmen Laforet's *Nada* (1945). This autobiographical novel about post-war Barcelona is, for Barea, "depressing and revolting", full of descriptions of mad and hysterical people. "The staggering thing about the book, apart from its popularity, is the cool acceptance of this sort of life as normal".[13]

It is interesting to compare Barea's approach with that of Jorge Semprún, then in his most Stalinist period of PCE militancy. Semprún flayed *Nada* for its nihilism and uselessness as a tool in the working-class struggle. Barea's more sophisticated appreciation is that, even in a decadent closed society such as 1940s Spain, good literature could be produced. Like Semprún, he is interested in the book for what it tells us about Spanish society; but his vision, unlike Semprún's, is not reductionist and mechanical. Barea does not think a book is only good if it is useful in the class struggle: a view of course that the later Semprún would share fully.[14]

Barea believed that a totally non-political novel like *Nada* nevertheless expressed the misery of post-war Spain:

> *She {Laforet} arrived in the city of the victors, and wrote down what she saw: the blurred picture of violence turned inwards.*[15]

Barea finds a kinship between this "blurred picture" and the "heaped-up horrors" of Cela's first novel.[16] The terrible tale of the impoverished and brutish Pascual Duarte is in the tradition of the Spanish satirists who described corruption at all levels of society whilst affirming, to cover themselves, that the book was meant as a deterrent. This "slashing social satire" describes, for Barea, "a deadly, impossible world in which the oppression became tangible and material".[17]

Barea is right, not only in his literary judgement in raising these two books above their contemporaries, but also in that, despite the censorship, they represented a truthful picture of a defeated country or one which had suffered "a deceptive victory, without faith and the fresh air of discussion".[18] Barea showed considerable maturity in his evaluation of what was being written in Spain, avoiding the pitfall of dismissing everything written inside the country as fascist. He perceived that literature even under mass repression could tell the truth about the state of society, and as such placed himself solidly in the line of social literary criticism. For Barea, a book's literary quality was neither reduced to what it explained about society, but nor was it separate or abstracted from this explanation.

Nevertheless, he showed disappointment with post-war literature from within Spain. He did not live to see a certain rebirth of the novel in the 1960s and '70s and, what would have pleased him even more, a huge expansion of the reading public in the 1970s and '80s, even though it was not to reach the working masses in the way that the explosion in reading and education had in the 1930s. He was reduced to pious hope that the "spiritual wound [of the war] will become creative art".[19]

Cela is praised in all of Barea's literary essays as "the only important novelist so far produced by the post-Civil War generation".[20] Barea was able to write the introduction to Cela's most famous novel *La colmena*, published in English translation in 1953 as *The Hive*, where he once again insists on Cela's place in the Spanish novelistic tradition, because of his grim realism, the picaresque pastiche and "the note of hunger" and fear which runs down the centuries through Spanish literature to Cela.[21] Barea quotes Cela as saying that novels in Spain today could only be written in the "slice-of-life" style of *La colmena*. Barea notes that this is a crude sort of realism, which clashes with his own view of a more psychological realism. However, he suggests, no other way of writing is feasible in present-day Spain:

> *Any modern Spanish psychological novel would be lopsided unless it included the harsh domination of hunger, misery and unsafety in their humdrum forms.*[22]

Cela's early books, for Barea, were masterpieces of bitterness and cries of protest against the conditions of life. Barea's way of evaluating them was to measure his response to their power: to let himself feel the truth of their descriptions. The degradation of Pascual Duarte is perhaps no greater than that of Viance in Sender's *Imán* (1930), only 12 years before. But Cela's books of "loss of human dignity" showed that nothing had changed for the better and gave Barea hope that great truthful literature (and thus hope) could be produced even in the darkest years of the dictatorship.[23]

Barea also wrote a long essay on the evolution of Spanish literature from the 1920s through to 1953.[24] This last critical article of his condenses his approach. He focuses on illiteracy and hunger. He discusses how, in the late '20s, cheap mass editions started to be available and sensationalist sex and violence novels began to be devoured by a newly literate working class. Also popular was "rebellion in any shape or form":[25] German and Russian novels of revolt poured out in bad translations. These translations were a large part of Barea's own reading matter, as well as the mass experience of a generation hungry for books. He connects this new mass literature to the marginalisation of the literary figures famous among the elite: Baroja, Azorín and Benavente, who by the late 1920s had no literary or cultural impact at all on the masses. "They were merely famous and successful," Barea comments with a dryness uncommon in him.[26]

This article also praises Sender and his "bizarre, harsh" language of "violent action" that succeeded in describing the new workers' movements of the 1930s.[27] In a separate essay on Sender he acknowledges his debt to the Aragonese writer, especially in relation to *Imán* (see Chapter V), though tantalisingly he hardly refers to the monumental *Crónica del alba*, so evocative of Barea's own work in its autobiographical account of a gifted, rebellious child. His essay on Sender ends with this conclusion:

> *His unique place in Spanish literature – and, so I believe, in the contemporary novel – {is due to} a fusion of the elements of naturalism, symbolism, and idealistic faith.*[28]

Throughout Sender's work there is a bizarre often vivid coexistence of realistic accounts with symbolic visions, the excess of which makes some of his post-war novels like *Epitalamio del prieto Trinidad* hard to swallow. This was the very novel whose English translation (*The Dark Wedding*) Barea's essay on Sender prefaces. Barea praised the development in Sender from 1930s chronicler of popular movements to what he sees romantically and impotently as "a modest hope born from a ruthless recognition of the ugliness and violence in our world".[29] Barea highlights Sender's post-war movement away from realism towards "idealistic faith".

Here is not the place to enter into the applicability of Barea's comments to Sender's work. In citing them, the purpose is to support the argument of Chapter VII that by the late 1940s Barea's thinking had developed away from a socialist belief in the possibility of collective struggle to change the *status quo* – a belief that infuses the early Sender and the Barea of the trilogy. Barea's comment on "hope born from . . . recognition of . . . violence" is reminiscent of the end of *The Broken Root* (see Chapter IX), where among death and despair some frail hope in human goodness arises. But, both here in talking of Sender and on the last page of *The Broken Root*, Barea's views are unconvincing. As he presents no concrete reasons for this hope, it becomes just wishful thinking. As he moved away from the socialist movement, his belief in a human future became more abstract. These comments on Sender and his own hollow attempt to express the same in *The Broken Root* demonstrate the creative and intellectual impasse that Barea had reached by the late 1940s. In this sense it is true to say, along with Marra-López:

> *Empty of his essence, {Barea} at his death was a writer without a future, who was trying, like a beginner, to stammer excessively ingenuous and clichéd words.*[30]

The reason for Barea's increasing recurrence to vague "universal values" lay in his progressive distancing from the impulse of revolt and rebellion which burned in the 1937–1944 period, in the trilogy and *Lorca*. His artistic sterility, shown in the decline from the trilogy to *The Broken Root*, was matched by an intellectual stagnation. He did indeed die as a "writer without a future".

Lorca: poet of class or race?

Before reaching this low-point, Barea wrote the best and longest of his critical essays, *Lorca, the Poet and his People*. Barea placed Lorca above all others of his contemporaries. He is clear why: "Lorca gathered the rich flow of popular expressions and transformed it into a rich flow of poetic images".[31] Barea, despite recognising Lorca's privileged upbringing, understood him as a poet with profound popular roots and impact on the semi-literate workers and peasants fighting fascism:

> *His songs . . . ran through the trenches in the mouths of men who were learning to read in the intervals between fighting. Among the Republican soldiers, he became common property in the way anonymous rhymes do, and much more so than the political verse of those left-wing poets who toured the front.*[32]

He wrote his major study on Lorca for *Horizon* and reworked it for publication in book form in 1944.[33] He was consciously seeking to explain Lorca to an English-speaking audience. As such, the book can be seen as an early example of cross-cultural studies, comparing different modes of viewing death and sex in Spain and Britain, and seeking to integrate them with their political context. The particular moment of politicised culture and Barea's position as an exile seeking to explain his own country combined to produce an excellent and intense book. Ramón J. Sender commented of it:

> *Barea made a brilliant analysis, disengaging himself from . . . wordy virtuosity.*[34]

Sender's point is true of all Barea's criticism: direct and unpretentious. In the sixty-five years since the publication of *Lorca*, a massive amount has been written about the poet, but Barea's book stands the test of time: both because it is source material, giving a first-hand reaction to Lorca, and because it avoids "wordy virtuosity".

Lorca is source material in the sense that it charts the reactions of Lorca's contemporaries to his plays and poetry:

> *I myself never knew Federico García Lorca, though he was of my generation. I did not belong to his set. But I belonged to his public, the people, and it is the people's Lorca whom I know.*[35]

Lorca opens by describing the special place of the poet in the minds of these peasants and workers, who, in taking up arms to defend themselves in 1936, opened their minds to political and cultural life. Thus, *Lorca* was a part of the task Barea set himself in *The Forging of a Rebel* of charting the life of his generation.

The brief 67-page *Lorca* has three chapters: *The poet and the people*, *The poet and sex* and *The poet and death*. In the first, Barea analyses the *Romance de la Guardia Civil española* in the form of an explanation to a *miliciano* of its meaning:

> *He {the militia-man} would produce a tattered copy of Lorca's* Romancero Gitano, *filthy with the grease of the trenches, and say: "Explain this to me. I can feel what it means and I know it by heart, but I can't explain it."*[36]

Barea's argument, in brief, is that Lorca had little interest in politics. Indeed his writings often have an apparently conservative message, yet Lorca's impact was not conservative:

> *. . . a great part of his work is "popular" in the sense that it touched his people as though with the full charge of their own half-conscious feelings . . . The emotional forces he released became part of the shapeless revolutionary movements of Spain whether he intended or not . . . his work became a banner to the Spanish masses.*[37]

Barea explains this conundrum through the concrete exegesis of the *Romance de la Guardia Civil española*, showing how the *miliciano* <u>felt</u> the romantic tale of the *Guardia Civil* and the gypsies as the clash between the State and the peasants:

> *. . . they {the peasants} came to hate the Civil Guard with that bitter personal hatred which it is difficult to feel for an impersonal system.*[38]

To illustrate how Lorca, without political comment or deliberate political intent, touched the emotions of workers and peasants, Barea looks at several other poems through the prism of their impact on semi-literate people he met during the Civil War. In a later essay, Barea made a telling comparison between Alberti who, despite his Communist ideology, lacked sympathy for the Spanish people (in Barea's view) and Lorca who had this ability to reach people through their feelings.[39]

Barea's second chapter *The poet and sex* comments on the plays, *Bodas de Sangre* (Blood Wedding) and *Yerma*.

> *Lorca . . . felt the emotions at the root of the Spanish sexual code so deeply that in his art he magnified them until traditional values came alive with disquieting significance.*[40]

Barea considers that the plays' productions overseas had failed because foreign spectators could only understand them intellectually and "not through the swift, piercing associations and sensations . . . produced in a Spanish public".[41] This chapter of analysis of the traditional Spanish sexual code, based on "masculine honour and [female] virginity", suggests that Lorca's plays are a *reductio ad absurdum* of Spanish sexual repression.[42]

> *I do not mean to convey that Spaniards are like this or that their sexual relations in everyday life conform to this pattern. But this is how the common Spaniard sees himself, and how he feels he is or ought to be. And here lies Lorca's immense power: he makes those obscure sediments of popular Spanish tradition visible with such an emotional impact that he clarifies them. It may be – perhaps – a step towards clearing them away.*[43]

After reading *The Forging of a Rebel*, one cannot read such a passage as this without thinking of Barea's own personal trajectory.[44]

The third chapter examines Lorca's treatment of death. Barea argues that in Spanish culture – perhaps we should read, "Andalusian" – the attitude to death is different from in England:

> *[In England] . . . everyday life is protected by a taboo on the mention of death . . . Perpetual consciousness of death gives Spaniards a deep interest in the manner of their death. They feel, like Lorca's gypsies, that they want to die in dignity.*[45]

Barea maintains that Lorca had to struggle against his fear of annihilation, exacerbated by his inability to accept the easy message of an afterlife.

> *Lorca did not even try to mitigate the fear and terror of individual death by the consolation of religion. In him the spiritual intimacy with death bred an utter clarity of vision – "the ice to his song", said Machado – which heightened his reaction to the living world but forbade him to blind himself to the finality of individual death.*[46]

Barea compares Lorca to Unamuno. Both had a religious sensibility, i.e. a desire for immortality, but without the ability to believe in an after-life:

> *{Unamuno's} . . . "tragic sense of life" made him equally incapable of resigning himself to his final death as an individual and of deceiving himself into believing in a survival or resurrection of his individual life.*[47]

Barea's line of criticism places him among those who were accused of using the dead poet for political or partisan ends. Lorca's friend Martínez Nadal had written as early as 1939:

> *No less to be censured is the tendentiousness of certain English circles, who seek to make of Lorca a* popular *poet in the class sense, instead of, as he is, the poet of the Spanish people, in the racial sense. No protest can be too strong against this use of Lorca's name for purposes of propaganda.*[48]

Later, an internal critic Ynduráin argued that:

> *{Barea in* Lorca*} wants to make out that the lamented poet from Granada is a poet of the proletariat in its struggle against oppression and cruelty.*[49]

In fact, Barea's critique is a curious mixture of the racial and class approach. When he is talking of a special Spanish understanding of sex and death, he is veering towards the folkloric "racial" Lorca. However, in his description of the impact of Lorca on the poor, Barea offers a "class" interpretation. It is a subtly made one, too, avoiding the pitfall of propagandistic distortion precisely because it bases itself on the impact of the poet on the doubly hungry people, thinking for the first time in the Revolution of 1936. Barea's concreteness again makes his case and avoids propagandism.

Unamuno: Bloody-minded independence

Barea wrote another short book of literary criticism: on Unamuno. At first glance, it seems unusual that Barea, a Republican exile, a UGT member close to the Communist Party during the first part of the Civil War, should take a positive interest in Unamuno. For at the outbreak of the war, Unamuno declared himself in favour of the military uprising, was stripped by the Republic of his public positions and at once confirmed as Rector of Salamanca University by the rebels. He became a target of hatred in revolutionary Madrid, all the more intense because he was seen as a traitor to the Republic he had fought for throughout his exile during the Primo de Rivera dictatorship.

Nevertheless, his famous speech of 12 October 1936, an act of legendary courage, again altered both the position and the popular perception of Unamuno. Face to face with Millán Astray (who in general, and very specifically for Barea – see Chapter 5 – incarnated reaction), Unamuno rose to attack the General personally and the military rebellion in general. He was stripped of his Rectorship by the rebels. It was characteristic of Unamuno's independence of mind that in three months he should be sacked by both sides. And he died in melancholy despair just 80 days later.

Despite Unamuno's contradictoriness (ambivalence is not the word, for Unamuno flung himself whole-heartedly at any position he adopted), he became influential after the war among Spanish exiles. There were several reasons: his own 1920s exile, precursor of their own; his very independence, which some exiles (Barea included) felt on reflection they themselves had not maintained among the Communists; and his identification with the quest to investigate the nature of Spain, given even greater impulse after the Civil War than 40 years previously after the defeats in Cuba and the Philippines.

Nevertheless, Barea's book (little more than an extended essay, 51 pages in the English version and 69 in the Spanish) is uninspired. The *TLS* reviewer commented that it gave an exact idea of Unamuno's writings but "rather a frigid picture" of the man:

> *He {Barea} obviously sympathises with him {Unamuno} much less than with García Lorca . . . We are not told of the powerful swing of the master's prose nor of the marvellous string of perhaps legendary anecdotes.*[50]

Unamuno reads like the commission it was: its lack of passion makes it unattractive and so a failure in its purpose of stimulating university students' interest in Unamuno. It reflects the drying up of Barea's imagination and the stultification of his political views, rather than any antipathy to his subject. For we have the word of Ilsa that Unamuno was an impassioned theme of Barea's conversation.[51]

Unamuno, like *Lorca*, is divided into three chapters. The first deals with Unamuno's background and upbringing and focuses on the 1890s, when Unamuno transcended the conflict in his mind between Spanish tradition and opening to Europe, by adopting the idea of fighting for a new Spain yet to be born. The second chapter tackles Unamuno's "tragic sense of life", which Barea defines as essentially the desire for immortality in conflict with the rational belief it does not exist. The third chapter, "The Poet in

Unamuno", explains Unamuno's desire to be a great writer and his realisation that his talent as a poet was slight. Barea maintains (and it is hard to disagree, though the *TLS* reviewer did) that the characters in Unamuno's novels are on the whole shadowy, little more than mouthpieces for his ideas.

Barea shared Unamuno's bloody-mindedness and independence. If Unamuno was talking to a monarchist, he would attack the King; to a catholic, attack the Church; to an atheist, praise God. This independence of mind, combining with great intellectual range and ability, is attractive – at a distance. Barea concludes conventionally that Unamuno's greatness resides in this awkward independence and his ability to reveal his conflicts "with moral courage and integrity". He was "a thinker who teaches how to turn conflict, contradiction and despair into a source of strength".[52] This final sentence of the book returns again to the terrain noted earlier, in connection with Sender and *The Broken Root*, of hope arising amidst the worst of circumstances. However, Barea signally fails to demonstrate this in the text. His views on Unamuno are commonplace and unobjectionable, but the book is not "source material" in the sense that *Lorca* is, and fails to show why Unamuno's stature was so great.

As well as *Unamuno*, Barea wrote a brief essay on two other contemporary thinkers, *Ortega and Madariaga*. It was part of a series in the Chicago *University Observer* to explain the renaissance of Christian Democracy as a political force in post-war Europe. Barea has no time for Ortega's conservative theories of how Spain could be saved by intellectual elites. He saw Unamuno's struggle for a new Spain as a much more honest and democratic enterprise. The apparently rational and liberal Ortega based himself on a traditional view of order in society, which bore no relation to modern realities such as big industry or mass movements.

He saw Madariaga, whom he visited once in Oxford, as an epigone of Ortega, trying to apply Ortega's general views more practically in the political arena. Both denied equality of opportunity for the poor on the basis that there was a natural order of things, a hierarchic principle, more important than class and economics in the structure of society. Barea concludes the essay with his usual reference to the touchstone of his own experience:

> *My own life – the memory of my uncle who had been a laborer and felt an almost religious reverence for the articulate knowledge inaccessible to him, and the memory of unlettered peasants and olive field workers who learned how to read and write in our trenches – makes me believe that Madariaga's passive people is a fiction, a fragment of his hierarchical beliefs.*[53]

Stories

During his years in England, Barea wrote a number of short stories, from *Mister One*, which dates from April 1939 (discussed in Chapter II), to *La lección*, written in Autumn 1957. Fourteen of these were collected by Ilsa Barea in *El centro de la pista* (The Centre of the Ring), published in Madrid three years after Barea's death.[54]

These stories have been barely mentioned by critics: not surprisingly, as they were published at a time (1960) when the impact of Barea's trilogy had waned and in Franco's Spain, where he was unknown except to a few hundred readers of works published abroad. They were not re-issued at the time of the first Spanish publication of the trilogy (1977) and were only republished in a limited edition in a series of Extremaduran writers (1988). Not until 2001, with *Cuentos completos*, did *El centro de la pista* reach a wider audience. *Cuentos completos* also includes an unexpected bonus: 14 stories not included in *Valor y Miedo* or *El Centro de la pista*. Some of these were previously unpublished. They show an unexpected side to Barea. As well as stories like the very interesting *Una paella en Marruecos* or *La Almenara*, which could have fitted perfectly into the trilogy, he tries a ghost story (*El callejón de Cristo*), a bullfighting anecdote (*Curro y la Triana*), a reflection on exile (*Teresa*) and various attempts at a futurist parable (*Bajo la piel*) – one version of which did appear in *El centro de la pista*. Such stories suggest a surprising restlessness as a writer, a readiness to experiment with various styles and themes.

El centro de la pista is different from Barea's other volume of stories *Valor y miedo*, in that its style is much more lyrical and subject-matter more varied. Its main problem, which it shares with *Valor y miedo*, is that very few of the stories are short stories in the proper sense of the word. Although they are usually longer and fuller than Barea's first book's sketches, they often lack the twist, plot, personality or ending that creates a satisfying short story.

La rifa, for example, describes how a young girl uses her mother's money to win a *duro* in the market lottery. It contains a subtle account of the relationships within a family; and, exception which proves the rule, is not autobiographical. Barea tells the story with considerable skill from the points of view of the 7 year-old girl, her older sister and her mother. The story as story, however, does not work because Barea does not know how to end it. The ending is sudden and confused. Thus it misses being a story and becomes more a slice-of-life chunk of description, just like the fascinating account of characters from his childhood, *Madrid entre ayer y hoy*.

In general, Barea did not have the particular gift of compression necessary in a short-story writer. He knew how to order material, indeed to express a lot in a very short space (see analyses of parts of *The Track* and *The Clash* in Chapters V and VI), but in the trilogy his effects are mostly created by contrasting events and contexts developed over many pages.

The stories of *El centro de la pista* are of great interest to anyone who has read *The Forging of a Rebel* and wants to delve deeper into Barea's mental world; and some of them are indeed accomplished. Nine of the 14 could have fitted into *The Forging of a Rebel*, mostly *The Forge* – which once again shows the unity of all Barea's work – just as most of the incidents of *Valor y miedo* would have fitted into *The Clash*. Like *Lorca*, the stories are footnotes to Barea's novelised autobiography, feeding from the same source of his life in Spain and, in most cases, of his childhood.[55]

El cono and *Agua bajo el puente* attack social injustice in the countryside. The events probably date (as there is no evidence he ever invented anything substantial) from Barea's time working with his brother as manager on a big estate in 1928 or his months at Novés in 1935/6. *El testamento* describes the folly of waiting to inherit wealth; *El huerto* attacks snobbery in Córdoba, where Barea had family; *Madrid entre ayer y hoy*, the social changes accompanying the introduction of running water in the first years of the century; *Física aplicada*, like the sinister *Las tijeras*, is about children playing.

I want to look closer at two contrasting stories, *La lección* and *Agua bajo el puente*. The seven-page *La lección* (Big Granny)[56] is a story like several in the volume, imbued with Barea's longing for the past, a longing expressed in its direct and colloquial language. Indeed it is directly autobiographical, with the names of his paternal grandmother Inés[57] and his sister Concha in the text. Its recreation of the Madrid of his childhood is told in a tone of tender memory, which contrasts effectively with Inés' crude, aggressive roughness. The longing is also expressed in the almost obsessive detail ("My sister Concha had her stiff little plaits tied with red ribbons") and the description of the railway station.[58] The cinematic intensity of Barea's externally seen, naturalist descriptions not only creates (as is to be expected) a vivid *costumbrista* picture of old Madrid, but also a subjective world of emotive memory. As in *The Forge*, the realist Barea at times seems closer to Proust than Baroja. The reason lies in this excess of vision, this extreme detail, which gives a subjective, emotional tinge to the descriptions. Barea combines a comic and affectionate tone about his grandmother with this intensity of description. The story ends satisfyingly with a twist; and then is beautifully and economically rounded off with the author's own later experience, when he put his grandmother's lesson into practice. Not many of Barea's stories are of this type, tied up with a sudden twist; and in this and a few others that are, such as *Cleptomanía* or *La plancha* (both in *Cuentos completos*), we see the qualities of a born story-teller, a man who loved to tell stories, in Ilsa's words, "mixing the crudities of a ruthless account with tender nostalgia".[59] Big Granny's lesson is a classic lesson of individualism and pride:

> *"Let it be a lesson to you, you snivellers. If you behave as if you were all sugar and honey, the flies will eat you. And if you want to get on in life, don't let anyone tread on your corns. It's the only way to make 'em respect you . . . "*[60]

If Inés is the toughest granny on the block, *Agua bajo el puente* is an altogether rougher and harder story. Also autobiographical, it is an excellent political story, beautifully and subtly written, which in eleven pages succeeds in explaining why the poor peasantry supported the Republic and would fight to defend their gains in the Civil War. Its style is more sober and spare than that of *La lección*, though it does not abandon the conversational, confiding voice common to several of the stories in *El centro de la pista*.

The story is about the change that the Republic brought. Set on a Spring day in 1931, it recalls the circumstances around the killing of a hated *cacique*, Don Antonio, several years previously. There are three versions of events, told as the narrator draws closer to the site of the crime: that of the self-satisfied right-wing magistrate with a "weak man's mouth", of the Civil Guard who does not like the new regime but is prepared to cut his coat to fit, and of the narrator's friend the shoemaker who is revealed to have played a decisive part in the killing. The magistrate is an appalling amateur writer, with a baroque style, so alien to Barea's spareness and directness. For Barea, such a style in itself is evidence of corruption.

The reason for Don Antonio's murder is clear (though a sharper sexual motive is also implied):

> *{Don Antonio} . . . manipulated wonderfully well the elections, the town councils, the police and those in a good position . . . In the village there was not a single man who did not hate Don Antonio with all his soul.*[61]

The skill of the story is that by gradually setting the scene through the different points of view, Barea succeeds in justifying the murder. Don Antonio's death is justified by the release of the water, whose loss was what had cast the villagers into debt and dependence on him in the first place. Symbol and concrete image mesh, both functioning perfectly at their own levels: the hopes of the new Republic flow with the water "snaking towards the tiny thirsty vegetable plots".[62] Barea understood all too well the value of water, as he had shown in *The Track* when he described the stubborn fig-tree fed by the spring. And he understood too the role of the all-powerful *cacique*, as he showed at the start of *The Clash* with another Don Antonio, Heliodoro the usurer of Novés. Politically and artistically *Agua bajo el puente* is a triumph: surely Barea's best story.

IX

Exile without Resentment

Arturo Barea lived the last 18 years of his life in exile. Though exile is always a painful state of statelessness, in Barea's case, paradoxically, his personal uprooting coincided with his greatest success. All his best work was written in exile: he became a well-known writer in exile [in Ynduráin's words: "our only writer born to Literature in exile"],[1] even though the process of his conversion from middle-class businessman, morally adrift, to a committed novelist had begun while he was still in Spain. The first part of this chapter deals with exile, *destierro (dis-earthing)* in the vivid Castilian term, and how it affected Barea; the second examines his novel on exile, *The Broken Root*.

Words lost in the wind

José Marra-López cites Barea as the outstanding example of the thesis of his pioneer book (it dates from 1963) on the Spanish novelists of the 1939 Diaspora, a theory worth examining for the light it throws on Barea's work.[2] Marra-López states:

> *As a writer, Barea, for better or worse, remained faithful to his Spanish roots, so much so that he is almost the only exile writer who never, in his entire writing career, strayed from his native soil.*[3]

In other words Barea wrote only about Spain. The sole exceptions in his published works are two brief stories: otherwise every single thing he wrote was set on Spanish soil or dealt with Spanish themes.[4]

Marra-López maintains that Spanish political exiles suffered particularly from enforced absence from Spain. They found greater difficulty than other exile nationalities in integrating into local society. In the 1939 exodus, the precarious economic circumstances of many exiles increased this isolation. Moreover, the historic magnitude of the Civil War and the subsequent length of exile and dampening of hope as Franco's regime consolidated itself after 1945 deepened the exiles' misery.

The most cursory look at the novelists Ayala, Sender, Chacel, Rodoreda,

Aub or Barea, or, in other fields, Sánchez Albornoz or Américo Castro, confirms that the writers of the 1939 Diaspora were obsessed with explaining Spain and its problems. If then the 1939 exile was unable to write of anything but Spain, a vital follow-up question arose for them: who was their audience? Marra-López cites Francisco Ayala, who wrote forlornly in 1948: "Who are we writing for? For everyone and for no-one, would be the reply. Our words are taken by the wind: we trust that some of them are not lost".[5]

The exile, continues Marra-López's thesis, has "eternal desperate longing" for Spain, expressed in constant awareness of his/her having been violently uprooted and an obsessive preoccupation with the fatherland (*la patria*). However, as time passes, the exile becomes steadily more distant from the reality of his/her own country. This process leads to the creation of "the invented Spain" by authors whose writing about the Spanish past is exhausted, but who no longer know what the Spanish present is like.[6] Increasingly the exiled writer runs the risk of writing for no real audience at all.

In the most extreme cases, the exile returns to a beloved and longed-for Spain, but that Spain imagined in exile no longer exists, just as the past no longer exists except in memory. Fictionally this occurs in Ayala's *El regreso* and Barea's *The Broken Root*, in both of which the returnee has little option but to leave again, feeling an exile in his own country.[7] As Barea's protagonist Antolin, in Madrid towards the end of *The Broken Root*, concludes:

> *"In London . . . I was always wondering if I would be less lonely among people who speak my language. That's finished now. Of course, I'll be a stranger in England all my life; but then, I'm a stranger here too, and that hurts more and is a worse kind of loneliness because it tears at me."*[8]

The case of Arturo Barea seems, indeed, to fit Marra-López's argument like a glove. Barea's exile was in England, a particularly lonely place within this Diaspora. His literary production, almost wholly produced in exile, is entirely about Spain. His greatest achievements, *The Forging of a Rebel* and *Lorca*, concern the Spain he knew intimately and then recalls in every yearning detail. His weakest book, *The Broken Root*, is precisely when Barea imagines the return to Spain he cannot actually make.[9] The titles of his books graphically make a very similar point about his uprooting. Barea tells us that he first thought of calling *The Forge*, *Las raíces* (Roots);[10] and of course *The Broken Root* is that severed root when Franco's victory chopped Antolin and the defeated Republicans out of their native land's contemporary history. The root was an image in Barea's mind at least from when he wrote *The Track*, where the fig-tree roots, so hard to break, represent underground resistance to reactionary Spain's imperial quest.

As further evidence in support of Marra-López's argument, we can point to Barea's virtual silence after this last novel.[11] The suggestive possibility that he started or planned another novel, but never got anywhere with it, confirms the withering of his inspiration, so fertile just ten years previously.[12] Moreover, though he could read English, Barea never learned to speak or write it well.[13] He was no Conrad, Nabokov or Koestler, who changed languages through exile and actually wrote their most famous books in English. And certainly he could never be accused of writing a novel or even a short story about his adopted country.

Closer examination, however, suggests that Marra-López's interpretation does not correspond to Barea's story. At a personal level, Barea integrated himself to a high degree into English life, in various ways which affect understanding of his work. Margaret Weeden, who shared the Bareas' houses at Fladbury and Mapledurham during the war years, wrote:

> *Arturo Barea was one of those people who are at home in any sort of company. He wasn't a bit interested in famous people, only in people as human beings. He was tremendously popular in all the country pubs that were the "local" in whatever part of England he happened to be living. He would drink beer and play darts with the farm labourers, tease the landlord, and somehow, even when supplies were at their lowest, always manage to wangle from that gentleman a generous supply of beer, wine and cigarettes.*[14]

Barea rapidly found his feet in England. The Puckeridge pub had been the basis for his first British article in 1939.[15] Pubs were the places he found most congenial throughout his years in England: perhaps in them he found some echo of Serafín's bar, which he had frequented in his youth and had become his refuge at crucial times of stress during the Civil War. In the 1950s he and his neighbour David Vine went together to pubs.[16] Pubs, too, supplied the basic material of anecdotes and personalities for his BBC broadcasts (see Chapter VII).

A second pointer to Barea's involvement in English life is his lack of relationships with other Spanish exiles. In the liberal exile of the 1820s, large numbers of Spanish intellectuals grouped together in London; but after 1939, most Republican exiles went to Central and South America, France or the Soviet Union and only a scattering to other places. Few reached Britain, partly because Britain was much harder to get into than it had been, especially for left-wing exiles. The Bareas were lucky to have found a sponsor.[17] Exact figures do not exist, but it would seem that out of some four hundred thousand exiles, who had left Spain by April 1939, only a small proportion (almost certainly less than ten thousand) found refuge in Britain.[18]

Among these there were relatively few artistic or political figures: the 1939 exile was unprecedented in Spanish history as a mass exodus. Barea describes briefly this world as the background to Antolin's experiences in *The Broken Root*.[19] In the Majorca restaurant, Barea met other Spaniards and discussed news from home (see Chapter VII), which he did with his customary gregariousness but without becoming politically involved.[20] In Madrid he had liked to chew over political ideas in bars, but detested the intrigue of committee and party politics. Impotent intrigue is of course the very essence of exile politics, where negative features of political discussion are exacerbated by the exiles' impotence.

Nevertheless, Barea was involved to some degree in exile politics in 1940/41. He wrote at least one article for *Españoles*, an exile magazine, and was present on the November 1941 anniversary of the Russian Revolution at the London inauguration of the short-lived *Hogar español* (Spanish House). However, his living outside London and starting to work for an organisation, the BBC, that frowned on political activity (except its own) contributed to his distance from exile politics.[21] His 1948 adoption of British nationality, his going to live in the country and his enjoyment of country life are additional pointers to his acceptance of England. Most of all, his explicit praise of England throughout his radio broadcasts go a lot further than merely formal courtesies (see Chapter VIII).

Barea involved himself in exiles' cultural activities even less than in their political life. Although he visited and spoke at Oxford University and lived briefly in Oxford, he was not part of the academic world.[22] Barea may have met the poet Luis Cernuda, who worked at Cambridge during the 1940s, but there is no record of any friendship between them, though Barea recommended Cernuda warmly for BBC work.[23] There was little Spanish cultural life in which he could become involved; and what there was, he avoided.

Barea's political apartness was in fact no different from his pre-Civil War attitudes: it had only been during that war that he had briefly moved to the centre of the political stage. Similarly, his aloofness from Spanish cultural circles was consistent with the previous pattern of his life. In this respect England represented not a rupture in Barea's attitudes, but continuity.

However, whereas exile might be expected to bring an ossifying of previous attitudes, especially in a man over 40 when he left his country, the reverse was true for Barea. After the initial shock of his first year, Barea relaxed in Britain and developed a more, rather than less, positive view to cultural reviews and figures. Chapter VII noted his contact with Ilsa's colleagues at the Monitoring Service, his connections with Brenan and Connolly, his meeting John Betjeman.[24] He knew too some of the people involved in the "Searchlight" series. All this was new to Barea: unlike other exiled writers, he had not experienced life in cultural circles before leaving Spain and so had nothing to miss, no sense of loss in this respect.

In beginning to write essays of literary criticism, Barea showed that his earlier antipathy to other writers and critics had softened. Previously, he had rejected cultural and literary circles, partly on account of their rejection of him when in 1913 he had attempted to enter Madrid's literary world.[25] Even more indicative of his previous approach had been his attitude to the *Residencia de Estudiantes* (Students' Residence), which in the post-First World War period became the base for one of the most brilliant literary and artistic generations of Spain's or any country's history. This was precisely Barea's generation: he was a year older than García Lorca, three years older than Buñuel, five years older than Alberti and Dalí. And yet he never met Lorca or any of them.[26] It is worth quoting at length what Barea has to say about the *Residencia*:

> *There existed a progressive cultural center in Madrid, Giner de los Rios' Institución Libre de Enseñanza. From there and from his Residencia de Estudiantes issued a new generation of writers and artists: my own way of thinking might have fitted in there. But when I probed the chances of entry I was confronted with a new aristocracy hitherto unknown to me, an aristocracy of the Left. It was as expensive . . . as to enter one of the luxury colleges of the Jesuits. There were free courses and lectures, but to follow them would have meant giving up the work I had to do for my living. I came to feel that the marvelous achievements of Giner de los Rios had a very serious defect, the basic defect of all Spanish education: the doors were closed to working people . . .*
>
> *There was no road for me there.*[27]

Unlike so many working-class children in this situation, Barea's desire to write was not totally extinguished. But it took the enormous upheaval of the Civil War, twenty-five years after the period he is writing about in the above extract, to stimulate him to start again.

During the Civil War, Barea recorded his continuing contempt for the majority of writers and intellectuals who passed through Madrid, including the famous participants in the Writers' Congress:

> *. . . the International Anti-fascist Writers' Congress, with its exhibition of intellectuals posturing on the background of fighting Madrid.*[28]

However, no-one, not even a relatively unpolished writer like Barea, can mature as a writer with infantile rejection of all other writers. He felt he had nothing to learn from Benavente or from the *gongoristas* of his own generation. And Barea preferred Serafín's tavern to Alberti, Malraux or lesser pro-Stalin propagandists of the Writers' Congress; with justice in terms of his own writing and personality, even if not without some inverted snobbery.

There were at least two writers he met and respected during the war: John dos Passos and Ernest Hemingway. Both were recorders of grim contemporary reality in prose, working outside the direct influence of Stalinist social realism. The "cinematic" effect that is evident in a number of sketches of *Valor y miedo* and in *The Forge* is close to dos Passos' techniques. Perhaps too the confidence to try and chronicle his age, mixing private and public events, owed a debt to dos Passos, even though the latter's collage way of doing this was different.[29]

Hemingway was more of a benchmark for Barea. As discussed in Chapter III, Barea went through a process of change and struggle in 1938 to move from the surface realism of *Valor y miedo* to the more sophisticated psychological realism of *The Forge*. Barea's 1941 essay on Hemingway implicitly summarises that process within a critique of Hemingway's romanticisation of Spain.[30] *Valor y miedo* may owe something to Hemingway in its baldness and directness of style. More than anything, however, friendship and discussion with such good writers gave Barea the confidence to start.

Though Barea was not averse to learning from writers, he went his own way and seemed unawed by reputations. It should be no surprise that in Britain he was no more interested in the literary world than previously, although now, as he was himself a writer, he met other writers. There was continuity in his attitudes. And where he changed, his attitudes were softened, rather than hardened as might normally be expected, by exile.

Arturo Barea ends *Lorca* by discussing what he saw as Lorca's panic, reflected in *Poet in New York*, lines which inspire reflection on Barea's own position as an exile:

> *In 1930, this poet from Granada, - the landscape of his mind alive with the silvery green of olive fields and white-washed little houses . . . finds himself in a street canyon of New York, on a volcanic floor of asphalt.*[31]

Barea describes the poet's "angry frustration" at being cut off from his Andalusian roots and the hatred that exploded within him. Barea asks why Lorca responded thus and suggests:

Lorca, like so many others, refused to become part of a world other than his own, and thus that other world seemed to him only a living death . . . {he} was now suddenly thrown back on his own weakness and loneliness . . . and his vision was no longer clear.[32]

This response, extreme as it is, is reminiscent of Barea's own first feelings on his exile during 1938 and 1939. Yet, unlike Lorca's panic in New York on losing touch with his familiar world, Barea's artistic vision was clarified and fed by exile. Barea's most productive years coincided with the first years of his exile. All his writing shows that Barea's heart and mind were fixed on Spain. But this did not stop him finding literary nourishment and maturity in England. His dispassionate objectivity and ruthless clarity, which were the necessary tools for his investigation of his own past and the causes of the war, were aided by his exile. He was able to overcome panic, to then look from a distance. His own past, Spain itself, he could perceive better from England.

The Broken Root: entering the beehive

Barea's last novel, *The Broken Root*, contradicts any idea that Barea had found full peace of mind in his last years. It is a painful, emotional book, which does indeed fit Marra-López's thesis of the exile out of touch with contemporary Spanish reality, writing compulsively about an invented Spain.

The Broken Root is Barea's only imagined novel, in the sense that he is writing a story which is not literally true and inventing fictional characters. And it is not a good book. It has suffered almost universal mauling from critics of both left and right, British, Spanish and South American.[33]

Its failure is double, technical and ideological. All in all, it forms a sad document.[34]

A highly-coloured work, bordering on melodrama, useless because it is not credible.[35]

. . . a failed novelist, as he deals in melodrama.[36]

The description of a reality he had not experienced and, therefore, assembled on four clichés lacking genuine representative value.[37]

These negative reactions cannot be called unfair, but (without going to the extremes of dos Passos' praise), I would like to rescue the novel from such universal condemnation. Curiously, critics do not focus on its greatest defect for a reader, its lifelessness: it lacks the sparks of vivid descriptions or anecdotes.

The key failure of *The Broken Root* lies in that there are not two struggling arguments, i.e. it is not dialectical but, rather, monolinear. Barea tilts everything to support his proposal: that it is impossible for his exiled protagonist to return to Spain. As such, the tension that arises from the struggle within Barea throughout *The Forging of a Rebel*, the dualism of the child caught between poverty and wealth, and of the man torn between honour and corruption or between union struggle and a comfortable job, no longer exists. There is indeed an anguished conflict within his protagonist Antolin Moreno: to stay in Spain or return to England. All the dice, though, are loaded in favour of the return. The situation is prejudged.

This is the central artistic failure of the novel. It represents a political failure too, for profound politics cannot emerge from Manichean board-games. But *The Broken Root* is not all dross. It is a painfully raw and honest book, written with Barea's characteristic sincerity. It is of a oneness with all his work, in that the subject is Spain and the state of Spain. Whereas *The Forging of a Rebel* examined the causes of the Civil War and *Struggle for the Spanish Soul* investigated the ideology of the victors, *The Broken Root*, almost the "fourth" part of the trilogy, seeks to examine the consequences of defeat and the reality of life under the dictatorship. Its mood is gloomy and static, similar to the chill and misery in *Nada*, a book which Barea admired (see Chapter VIII). It is not so distant from the stifling, nihilistic mood of Cela's *La colmena*, published at much the same time (just as Cela's *Pascual Duarte* and *The Forge* had been contemporaries). The image of the beehive in Cela's novel and in Víctor Erice's film (*The Spirit of the Beehive*, 1973) two decades later, to represent a closed and isolated society, would be appropriate too to Barea's novel. Barea's achievement in creating this remote, closed, oppressed society into which irrupts a man from another world is real and should not be ignored because of other defects.

In three specific ways *The Broken Root* can be read as a sequel, or rather a melancholy coda, to *The Forging of a Rebel*. First, it seeks to continue the story of Madrid up to 1937 contained in the trilogy with a portrait of the hunger, repression and black market of Madrid in 1949. Secondly, Barea maintains the balance between the social and psychological, which, as he had theorised throughout the 1940s, made him the kind of realist who was not content just to seek social explanations, but investigated the psychology of his characters. And thirdly, Barea repeats in *The Broken Root* his use of a large cast of secondary characters, with which he seeks to illuminate the various classes and tendencies in society.

The Broken Root has three principal differences from the trilogy. First, the novel is written not through the eye of the first person narrator, but from a position of authorial omniscience, entering not only into the thoughts and feelings of Antolin, but also into the minds of other characters, especially Antolin's children Pedro, Juan and Amelia. Secondly, Barea is not writing about a Madrid he knows. The Madrid of *The Broken Root* is the Madrid Barea knew plus ten years of imagined change. For a writer as fresh and descriptive as Barea, this lack of direct knowledge of the 1949 city is damaging. During the writing of the book he talked closely with his nieces Maruja and Leonor, who came to live with him in 1947,[38] but the directly seen vividness of detail so important to Barea's writing in *The Forging of a Rebel* is missing. The third important difference is that the novel is too schematic: many of the characters are only there to represent abstract ideas. This point I will return to later.

The plot is strong in two respects. It is similar to *The Track* in that it is naturally framed by the protagonist's arrival in and departure from a foreign country; and, second, it opens clearly, defining the different characters in their backgrounds during the first five chapters. Antolin returns to Madrid from exile in London ten years after the end of the Civil War. He wants to see his wife and three children, whom he had left behind, and to sort out whether to stay with them or return to live with Mary in England. He is moved both by a sense of responsibility and also, more selfishly, by his loneliness in England. His arrival is the catalyst for explosions in his family. His wife Luisa has retreated into bitterness, snobbery and spiritualism; one son, Pedro, is a pimp and black marketeer well in with the Falange; the other, Juan, is a Communist factory worker; and his daughter, Amelia, is under the control of another of Barea's long line of nasty priests, the unctuous Father Santiago (see Chapter 4).

After the first five chapters of exposition, the plot runs into problems, as Barea's admirer Marra-López denounces:

> *. . . in a series of "coincidences" that are truly ingenuous in novel-writing terms . . . more characters of the tale begin to appear, linked to each other like a string of sausages.*[39]

One could say the plot works like clockwork: each coincidence is fully justified. Conchita knows Eusebio because she is his masseuse; Caro knows Pedro because they both visit the same brothel; Conchita knows Luisa because she is Américo's medium. However, whereas one coincidence is realistic enough and two acceptable, such a lengthy succession of them (*a string of sausages*) undermines any semblance of verisimilitude.

Antolin sees his family in action, as Pedro and Amalia denounce Don

Américo the spiritualist and Juan, who are both killed, to the police and church, respectively. Disgusted, he feels conveniently relieved of any responsibility for these children and, after managing to fix up Amelia in a convent and Luisa with Conchita's mother (another improbable coincidence), he decides to return to England. To escape the police and get Lucia, his dead son's girl-friend, out of the country, he has to dirty his hands and use the services of the black-marketeer (*estraperlista*) Colonel Caro.

Stranger in his own land

The theme of exile pervades the novel. From the first page, when Antolin is dozing in the train drawing in to Madrid and "memories of innumerable trips to the sierra rushed to his mind",[40] Barea is in the terrain of nostalgia for the past. Antolin then misunderstands the reason for the four young men jumping from the moving train. He thinks they are young bull-fighters without tickets, whereas in fact they are smugglers. From general dreamy nostalgia for a lost past, Barea has shifted the reader rapidly into a rough present: Antolin no longer understands what is going on in his own country. He is an exile in his own land. As Antolin leaves the train, he bumps into someone on the platform and says "I'm so sorry" in English. Embarrassed, sticking out with his clothes and manners as a foreigner, he moves away down the platform, "wishing to disappear among the people".[41] He will not be able to. He is decisively different, as his first meeting – with his old friend Eusebio – rapidly confirms.

These strong opening pages of *The Broken Root* set the scene with Barea's customary care. The basic thematic question of the novel is clearly expounded: whether Antolin will stay or go, whether he will "disappear among the people" or remain an exile. This failed novel confirms once more that Barea is a much more careful writer in his composition, plotting and juxtaposition of themes than he has usually been given credit for.

Just as Barea had in *The Track*, here too he uses imagery of roots (mentioned at least 20 times in the novel) to underpin his theme. Antolin was uprooted by the war.[42] Pedro, his criminal son, has his roots covered in slime.[43] As the novel moves towards its climax, Antolin tries to work out his position in the following scene with his confidante and landlady Doña Felisa:

> *"Most people I've met in Madrid . . . are just as much uprooted as I am, though they didn't go into exile. In fact, they're rootless. What is it that has gone so*

wrong? . . . Of course, I know everybody in this country's poisoned by the corruption and the violence of the last ten years."[44]

Barea's argument here contradicts his previous image of roots being severed by exile and the war, for Antolin says there is something more than Francoism which has uprooted everybody. This echoes the words of Barea's frontispiece to the novel:

In telling a story about Spaniards living in Madrid in 1949, I have tried to give shape to human problems which are universal and by no means confined to a particular country.[45]

In so extending the idea to include all humanity, he falls into a kind of superficial existentialism, i.e. that everyone in the modern world is rootless. This makes the image of roots and rootlessness too general to have any specific weight. It blunts the sharpness of his critique of Franco's Spain.

Conchita, the *deus ex machina* who extracts both Barea the novelist and Antolin the protagonist from their problems, contradicts both the author's frontispiece and protagonist by returning the image of uprooting to its more specific use of "here" and the victims of the dictatorship. When Antolin is worrying about taking Lucia, his replacement daughter, out of the country, Conchita tells him:

"Don't talk nonsense, Antolin, we're all uprooted. And what sort of home have we got? Most young people would give anything to get away to America because there isn't any hope for them here."[46]

Barea's final mention of roots comes on the last page of the novel, where he wants to indicate at the bitter moment of Juan's funeral a message of hope for the future. This hope is personified in decent people like Rufo the UGT man, Conchita the independent spirit and Lucia. But the message is unconvincing, given the uniformly pessimistic tone of the novel, from which one can only extract the conclusion that all the Spanish can do under Franco is emigrate. The message of hope and renewal is merely tacked on. A grave-digger explains to Antolin and Lucia that what looked like "a heap of grey, fretted and splintered bones" are in fact broken roots, which refuse to die.

. . . small bundles of whitish fibres sprouted from odd patches of wrinkled root, lay like floss on the dark earth and seemed to cling to it with weak tenacity.

> *"If we dug them in where the ground isn't sour, and if it rained for three days, the young shoots would start growing," said the man with the spade.*[47]

Just as, on the last page of *The Track*, Barea used the mad blind Arab to mock the pretensions of the imperial road-builders; at the end of *The Broken Root* he uses the grave-digger to affirm faith in the future against the same dark forces. The problems are that in the latter case the argument is not shown and developed artistically; the "roots" image does not arise from the action. And besides, the "roots" image is confused, used to mean different things at different points.

Symbolism of this sort was not Barea's forte. Barea's strengths, as *The Forging of a Rebel* shows so well, were vivid description, especially of working-class life, the quick movement of feelings provoked by a concrete situation, his honesty of observation and response. These strengths are marred, but not totally obliterated, in *The Broken Root*. Chapters 12 and 13 are full of action and succeed in involving the reader in the destiny of Juan and then his father. The opening chapters, where Antolin remembers and describes England to Eusebio, are rich in description and set up well London and Mary as counter-weights to Madrid and Antolin's family. The scene-setting of Antolin's family which follows is strong, too. Descriptions of the family's tenement or Doña Felisa's *pensión* live with the vividness of things Barea had known or seen. Many of the secondary characters are well-sketched: *La Tronío* the brothel-keeper, Doña Felisa, Don Américo the spiritualist, Juan and his girl-friend.

However, the book is very uneven. Other characters, such as the police chief or Colonel Caro, are plucked straight from a rogues' gallery. Ynduráin justly criticised Barea for his black or white characters, both secondary and principal:

> *If some characters are so irredeemably hateful and the others have such moral beauty, there is no way any general consequences can be drawn.*[48]

Of the main characters, the weakest of all is Conchita, who colours the book with sentimental yearning. She is the tart with a heart of gold, the tough woman who has retained sensibility in a bitter world, in short Barea's fantasy of the ideal Spanish woman he would have liked to know. Amalia and Luisa are also unconvincing caricatures. Yet Juan and Pedro are much more rounded and credible. Possibly this had as much to do with Barea's difficulty in drawing female characters as with his Manicheism.

Manicheism is the main criticism arising from the woodenness of these characters made both by Yndurain and the novelist Anthony Powell, for whom "the characters tend to represent an abstract idea" in the style of Koestler.[49] And so Antolin, a more rounded figure, is judged by different standards to those who represent for Barea the various evils of the Francoist state: Father Santiago and Antolin's *beata* daughter (Church), the black marketeers and Pedro (Corruption), the policemen (Repression). This is a fatal weakness in the novel.

However, the book is not just an autobiographical projection of how things would have been, had Barea returned to Madrid to see his family. There is, of course, a lot of this: for example, Luisa's spiritualism is not so distant from the involvement of Barea's first wife, Aurelia, in a sect.[50] But the character of Antolin himself is not similar to what we know of Barea's. Both Antolin's indecisiveness and his recognition of the phlegmatic "Englishness" of his own character as against the passionate "Spanishness" of Eusebio and others have little to do with Barea's traits. Antolin does share many things with the author: big things such as his age, his exile, his attachment to England combined with the pain of exile, the contrast in his attitude to women and marriage with his own previous attitude; and lesser details like his eye for pretty women.

Nevertheless, in creating the character of Antolin, Barea sought not to project himself, but rather to get away from himself.[51] He tried to imagine a man with different traits to himself in Madrid: for this, he gave Antolin a different background (he is a hotel-worker, he has an English lover with whom he shares no passion and no commitment) and a more analytical, phlegmatic character. And in doing so, Barea seeks to subject Madrid to a rational, dispassionate inquiry. However, he imagines Antolin insufficiently. Life and spark is lacking.

Ortega described the novel with words such as "falsification" and phrases like "the lack of authenticity between the lived and the written".[52] These terms are too strong, in that they imply intention to deceive: the novel is honest in its intention. But the contrasts and conflicts are stereotyped in terms of nationality (English/Spanish) and character (the bad falangist), features too of his radio broadcasts of the time (see Chapter VII). Barea showed conclusively he was not able to imagine a world and a protagonist different from his own and himself. The criticisms that Barea's information about Spain was deficient seem of scant importance. If the characters and their problems had come to life, no-one would worry that a price here or a detail there was not right.

Into *The Broken Root*, a critique of Franco's Spain, politics inevitably enter. But Antolin himself is not a political animal; and, as in *The Clash*, there is a startling absence of political comment, despite the book being manifestly a denunciation of the Franco dictatorship. The dull Antolin is profoundly disappointed by the failure of political action[53] and, like Barea himself, sees no perspective other than trying to behave decently on a personal level. The PCE, as incarnated in Juan and his link Ramon, is caricatured as dogmatic, moralistic and ineffective. Barea's own union the UGT, in the shape of Eusebio and Rufo, is seen as warmer and nicer, but does nothing.

This leads Barea to put most weight on the activities of Conchita, vaguely linked to the UGT through her husband who had been shot. She uses her contacts and wiles to manoeuvre in favour of decency and hopes to make life difficult for the likes of the police chief. Personal gestures such as these do not add up to a political perspective. In the end, the novel lacks ideas. Barea is pessimistically reduced to the empty hope of roots sprouting in the graveyard and the pious aspirations to universal truth expressed in the frontispiece.

Loneliness of exile

The novel's stereotyping, weaknesses of characterisation and plot, and failure of imagination were all used by Spanish critics in the 1950s as a stick to beat Barea with: a small stick, for one can hardly imagine more than a few dozen people in Spain reading *The Broken Root* in its British or Argentinean editions. Professor Ynduráin, writing in 1953, considered: "[*The Broken Root*] is most barefacedly sectarian, much less human and authentic than his trilogy".[54] In an obituary notice, Angel Ruiz Ayúcar sneered:

> *An English writer . . . His work . . . is characterised by his virulent sectarianism towards Spanish problems . . . but, in short, it will be his compatriots who have to decide whether Barea's death means or not a serious loss to English literature.*[55]

As in the Embassy-sponsored attacks in South America on the 1956 trip, Ruiz Ayúcar uses Barea's English citizenship and praise of England in *The Broken Root* to discredit his work. For these critics, the Civil War was still being fought and they revelled in the weakness of Barea's novel. José María Castellet wrote in the same month as Ruiz Ayúcar the first article published in Spain to praise Barea. His calling Barea "a Spanish writer [with] deep Iberian roots" was, in the codified language common under dictatorship, an implicit rejection of Ruiz Ayúcar's *ad hominem* sneer at the "English writer".[56] Castellet found Barea's work "unequal, but all of it sincere and passionate".[57] But he too can find little to praise in *The Broken Root* but honesty:

> *Barea's mistake was to write a novel,* The Broken Root, *that he placed in a Madrid he did not know and did not know how – because he couldn't know – to reflect accurately, despite his good intentions.*[58]

The Broken Root is an anguished and serious attempt to discuss responsibilities and commitments within the terrible dilemmas of exile. Castellet saw Barea as, above all, a lonely writer – or a writer about loneliness. He suffered "generational loneliness," because he had no literary relationships with his generation; "the tremendous loneliness of exile"; and "this solitary character of his life [in England]". And most of all, his constant rebellion against injustice made him lonely.[59]

As has been argued, the facts of Barea's life do not fully bear out this romantic image of him. Nevertheless, *The Broken Root*, in charting Antolin's conflicting feelings, reveals a great deal of depression and pain about the situation of exile. Antolin is a man weighed down by the impossibility of acting to change anything in his Madrid family or Spanish society. He was defeated in 1939 and in 1949 remains defeated. Only the partial solace of material peace and lack of disturbing passion in England weighs against this terrible defeat.

Barea's loneliness as an exile was real. It is apparent in his writing, as it was in his spoken words (see Appendix 4). Troubled though he was at times, yet loneliness did not hinder his reaching literary maturity in his English exile, and drawing from it nourishment and some peace of mind. He said about the generic village of his broadcasts:

> *The affection they had given me, the help everyone lent me, everyone's delicacy so that help would not look like charity and make me feel ashamed, had staunched the painful wounds of my tragedy, had cut through my hostile feelings and, still more important, had incorporated me into human society.*[60]

Barea's participation in English life gave him the environment within which, without the resentment into which, as an uprooted exile, he could so easily have fallen, he could write about his anguish concerning his family and Spain.

Conclusion

Unflinching Eye of a Working-Class Writer

Arturo Barea was a writer within the Spanish realist tradition reaching its peak with Pérez Galdós and the more low-life books of Pío Baroja. He was an innovator in his use of autobiography, an intimate form of writing linking him, at first glance surprisingly, to modernist investigations (e.g. Joyce, Proust) of the writer's own past. This book has tried to place him in the context of the first forty years of the century, which formed him, and whose interpretation is, in turn, assisted by his work.

There is extraordinary unity to Barea's work. It is all focused towards the aims he set himself. He wrote the same at the end of *The Clash* and in the introduction to *The Track* during the early 1940s and then again on the Córdoba tape the year before he died. He sought to use his own life and experiences as a touchstone, to explain the tremendous upheavals he had lived through.

This thematic unity contributes to the high intensity in Barea's work. Many people have written books twice as long on Lorca and said half as much. He condenses and packs in what he has to say. The same is true of the trilogy: it is not really long for the amount of incidents and characters covered. Such intensity is seen in the freshness and sharp colour readers find in Barea and is a suggestive reason why his creative flame burnt out rapidly.

Arturo Barea's political views were of no great depth. His personal behaviour and tastes were ordinary. There was nothing exceptional about his circumstances. He could easily have faded away into a discontented, grumbling middle-age, spending too little time at home and too much in bars. The Civil War made him a writer. It released his potential. Of no other Spanish writer can this be said in the same way. All Barea's generation and the subsequent ones have had to come to terms with the Civil War. Only of Barea could it be said that his experience of the war completely altered his trajectory and made him an artist.

The limitations in his writing have been discussed here: his difficulties with fictional creation, his sentimentality, his lack of political analysis. What it has not been possible to transmit is the vividness – the word sounds poor, repeated yet again on the page – of his finest writing.

Brutality, honesty, sincerity, crudity . . . all these words cited throughout this book are related to his vivid intensity. He is the writer of scenes, of pictures, of a character glimpsed – pity he never reached Hollywood!

The most powerful central image of Sender's first novel *Imán*, the wonderful story of Viance, the magnet who attracted all misfortune, is when Viance shelters from the battlefield carnage inside a dead horse. It is a resonant symbolic image, which Sender exploits for all its worth: the poor, ignorant, lost soldier returning to life after his night protected by death. Barea could not have written it. He wrote of war and death; he wrote of a dead mule putrefying in a trench wall, of flies feeding on the dead's spattered blood, but not of Sender's horse. Viance's feat is too implausible. Barea was a realist: his psychological truths came from penetrating the core of a situation, not from symbolic representation. Barea's gift was neither symbolic nor intellectual. His gift was to see. Differences in talent accepted, his eye is reminiscent of Goya's: direct, unflinching and honest. And he worked at his technique and material so that he was able to set down what he saw.

Barea's reputation today is contradictory. He is frequently found on reading lists of university courses in the UK and US, but this is more for his testimonial descriptions of the Civil War. In Spanish academia and in the literature faculties, he continues to loll in the doldrums. Jean-Pierre Ressot in a recent authoritative history of Spanish Literature really went to town on him:

> *Critics coincide in thinking that Barea's work is below his reputation.* The Track *and* The Clash *drift towards the grandiloquent sentimentalism of bad literature engagé . . . Barea is one of those writers who use literature to settle accounts with history.*[1]

It depends! It depends on what your view of literature is. If the role of a writer is precisely to engage with his/her historical time and attempt to explain it, Barea's work is of prime interest. For, scrupulously, he sought to write political literature without being propagandist, successfully avoiding crude naturalism, socialist realism or flat dry realism, on the one hand, yet never in his skilful descriptions of psychology losing sight of the impact of society on his characters on the other. His reputation lolls in the doldrums because he is consistently judged by other standards.

Barea was not an ordinary writer. The autobiographical form of the novel he adopted was original. Barea has to be understood as a working-class writer, both in his origins and in what he wrote about. His generational isolation, the fact that he used slang and incorrect forms, the undervaluing of his work because it was first published abroad, the failure of critics to understand his aims and the care put into his writing – all these are related to his being a working-class writer who wrote about the working-class.

This should not be taken as special pleading, for Barea's defects are evident and not glossed over in this critical biography; but, rather, as a basic point that must be borne in mind when reading him. Barea's focus was on the millions who live history without a voice. He examined unflinchingly the impact of the key event in modern Spanish history – the Civil War – its antecedents and effects, on those millions. He fulfilled his own aims.

Appendix 1

Publishing History

The unusual circumstance that nearly all Arturo Barea's work was first published in English, although he wrote in Spanish, is the cause of inconsistencies in his Spanish texts. This has given rise both to ignorance by readers and critics of much of his work and to controversies about his writing ability and methods of composition. Appendix 1 aims to set the factual record straight and to challenge the more prejudicial comments arising from this situation.

Early Work

Arturo Barea tells us that, when at school, he had a number of poems published in *Madrileñitos*, a magazine of the *Escuelas Pias*, and some unpaid articles in newspapers during 1913 and 1914.[1] Later, while in Morocco, he contributed to an Army magazine, *El Defensor de Ceuta*, and earned a few *duros* writing couplets and *pasadobles* for the "artists" of Ceuta's *Café Cantante*.[2] In 1940 Barea mentioned in his "Historia Literaria" that he had had two short stories published when he was in his twenties, one when he was at Guadalajara and the other in Morocco.[3]

The record of Barea's mature work begins with an unpublished piece written for the journal of the XIIth International Brigade early in the Civil War. Then, in June 1937, he wrote an article on the fall of Bilbao.[4] Its publication in the *Hoja de Lunes*, at that time the sole newspaper published on Mondays, signalled a victory for Barea in his fight with the Government to let more of what was true, even news of a terrible Republican defeat, pass through the censorship, and led too to his starting to broadcast on the radio.

Barea's first paid story was with the help of English journalist Sefton Delmer, who arranged for *The Fly* (later part of *Valor y miedo*) to be published in the London *Daily Express* in August 1937.[5]

Barea's first book *Valor y miedo* was published in Spring 1938 in Barcelona by *Publicaciones anti-fascistas de Cataluña* at twelve pesetas. It had a photo on the front, another on the back and at least one other photo along with several pen and ink drawings inside. The small print run is not known and a large number were sent to Barea in Paris. Several of the stories in *Valor y miedo* were translated by Ilsa in Paris, and sold to French magazines (including *La Nouvelle Revue Française*) and Swiss and Swedish socialist magazines.[6]

England

Barea's second book, and his first in England, was published by Secker & Warburg in July 1941: *Struggle for the Spanish Soul*. This is No. 10 of a series of pamphlets in the "Searchlight" series, by a number of well-known writers from the non-Stalinist left. Joyce Cary, "Cassandra" and George Orwell were other "Searchlight" authors. *Struggle for the Spanish Soul* was to have been published in May 1941, but the typescript and first proof were "destroyed by enemy action" (fitting trial for an anti-fascist broadside) and it did not actually come out until July, after *The Forge*.[7]

The year 1941 was Barea's breakthrough year. Cyril Connolly's *Horizon* published both *Not Spain, but Hemingway,* Barea's original article on *For Whom the Bell Tolls*, and the horrific short story *The Scissors*. There would have been therefore some expectation for the release of *The Forge* by Faber & Faber on June 12, 1941. The volume was widely reviewed and praised, but in its first year sold only a modest 1,027 copies at 10s. 6d.[8] It was Faber's most distinguished editor, T.S. Eliot, who dealt with this and Barea's subsequent publications.[9] The first edition was translated by Sir Peter Chalmers-Mitchell, British ex-consul in Málaga, who probably assisted in Faber's acceptance of the book.[10]

The Track was published two years later, on July 9, 1943, also priced 10s. 6d. This did a lot better and sold 3,911 copies in its first year. On March 3, 1944, Faber brought out *Lorca, the poet and his people* at 7s. 6d., which sold a respectable 1,495 copies in the first year. In the same year, the Readers Union published in a cheap edition of 20,000 copies *The Forge*, in Chalmers-Mitchell's rather than Ilsa's translation.[11]

The Clash was published on February 22, 1946, and was the most immediately successful of Barea's books, selling 6,021 in the first year at the price of 12s. 6d. The books continued to sell after the first year, but no figures of sales are available.

A new version of *The Forge*, translated this time by Ilsa, had been brought out in 1943 and was reissued on May 1, 1946, after *The Clash*. This reissue sold 1,109 copies in 12 months at 10s. 6d. The same year, *The Forging of a Rebel* was published in an omnibus edition in the United States by Reynal & Hitchcock. The first paperbacks were to be in 1958 at 2s. 6d, an edition which Roland Gant and Ilsa pressed on Four-Square. *The Forging of a Rebel* was translated to at least ten languages.[12] It is curious to note that Barea's total book sales for the five-year period between 1948 and 1952 placed him fifth in the list of the most translated Spanish authors, behind Cervantes, Ortega y Gasset, Lorca and Blasco Ibañez. Barea was for those few years ahead of Santa Teresa, San Juan de la Cruz, Unamuno and Cela.[13]

Articles of literary criticism by Barea were published in a number of different magazines, and in two cases as introductions to books, between 1941 and 1953. He also wrote, by Ilsa's count, about forty short stories.[14] In 1945, Barea co-authored with Ilsa a political pamphlet, *SPAIN in the post-war world*, sold by the Fabian Society at one shilling. This sober Labour Party briefing was possibly commissioned by Lord Faringdon, a Fabian luminary and Arturo's landlord-to-be.[15]

In 1951 the trilogy was published in Spanish for the first time: in three volumes by Losada in Buenos Aires. This opened up Barea to a broad Latin American public, who already knew him well as *Juan de Castilla*, under which name Barea not only broadcast but wrote several articles, and for the first time to a narrow Spanish audience, confined to literary critics, dissidents (the trilogy did circulate underground in Spain) and exiles.[16]

Was the trilogy written in English?

The 1951 Latin American publication led to a controversy over the genesis of the trilogy, which stemmed from the unusual publishing sequence of Barea's books and was compounded by the poor quality of the Buenos Aires text.[17] It is a controversy that rumbled on into the 1990s.

In the Buenos Aires edition, there are frequent linguistic errors, similar to those in *Valor y miedo*: "*la-ismos*", the use of "esto" for "eso", etc. In addition, there are anglicisms: for example, the omission of the relative article and use of English-influenced vocabulary. "*Realizar*" is used in its English sense of "realise" (*darse cuenta*) and not in its Castilian meaning of "bring about" (*llevar a cabo*); "José *produjo* una botella" instead of *trajo* or *presentó*; *refrán* instead of *estribillo*; "le fascinaba el *sujeto*" instead of *tema* etc.

Another fault found was with Barea's originality in punctuation and use of popular language, neither of which were acceptable to critics taking their lead from the *Real Academia de la Lengua Española*.[18] It is interesting that Fernández Gutiérrez and Herrera Rodrigo, when defending Barea on his use of slang as recently as 1988, felt the need to go to great lengths to justify Barea's *la-ismos* and *le-ismos*.[19] Many, though not all, of his "errors" are deliberate colloquialisms, as argued in Chapter II.

However, Spanish critics who were politically hostile to Barea could use these three elements – carelessness in the text, anglicisms and originality of expression – to insist that Barea was a bad writer. Ynduráin argued these points to conclude that Barea's reputation had been artificially inflated by anti-Franco interests;[20] other critics of the 1950s dismissed him as a minor "English" writer.[21] This type of attack is only interesting as a reflection of cultural life under the dictatorship and need not now be taken seriously.

However, the assertion that Barea was a careless and sloppy writer should not be so easily dismissed. Marra-López cites this typical syntactical error from *La Forja*: "Esta es una de las cosas porque yo quiero mucho a mi madre" (*This is one of the things because I love my mother a lot*).[22] On this error (if indeed it is an error: one must remember that Barea narrates *The Forge* through a child's voice), Marra-López then comments:

> *[This is] . . . one of the many grammatical errors that the splendid and intuitive Barea commits. Adding them all up would take ages.*[23]

Marra-López is wrongly assuming here that Barea's sloppy grammar is an integral part of his freshness and intuition. Later in the same article, Marra-López adds: "[*The Broken Root*] . . . is vilely written or retranslated . . . just like his earlier books."[24]

However, the critique is misplaced. What actually happened was that Barea wrote in Castilian; the books were translated into English, then published. When the time came for the Spanish-language version of *La forja de un rebelde*, Barea's original version either no longer existed or only existed in part. Therefore, Barea's sloppiness in writing is, in the case of *La forja de un rebelde*, not because of his fresh spontaneity, but because he was sloppy in writing the re-translation, the second Spanish version reconstructed by him and Ilsa from the English version. That this is what occurred is supported by the fact that there is no translator credited for the Losada 1951 or subsequent editions.

Owing to the non-existence of the original Spanish-language manuscripts, there have long been insinuations, both innocent and malicious, that Ilsa co-wrote the trilogy. This can be directly rebutted by the evidence of Olive Renier and Margaret Rink (later Weeden), Ilsa's translation assistants.[25] Moreover, in her preface to the Argentinean edition of *Unamuno*, Ilsa explains that there never was a full Spanish-language manuscript of this work: this was, she goes on, because she and Arturo co-authored *Unamuno*, but this collaboration was completely different from Barea's practice with his earlier books.[26]

A final insinuation is that it was not Arturo Barea at all who wrote the trilogy, but Ilsa alone. This is implied, though with no malicious intent, in Giménez-Frontín's repetition of earlier rumours in a 1986 newspaper article: "[The trilogy was] . . . originally written in English."[27] Barea of course could not have written it originally in English. The source of these persistent rumours is almost certainly Rafael Martínez Nadal. Martínez Nadal worked for the Spanish Section of the BBC, in a Wood Norton pre-fab close to where Ilsa worked in the Monitoring Service. In his 1995 two-page memoir of Ilsa and Arturo, he explained:

As the autodidact that he was, Arturo lacked the most elementary cultural training or suitable reading.[28]

Martínez Nadal portrays Ilsa as the mother–wife who gave birth to Barea's literature, to the extent of supplying him with a reading list and obliging him to read each day. His sketch culminates with Ilsa telling Martínez Nadal in about 1941:

*" . . . the best – Ilsa insisted – is hearing Arturo express, in his rough language, the sharpest, most unexpected observations. So strong, so vivid and so vital that I am now taking notes in English every night of what he tells me in Spanish. Then the girl who shares our house (*compañera de casa*) checks them for me and we find we have pages of a possible autobiography by Arturo written in a language he does not know."*[29]

Martínez Nadal is a writer for whom the well-turned anecdote is more attractive than the literal truth. I had the good fortune to be able to put this version of how *The Forging of a Rebel* was written on several occasions to Margaret Weeden (the *compañera de casa* to whom Martínez Nadal refers) and to Olive Renier. Both the following quotes are from Margaret Weeden, the main authority on this question.

Firstly, the question of Arturo's authenticity: I am absolutely appalled to think that this is still being questioned. I thought that stupidity had been quelled long ago! . . . I shared a house with the Bareas for nearly 5 years and typed out a major part of Ilsa's translations! . . . I can still see in my mind's eye the thick wad of quarto paper on which Arturo had typed out The Forge *in Paris and which was used by Sir Peter Chalmers-Mitchell for his first translation, and, later, by Ilsa to do the re-translation.*[30]

Of course Arturo wrote his books in Spanish! Just like his charlas *{talks}: he suddenly went and sat down and typed out pages.*[31]

The oft-repeated direct evidence of Ilsa Barea's closest collaborators on the translation of *The Forging of a Rebel* has to be conclusive. This is not to say that Ilsa did not look after Barea, seek books for him, care for him during his nervous attacks, encourage him to write and of course translate his work. However, Martínez Nadal's version of events lacks credibility: the ghostly rumour he propagates, one that has wandered round the fringes of the literary world for five decades, should now be finally buried, stone dead.

It should also be noted that Barea was by no means as uncultured as Martínez Nadal makes out, and that *The Forge* was written before 1941. In addition, there is sufficient internal consistency between *Valor y miedo* and *La forja de un rebelde* to show that the author of the two was the same person.

Last books

Barea's last published novel – for some critics, his first and only – *The Broken Root* was issued by Faber at 15/- in 1951 and sold 1,982 copies in its first year. It was published soon after in the United States and in Denmark. Losada issued a Buenos Aires edition, *La raíz rota*, in 1955. On March 9, 1951 Faber issued a cheap (5/-) edition of *The Forge*, but it sold only 199 copies. Barea's moment of popular glory had passed.

In his obituary of Barea, Joan Gili referred to another novel Barea was working on.[32] And as early as 1951, Mario Benedetti reported a title, *Los guardianes de sus hermanos*.[33] There is no evidence that Barea ever wrote anything of this projected novel. It is of interest that he wished to write another book. That he failed to do so supports the impression given by *The Broken Root*: Barea was burned out as a writer. He had covered the subject matter that stimulated him and had lost the necessary imaginative intensity. Only three stories of his were written after *The Broken Root*.[34]

Barea's last book published in his lifetime was *Unamuno*. This short sixty-one page study of the thinker was issued by Bowes & Bowes in 1952 as part of a series "Studies in Modern European Literature and Thought". It was commissioned, *via* Ilsa, by the series' editor Erich Heller, a Cambridge professor of Austrian origin, who offered Barea the choice of Unamuno or Ortega y Gasset.[35]

Posthumous: too full of light

According to Ilsa, Barea often intended to collect the stories he liked, but never did.[36] After his death, she selected the contents of the collection *El*

Centro de la Pista (The Centre of the Ring), which was published in Madrid by Cid editions in 1960. *El centro de la pista* is a minor landmark in Spanish publishing history. It was the first post-war work of fiction published within Spain by a Republican supporter who had gone into exile at the end of or during the Civil War. A twenty-one year silence was broken. The Franco censorship had never been fully consistent and, as political circumstances forced a slight thaw, it became in the 1960s even less so. Cid editions seem to have been able to publish Barea without problems. The publication of Marra-López's book in 1963 was another indicator of changes in cultural climate. Marra-López and literary critics such as Alborg, Castellet and Nora, as well as publishers, were interested in getting Sender, Rodoreda, Aub, Alberti, Barea and other exiles read within Spain.

The fact too that *El centro de la pista* was a minor book by a dead writer made publication easier. It is highly unlikely that *La forja de un rebelde* could have been published within Spain in 1960; and even less so, had Barea been still alive to broadcast and write on the fact. It was not until 1977, twenty years after Barea's death, and also after the dictator's, that the readership he had written for could finally have full access to the trilogy. However, despite subsequent reprints in Spain and England, and in spite of a six-part nine-hour television series of *La forja de un rebelde*, broadcast in 1990, Barea has not been widely read.[37] *Lorca*, *Unamuno* and *La raíz rota* have never been published in Spain.

The reasons for this relative neglect are various. Giménez-Frontín suggested that:

> *. . . incomprehensibly, Barea was not "recovered" in the historical moment when in all justice he should have been . . . Perhaps, all in all, Barea was too rough a diamond (*un plato demasiado crudo*), too full of light to find a publisher in those years (from the mid-60s to mid-70s) of self-controlled and restrained liberalisation.*[38]

Moreover, Barea died relatively young, so could not be one of the exiles publishing articles in the Spanish press from the late '60s on. And, unlike many of his contemporaries, he was unable to stimulate interest in his work by actually returning from exile and being interviewed in the media.

Further factors in the neglect of Barea are that his work is hard to classify: fiction? autobiography? Its standard is uneven. He did not belong to any school. He did not have the status of a "modern classic". Nor did Barea fit easily into any political slot: despite his PCE sympathies just before and at the start of the Civil War, *The Clash* is implicitly critical of the PCE, and *The Broken Root* explicitly so. Barea's political path was too independent for the PCE to want to promote his re-publication. Nor did the UGT, to which Barea gave his most consistent political loyalty, and the PSOE involve themselves in promoting their past. The period when Largo Caballero spoke of Marxism and Revolution fits ill with the modern, neoliberal, social democratic party of Felipe González and his heirs.

Despite the television series, by the end of the 1990s Arturo Barea seemed forgotten. The problems he tackled were no longer of such burning immediacy to Spanish readers keen to forget their past. And both politically and academically he remained a "rough diamond" and difficult to define. There was still little room for the self-taught son of a laundry-woman in Spanish letters.

However, in recent years, the first years of the twenty-first century, Spain has lived through intense changes in the way its past is viewed. The diverse movements to recover historic memory – in reality, to fight for historical justice – have broken through a wall of silence about the Civil War and dictatorship. Debate's fine publishing project of three Barea volumes in 2000/2001 (a revised version of the trilogy, *Palabras recobradas* and the Collected Stories) seems now prescient, making Barea available at just the time this movement was taking off. Part of this process, too, is the annual Arturo Barea Prize for Historical Research, awarded by the *Diputación* (Regional Council) of Badajoz, his birthplace, since 2001.[39] Fittingly, for Barea's work is a conscious effort to recover historical memory, only the first year's Prize was awarded to a study of Barea. Since then, the prizes have been awarded for research into disinterring the buried truth of the dictatorship's crimes in Extremadura's towns and villages.

Today, unlike ten years ago, one could say that, inasmuch as any novelists of his generation are known or read, Barea has lasted.

Appendix 2

Chronological Table of Barea's Books and Articles

1 Chronological table of the editions in English and Spanish of Barea's books.
2 Chronological table of stories and articles published by Arturo Barea.

1 Chronological table of the editions in English and Spanish of Barea's books

Date	Title	Publisher	Place of publication	Other info
Summer 1938	*Valor y miedo*	Publicaciones Anti-fascistas de Cataluña	Barcelona	With 12 prints
12 June 1941	*The Forge*	Faber & Faber	London	Translated by Sir Peter Chalmers-Mitchell
July 1941	*Struggle for the Spanish Soul*	Secker & Warburg	London	Searchlight pamphlet 10
1943	*The Forge*	Faber & Faber	London	Translated by Ilsa Barea: reprinted 1946 & 1951
9 July 1943	*The Track*	Faber & Faber	London	Foreword by Barea
1944	*The Forge*	Readers Union	London	Club edition in Chalmers-Mitchell translation
March 3 1944	*Lorca, the poet and his people*	Faber & Faber	London	
August 1945	*Spain in the post-war world*	Fabian Publications	London	Written with Ilsa Barea
22 Feb. 1946	*The Clash*	Faber & Faber	London	
1946	*The Forging of a rebel*	Reynal & Hitchcock	New York	Trilogy in one volume
1949	*Lorca, the poet and his people*	Harcourt & Brace	New York	
1951	*La forja, La ruta, La llama*	Losada	Buenos Aires	Reprinted in 1954, 1958 & 1966
20 April 1951	*The broken root*	Faber & Faber	London	
1952	*Unamuno*	Bowes & Bowes	Cambridge	With Ilsa Barea

1953	*Unamuno*	Yale Univ. Press	New Haven, USA	
19 Aug. 1955	*La raíz rota*	Santiago Rueda	Buenos Aires	
1956	*Lorca*	Losada	Buenos Aires	
1958	*The Forge, The Track, The Clash*	Four-Square	London	First in paperback
1959	*Unamuno*	Editorial Sur	Buenos Aires	Translated by Emir Rodríguez Monegal
1959	*La forja de un rebelde*	Ediciones Montjuich	Mexico City	Reprinted in 1965
1960	*El centro de la pista*	Ediciones Cid	Madrid	No. 26, Colección Altor
1972	*The Forging of a Rebel*	Davis-Poynter	London	Omnibus edition
1973	*Lorca*	Cooper Square	New York	
1974	*The Forge, The Track, The Clash*	Quartet	London	
1975	*The Forging of a Rebel*	Viking	New York	Omnibus edition
1977	*La forja, La ruta, La llama*	Turner	Madrid	First Spanish publication – reprinted 1984
1980	*Valor y miedo*	José Esteban	Madrid	
1984	*Valor y miedo*	Terceto	Barcelona	Reprinted by Plaza & Janés 1986
1984	*The Forge, The Track, The Clash*	Fontana	London	Flamingo paperback
1985/6	*La forja de un rebelde, La ruta, La llama*	Plaza y Janés	Barcelona	Despite title, first volume only contains *La forja*. Reprinted in 1990
1988	*El centro de la pista*	Diputación de Badajoz	Badajoz	Introduction by María Herrera
April 1993	*La forja, La ruta, La llama*	Plaza y Janés	Barcelona	Number 154, Biblioteca de Autor
April 2000	*Palabras Recobradas*	Debate	Madrid	BBC talks, essays & letters from the archive of Uli Rushby-Smith
April 2000	*La forja de un rebelde*	Debate	Madrid	Omnibus edition, with several errors and anglicisms corrected

April 2001	*Cuentos completos*	Debate	Madrid	Contains *V & M*, *El centro de la pista* and a number of previously unpublished stories from Uli Rushby-Smith's archive
2001	*La forja de un rebelde*	Bibliotex	Madrid	Printed in 3 volumes on successive days as one of *El Mundo*'s "100 best twentieth-century novels in Castilian"
July 12 2001	*The Forging of a Rebel*	Granta	London	Paperback edition, with introduction by Nigel Townson

2 Chronological table of stories and articles published by Barea

Date	Title	Where	Type	Comment
1918/20		*Blanco y negro*	Story	Winner of a competition, according to AB in PR, p. 659
1920/23	El moro ciego	Military journal	Story	AB, PR, p. 660
June 1937	La caída de Bilbao	*Hoja de Lunes*, Madrid	Article	
17 August 1937	The Fly	*London Daily Express*	Story	Published through Sefton Delmer
11 August 1939	A Spaniard in Hertfordshire	*The Spectator*	Article	
1938/40	Various . . .	*La Nouvelle Revue française*	Stories	Translations of stories from *VM*
23 Feb. 1940	Kleptomania	*John O'London's Weekly*	Story	See *Cuentos completos*, p. 94
1940	Brandy	*Penguin Parade*, 7	Story	Translation of *Coñac* from *VM*
19 August 1940		*Reynolds News*	Article	On the Fifth Column
16 Nov. 1940		*Time and Tide*	Article	On Morocco (PR, p. 664)
1941	The Scissors	*Horizon*	Story	Reprinted in Horizon Stories, 1943
May 1941	Not Spain – but Hemingway	*Horizon, III, 17*	Lit. Crit.	
Dec. 1941	Unidad	*Españoles, 6*	Politics article	Exile journal in London

March / April 1942	Lorca	*Horizon, V, 27 &28*	Lit. Crit.	In two parts
February 1943	The Man in the Wine Cone	*Lilliput*	Story	See CC, p. 268
April 1943	Foreword to *The Track*	Faber & Faber		
Aug. 1943	The Beacon	*Lilliput*	Story	See CC, p. 21
Sept. 1943	The Spanish Labyrinth	*Horizon,* VIII, 45	Book Review	
1944	Paris, 1938	*The Windmill*	Story	See CC, p. 274
1945	Las raíces del lenguaje poético de García Lorca	*Bulletin of Hispanic Studies*, Liverpool, volume XXII	Based on a speech given on 17 Nov 1944	Later published in *Marcha*, 814, Montevideo
April 1945	The Indivisibility of Freedom	In: *Freedom for Spain*	Speech, London, 31 March 1945.	*Socialist Vanguard* pamphlet
August 1945	The Orchard	Lilliput	Story	See CC, p. 251
1945	Mr. One	*Voyage: an anthology*	Story	Edited by Denys Val Baker. See CC, p. 256
Autumn 1946	Ramón Gómez de la Serna	*Phoenix*	Lit. Crit.	
Winter 1946	New writing in Franco Spain	*London Forum 1.i*	Lit. Crit.	
1946	Federico García Lorca	*Writers of To-day*	Lit. Crit.	Anthology edited by Denys Val Baker (PR, p. 20)
1946	Realism in Modern Spanish Novel	*Focus 2*	Lit. Crit.	In Spanish in *Palabras recobradas*
Winter 1947	Ortega and Madariaga	*University Observer* (Chicago)	Politics article	"A journal of politics"
Late 1947	The Spanish Mind	*World off duty*	Lit. Crit.	Anthology published by Contact Books
1948	Intro. to *The dark wedding* by Ramón Sender	Grey Walls Press, London	Lit. Crit.	
6 May 1948	An Andalusian poet	*Times Literary Supplement*	Lit. Crit.	On Rafael Alberti
November 1949	Madrid Between the Old and the New	*World Review, Nº 9*	Story	United States. See CC, p. 233
Spring 1950	Applied Physics	*Everybody's*	Story	See CC, p. 240

21 July 1950	Un grupo de inefables viejecitos	*El Mercurio*, Santiago de Chile	Anecdotic article	Similar to his BBC talks
November 1950	The Blessings of Non-Stop	*Go,* vol III, Nº 3	Story	See CC, p. 280
1951/2	El poeta y el pueblo	*Número,* 15, 17 and 19, Montevideo	Lit. Crit.	Chapter One of *Lorca, the poet and his people* (PR, p. 20)
Spring 1953	A quarter century of Spanish writing	*Books Abroad* xxvii, New York	Lit. Crit.	
1953	Introduction to *The Hive* by C.J. Cela *	Victor Gollancz	Lit. Crit.	*The Hive* was translated by J.M. Cohen "in consultation with" Barea
12 Feb. 1954	Don Quijote	*The Radio Times*	Lit. Crit.	Introduction to a radio adaptation
8 July 1956 to 28 Dec. 1957	63 articles	*La Nación,* Buenos Aires	Anecdotic articles, mainly on politics.	In *Palabras recobradas*
1957	La Lección	*La Nación*, Buenos Aires	Story	Broadcast on BBC, 28 November 1958
Nov. 1964	Big Granny	*Argosy*	Story	Translation of *La lección*

* Following Cela's Nobel Prize (1989), this translation was issued in paperback by Sceptre (London) in 1992, without Barea's introduction, but with his help in the translation acknowledged. Given his reduced participation, his name was aptly reduced to "Arturo Bare".

Notes

1 I have omitted from this list the several translations of stories published in Germany, Scandinavia and Argentina.

2 A number of Barea's radio broadcasts as *Juan de Castilla* were spoken essays about writers and writing. He spoke about at least the following: Gabriela Mistral (12/9/44); *Don Segundo Sombra* (7/11/44); Carlos María Ocantos (1944); Ciro Alegría (10/4/1945); Rómulo Gallegos (22/5/45). These are published by Nigel Townson in *Palabras recobradas.*

3 More than one of Barea's stories were also broadcast on the BBC. Barea sometimes referred to his more anecdotical war-time broadcasts as stories.

Appendix 3

Ilse Pollak/Ilsa Barea (1902–1972)

Background

Ilsa's background was very different from Arturo's. She came from a comfortably-off and cultured family. Whereas Arturo came to politics by his own experience as a worker, Ilsa's family was liberal and she became involved with the left during her time at University. She was born in Vienna on September 20, 1902, five years to the day after Arturo Barea.[1] Her father was Jewish, but non-practising; her mother from a Lutheran and military background. Such a meeting of opposites was not infrequent in the liberal Vienna of the late nineteenth century. In her adult life she never practised Lutheranism nor Judaism, though that was not to inhibit the Duke de Primo de Rivera, brother of José Antonio and Spanish Ambassador in London, from referring to her in a 1956 report as "a Jewish refugee".[2]

Though Ilsa's mother, Alice von Zieglmayer, had a "rose-coloured" memory of past imperial glory, Ilsa tells us she herself was Republican from her teens.[3] Her father, Dr Valentin Pollak, was born in 1871 and had some fame as co-author of a literary reader "Pollak, Jellinek and Streinz" in common use in schools in the 1920s. He became the Principal of a well-known boys' school in Vienna, and spent long years accumulating notes for a history of education in Austria, the notes for which he had to abandon when fleeing Vienna in 1939.[4]

The Pollaks arrived by train at Liverpool Street Station five days before the start of the Second World War. They then lived with Arturo and Ilsa from late 1939 until their deaths in Faringdon in the late 1940s. At Fladbury they were an integral and active part of the household, "Mama", as everyone called affectionately Ilsa's tiny mother, doing the cooking with Arturo. They were both buried on wet Autumn days in the annex to Faringdon churchyard.[5]

Ilsa was to dedicate to their memory the only book she published solely in her name: *Vienna*.

Communism and Socialism

Culturally, Ilse Pollak (born Ilse, she became widely-known as Ilsa after 1936: herself often using the name) was formed by the great Communist movement that swept across Europe after the First World War. She was also, in her own view, of a generation that was the last to feel the revolutionary breath of 1848. She went to University in Vienna after the world war and did not finally graduate in Economics and Sociology, for from *circa* 1918 on she was a full-time political activist.[6] She plunged into student debates, agitations and disputes; and at University, though whether as a founder member or not is unclear, joined the new Austrian Communist Party.

Without becoming a central leader, she was in the 1920s a prominent member of what was always a small party. She wrote articles for its press and may have been for a while a full-time worker for the party. In 1925 she was sent to Budapest on a Comintern mission to channel funds to a Romanian opposition leader. Something went wrong and Ilsa spent four months in a Hungarian jail, during which she suffered bronchitis, an ailment that was to assail her all her life. She left the Communist Party after her release. She believed the Comintern should have helped her more and at least paid her legal expenses.[7]

Back in Vienna, she became active in education and propaganda work on the left wing of the powerful Social Democratic Party. She spent time in England giving lectures during the late 1920s or early '30s, which accounts for her good English, though it is not clear on what subject she talked or how long she was there. The early thirties was the period of increasing Nazi pressure on Austria and the growth of an indigenous fascist movement, the *Heimwehr*, within the country. The Social Democrats had governed Vienna since the First World War and had instituted a massive programme of "municipal socialism". Hundreds of thousands of working-class people had been re-housed in tower-blocks, where services were cheap and facilities numerous. This was one of the most far-reaching attempts to build a socialist "island" within a capitalist state; and the principal reason why the Austrian Communist Party remained relatively small.

Ilsa had at least two close emotional relationships during this period; one with Kolamar Wallisch, a leader of the Schutzbund workers' self-defence organisation in the Viennese suburb of Styria. He was hanged by the Dollfuss regime after the final defeat of the workers during the "February events" of 1934.[8] At some stage, probably in the early 1930s, she married Leopold Kulcsar, also a working-class leader. We are indebted to Arturo Barea for a description of "Poldi" in Barcelona shortly before the latter's sudden death in 1938.[9] Kulcsar and Ilsa became leaders of a small underground current within the Social Democratic Party, called "The Spark". The name was taken from the faction Lenin had led (*Iskra*) within the Russian Social Democratic Party thirty years before; and suggests that Ilsa's early abandonment of the Communist Party permitted her to maintain a fighting communist line, whereas those who stayed within the Party to follow the vagaries of Stalin's foreign policies were often immobilised as revolutionary fighters.

"The Spark" started to organise in 1932/3 a military and political resistance within the Social Democratic Party as an alternative to the Bauer and Adler leadership's passive response to the imminent threat of the right's dismantling the party and its achievements. On February 12, 1934, the Government moved against the workers' organisations: there were tens of thousands of willing fighters in the Social Democratic ranks, but Bauer's pacifist policies had left them with neither political nor material means to defend themselves. Small bands of armed fighters, some organised by "The Spark", attempted to organise resistance. With workers' leaders detained, women desperately dug up the gardens of the council flats to search for buried arms. The armed fighters fell back on these blocks, but Chancellor Dollfuss brought up cannon, shelled the tenements and then gave the Heimwehr free rein to rampage through the blocks. Resistance was crushed and the survivors driven underground.

Leopold Kulcsar was one of those arrested; and Ilsa was on the run. For a time (in a curious minor twist of history) she took refuge in the one-room flat of Hugh Gaitskell. Gaitskell, Dora Gaitskell, Kim Philby and Stephen Spender were just some of the many English socialists attracted to "Red Vienna" during this period after Hitler's coming to power, whom Ilsa met.[10]

Ilsa stayed in Vienna for several months after the February events, probably until her husband left prison. She rented a large flat (with her parents' money?) in the Herrengasse in a big block with several entrances, where Gaitskell and Dora rented a room for a period. She did underground political work, which consisted mainly in trying to hide activists from the police: many were wounded, all were destitute, many had to hide in the sewers for several weeks (surely the source of Graham Greene's *The Third Man*). Finally, in late 1934, Ilsa left the city for exile in Czechoslovakia, where the great majority of Social Democratic leaders who had escaped were attempting to reorganise.[11] In Prague after the Austrian defeat, there was a massive swing from the Social Democrats to the Communists among the exiles. Kulcsar was one of those who joined the Party, and one may trace in his excessive rigidity, as Arturo and others portray him, some of the zeal of a reformed Austro-Marxist to prove himself before the Comintern.

It is clear that in the 1920s Ilsa had left the Communist Party without renouncing Communist ideals, which, as in the case of other left-wing Austro-Marxists, laid her open to persecution by the Stalinists. Arturo Barea tells us, in *The Clash*, that an important factor in his and Ilsa's exclusion from influence in Madrid in 1937 was the whispering campaign that Ilsa was a Trotskyist.[12] The exact political reasons for Ilsa leaving the Communist Party in the 1920s are however not clear. The underlying reason, if not the immediate, was probably the Party's failure to take root in Austria. But she did not become a Trotskyist, nor ever a public critic of the Communists either in Prague or Madrid, or later in England.

Her experiences in Spain, which she talked about frequently in Britain during the 1940s and '50s, do not appear to have led to any overall critique of the Soviet Union. Indeed, she sometimes liked to talk of her friendships with Russian generals.[13] However, she "never denied the existence of Stalinist terror".[14] Like many people moving away from political militancy, the question became less urgent for her. The contradiction between her own experience and what she thought was not put under pressure.

"Ilsa de la Telefónica"

Ilsa arrived in Madrid from Valencia without her husband and on borrowed money in early November 1936. She had used contacts in socialist papers in Norway and Czechoslovakia (in 1935/36 she edited one in Brno) to somehow persuade the Spanish Embassy in Paris to pay for her to come to Spain to assist in the Press Department.[15] She was a very insistent and determined person. And like many of her generation, especially the Germans and Austrians, she recognised in the Spanish Civil War another, and possibly the last, chance to combat fascism.

For the next 21 years her life was to be totally involved with Arturo Barea. But their meeting was not auspicious. Barea was exhausted and irritable, after weeks with little sleep. The Government had fled to Valencia during the crucial early November days of the siege of Madrid. Ilsa, just arrived, was at once evacuated to Valencia along with the rest of the Press Department. She managed to get back rapidly to Madrid from Valencia, on the grounds that her presence in Madrid would mean there was at least one left-wing journalist there. But Barea was ill-disposed to anyone who had fled to Valencia and describes their first meeting with his customary (till then, at least) disdain for women:

The woman sat down at the desk: a round face with big eyes, blunt nose, wide forehead, a mass of dark hair . . . She was over thirty and no beauty. Why in hell had those people in Valencia sent me a woman, when I had my hands full with the men anyhow? My feelings towards her were strictly unfriendly.[16]

Disciplined militant, Ilsa did not quarrel with his "strictly unfriendly" tone and began to use her knowledge of English, French, German and Italian to collaborate with the foreign journalists. At his boss's Rubio Hidalgo's telephoned suggestion from Valencia, Barea offered her a job in the Press Censorship. The rest, as they say, is history . . . Arturo's "feelings" changed. Ilsa's *sang-froid* before the shelling and bombing, her dedication and competence, her "delightful mouth" drew Arturo to her.[17] There is no direct evidence as to Ilsa's feelings. By Arturo's account, they spent all their time together; working night and day, eating together and sleeping on the camp beds in the *Telefónica*. They spent their limited moments of free time together too and within a few weeks were lovers.

Ilsa telephoned, then went to see, her husband, the ill-fated Leopold Kulcsar, in Valencia or Barcelona. Kulcsar, with dignity, agreed to a divorce, though told her he hoped to win her back. Kulcsar himself later confirmed the strength of Ilsa's and Arturo's relationship:

{Poldi} told us that he had found {Ilsa and Arturo} as happy as children; it was moving to see how entranced they were with each other.[18]

Ilsa Kulcsar rapidly became a famous figure in the *Telefónica*, her finest hour.[19] She had an endless capacity for work and was domineering and "bossy".[20] Peter Heller, who worked with her a few years later in the BBC, described her as "dominant, not domineering . . . She didn't let things rest".[21] To her friend Olive Renier, she was "very dominating, but good value . . . very serious . . . of sterling character, very brave, intelligent".[22] Journalist Sefton Delmer, who knew her in Madrid, thought she was "highly intelligent".[23] Intelligent and dominating are the adjectives that consistently crop up in people's comments about Ilsa. Although formally Barea's assistant, Ilsa had more contact than he with the foreign journalists. She had more sophisticated social skills and spoke several languages. The journalists were respectful and very careful of Ilsa, who was aware of her power.[24]

Arturo and Ilsa worked together in the censorship for ten months. They were in some ways a strange couple. The rather cadaverous, haunted-looking Barea and the "short, plumpish, ungainly" Ilsa.[25] The Spaniard who had not found himself, socialist but with traditional ideas about women; and the Austrian life-long Communist/Socialist militant.

After New Year 1936/7, Ilsa officially became Arturo's deputy in the press censorship, work which they both found of consuming interest. They believed in its value. While Arturo won his battles to tell the truth about Republican defeats and not just present the rosy picture, Ilsa often supplied the original ideas, was tireless in pursuing useful contacts and pushed Arturo forward. Neither of them had much liking for the jaded alcoholic worlds of journalists and Soviet commissars in the Hotel Florida. They preferred their own company.[26] During this period, both Ilsa and Arturo lived under the most intense pressure: of work, of the closeness of death, and also of the harm they were doing to their respective husband and wife.

In Autumn 1937, with Arturo's health deteriorating and a political campaign starting against them, the couple went on leave to the Levante. On their return, things had changed. They had lost their jobs as censors: and the plausible, given her past, but false campaign that Ilsa was a Trotskyist was in full swing.[27] In fact, Ilsa decided not to, and persuaded Arturo not to, fight these attacks, on the grounds that any public row could only give solace to the Republican side's enemies.

It was a mistaken policy to keep silent, something easier to perceive with 60 years' hindsight. Many people did speak out against Stalin and the PCE's disastrous policy in Spain: dos Passos (whom Ilsa knew) and Orwell were two famous foreign journalists who did. The POUM and the anarchists of course also did. But Hemingway, Gellhorn and Ilsa and Arturo were among the majority who opted for silence (see further discussion on this in Chapter VI).

Ilsa showed her strength in another way. It was her determination that dragged an increasingly fatalistic and depressed Barea out of Spain, before they were killed or arrested. The story of that trip is told in *The Clash*. It was, first, Ilsa's ability to pull strings with the powerful Comintern interrogator Kulcsar, and then various friends of Barea, that achieved on 22 February 1938 her and Arturo's exit from Spain, *via* La Jonquera in Catalonia.[28]

With Arturo, Ilsa spent almost a year living in Paris in poverty under the hanging sword of the impending war. She lived by occasional translations, including some of Arturo's stories, and selling her own articles. She wrote several for the review of a British economist Norman Angell. She was not well in Paris, suffering from the nervous reaction to her supreme efforts over the previous 18 months and from the sudden death of Kulcsar on 28 January, which had allowed her and Arturo to marry a week before leaving Barcelona. *The Clash* describes the guilt she felt at having left Kulcsar. His death meant the end of her youth, she told Barea.[29]

In Paris, she suffered rheumatic pains, bronchitis and often lay in bed with a temperature. Working for more than half an hour at a translation brought tears of pain to her eyes. Her malnourishment would not have helped: " . . . we often went hungry," Barea reports baldly.[30]

Listening to Hitler

Ilsa Barea went to work for the BBC Monitoring Service at Wood Norton in August 1939. She found a large, hundred year-old house *Brooklands* in the small village of Fladbury, four miles from Evesham and two from the BBC, where Arturo, her parents recently released from brief internment and Margaret Weeden joined her. The Monitoring Service was in rapid expansion, spurred by the imminence of war. Its function was to listen to and transcribe broadcasts from other countries. As the war developed, the Service's reports became a key element in helping to shape British foreign policy.

Ilsa spoke five European languages, though in all of them, despite her fluency, she had a Viennese accent. Many of the Service's new recruits were exiles from Central Europe. Ilsa was effective at her job, as Margaret Weeden, who was to become a close friend for the rest of her life, recorded:

> *I found myself sitting beside a short, heavily built woman with a large mop of rather frizzy hair who at once addressed me in German, to my fury. Fortunately, Ilsa Barea's smile and charm soon overcame this bad start, and it did not take long to realise that here was someone of quite exceptional ability. When the first German news bulletin was broadcast I remember watching with amazement as she scrawled a few odd words or phrases almost at random across page after page, while I struggled with shorthand. Then I watched with even greater amazement as she typed out an almost verbatim translation.*[31]

Among other broadcasts, Ilsa Barea often monitored the radio speeches of Franco and Hitler:[32] her information is reflected in Arturo's radio broadcasts, where his parodies of and comments on the Nazi leaders often show detailed knowledge of what they actually said. Ilsa was an important monitor. Her memory was good and she could write up a speech rapidly from minimal notes. Like Arturo, she was quick-witted and quick-fingered, her thoughts passing directly from her fingers onto the page without need for correction. She started on the eight-hour night shift, but was moved to the 4 p.m. to midnight shift, both because most of the interesting broadcasts were during these hours and because she was not strong. In winter she found walking the two miles from the BBC to Fladbury too much.[33]

The Monitoring Service shared premises during the first two years of the war with some units of the BBC's also fledgling foreign language broadcasts service. Ilsa's contacts with people in the Latin American Service eventually got Arturo some broadcasting work, which was to develop into the *Juan de Castilla* talks (see Chapter VII). Since leaving Spain, she had been the couple's major bread-winner; but this situation shifted as Arturo got more and more work with the BBC.

In 1941, Ilsa became involved in a controversy, interesting in itself and also for light it throws on her personality. She spoke out in criticism of the Spanish Service, calling those in charge "crypto-fascists" because of the content of the broadcasts to Spain (see Chapter VII). Ilsa must often have had to use her training in politics to help her bite her tongue, in order not to compromise longer-term aims of fighting fascism by short-term outbursts at some of the reactionary politics of the BBC hierarchy. The outburst mentioned above, made by a foreign refugee in a time of war about a part of the BBC other than the part she was working in, was risky for her own position and must have been provoked by considerable tension. On the question of Spain, it was clearly impossible for her to always keep silent. She and Arturo were both caught in a contradiction working for the BBC. It is a constant tension in Ilsa's letters.[34] She felt this contradiction more acutely than her husband: she was more of a political thinker than him and she was more to the left.

The letter of application she wrote to the BBC on behalf of Arturo in 1939 (see also Chapter VII) displays a trait which runs through all her letters, and which those who knew her recall from her speech: she was verbose and at times didn't know when to stop talking.[35] As in this letter, she frequently betrays her fears or desires by saying too much, even though at work in the *Telefónica* and at the BBC, and in her book *Vienna*, she showed she knew how to be self-disciplined.

Ilsa moved with the Monitoring Service to Caversham in 1943, then left the Service towards the end of the war. A valued monitor, she left of her own free will. As the war drew to a close, there was no longer a pressing justification to stifle her opinions. She looked forward to a career as writer and translator.

Translating

During the war, Ilsa continued her literary translations. Her first work in this area had been in Barcelona and Paris, then in England, translating Arturo's stories and articles.[36] The first book she tackled was *The Track*, the second volume of Arturo's trilogy, in 1942. She went on to translate *The Clash*, then to re-translate *The Forge*, originally translated by Chalmers-Mitchell. Ilsa collaborated on the trilogy with two English friends, Olive Renier, who read galleys and typescripts, and with Margaret Rink (Weeden), whose role was "more basic . . . helping with the translation".[37] Ilsa also had of course the great benefit for a translator of being able to consult the author whenever she wished.

Her strength as a translator is not that she always understood correctly the Spanish. However, the errors in her translations are of little consequence: in itself a rare achievement for a non-native translating between two second languages. Her greatest strength was that she was an excellent translator of literature, by which I mean three things: she had the capacity to express tone and nuance across a change in language; she had a beautiful style in written English; and third, she did not use these abilities to write in a vaunting way, but subordinated her language to that of the writer she was translating.

There are of course difficulties in assessing Arturo Barea's work, which relate to the fact that nearly all his books were first published in English, after being written in Castilian. The translation by Ilsa of the trilogy is a far more fluent and polished work than the "original" or re-translation, which Losada published in Buenos Aires in 1951 (see Appendix 1).

The easiest way of suggesting Ilsa's competence is to compare Chalmers-Mitchell's and her translation of *The Forge*. For example, Chalmers-Mitchell, over 70 when he translated *The Forge*, used slang out-of-date even at the time ("These military blighters are all the same");[38] whereas Ilsa often wisely leaves a term in the original.[39] Her treatment of the *voice* of a slum child is better. To give one small example, she writes: "heaps of rubbish which they would be able to sell for a few coppers . . . ";[40] rendered by Chalmers-Mitchell as: " . . . the vendible remnants from which they can gain a few coppers . . . ".[41]

The other great innovation Ilsa made was to tell the whole book in the past tense rather than in the historic present: an unexplained change inasmuch as Barea retained the present in the 1951 edition. However, it is a change which reads well and in no way impairs Barea's re-creation of a childhood world.

An example of the third and most difficult translating virtue, i.e. fidelity to the original through the process of transformation to another language, is shown through the following passages from *La ruta/The Track*:

Antonio, el cantinero, vino despacito, echó una ojeada y se volvió a su cantina. Regresó con el cuchillo de cortar el jamón.

– Cogedla unos cuantos y sujetadla contra el borde – dijo.
Veinte manos se apoderaron del cuerpo ahora limpio y metálico manteniéndole contra el reborde de cemento, y Antonio comenzó a cortar lonchas blancas, con una gota de sangre roja en el centro que al caer en el agua se disolvía lenta.
Antonio me pagó treinta pesetas.[42]

Ilsa's rendering:

Antonio, the canteen-keeper, came, looked and walked away to his canteen. He returned with a big knife for cutting ham. "Catch hold of it, some of you, and put it here on the edge," he said.
Twenty hands held the body, now clean and shining, against the edge of the trough. Antonio began to cut it into slices, which slipped back into the water, each with a drop of red blood in the centre, which slowly dissolved.
Antonio paid me thirty pesetas for it.[43]

Every translation involves a set of choices. Some of Ilsa's choices in the above extract illustrate the quality of her work:

(a) With her sparse three verbs: "came, looked and walked away," she catches the figure of Antonio, silent but for one spare sentence and dominant in the scene.

(b) She is skilled in her use of colloquial phrasal verbs, both in narrative and speech. Examples here are "catch hold of" and "hold against".

(c) She changes the order of words in the phrase starting "y Antonio comenzó a cortar . . . ", omits some words altogether ("blanca") and introduces the term "slipped back." Thus she succeeds in the translator's aim of transmitting the image and feel of the original: in this case, of blood dripping into the water.

There are some infelicities, especially in *The Track*, her first full-length translation. One small example:

. . . The kitchen yields me about ten pesetas a day. And there's always something to be got out of the clothing, even if I must leave the quartermaster-sergeant his portion. And my food is thrown in gratis: where sixteen eat, seventeen can be fed.[44]

The original reads:

La cocina me da unas diez pesetas al día: y siempre se saca algo de la ropa, aunque haya que dejarle su parte al suboficial. Y la comida me sale gratis; donde comen dieciséis, comen diecisiete.[45]

"Yields" and "must" are both awkward in the mouth of the mess sergeant. The first should be "gives," a more common word. "Must" should be "have to". Thirdly, "thrown in" for "me sale" is incorrect: the mess sergeant is talking about robbing the people who eat in his canteen, whereas "thrown in" implies that the food is his right as part of his earnings.

These points are quibbles. In general, Ilsa's are fine translations. They are not as brutal, as crude as the language of the originals. But Castilian is a harsher-sounding language in many ways; and Barea's prose some of the harshest written in that language. His ungrammatical use of some terms, which gives at times a colloquial, rough edge to the prose, is also something impossible to reproduce fully in translation.

Ilsa went on to translate all of Arturo's subsequent work that was translated, as well as co-authoring with him the 1945 Fabian pamphlet and almost co-authoring *Unamuno*. She wrote in the introduction to the first Spanish-language edition of this latter book:

> *Of course, our long discussions on the subject had a certain influence on the essay, but only on its expression, not on its essence.*[46]

Ilsa is being too modest about her role. Nevertheless, their method of mutual discussion, of intensely living the composition of Arturo's books (people who knew them say they worked at the same table in both Fladbury and Middle Lodge) would have greatly assisted her in finding *le mot juste* in her translations. She mentions in another context:

> *I vividly recall how often I asked Arturo for descriptive details on translating a sentence of his that had one of these allusions, which were incomprehensible to me and of course for so many other foreigners.*[47]

It was not only Arturo Barea's works which Ilsa translated. The trilogy was the first of about 20 full-length books that Ilsa was to translate from both Spanish and German into English over the following 25 years. The books are varied, and range from commissions she may not have felt much sympathy with, such as de Lera's bull-fighting novel *The Horns of Fear*, to books whose culture and/or politics she shared. The translations from the Spanish are high-quality. Those from the German are often complex, such as Schnitzler and Holderlïn, and have a good reputation as accurate.

Her most political translation, apart from Barea's books, was of the ghosted autobiography of the Civil War general, Valentín González. His book *Life and Death in Soviet Russia* is a powerful (though highly unreliable) testimony of an uneducated, but intelligent figure. According to his account, González, exiled in Moscow at the end of the Civil War, rebels against Stalinist restrictions, is imprisoned, escapes, is caught and ends up working as a labourer building the Moscow underground in the late 1940s, before finally fleeing the country. It is a book against Stalinism, written before 1956 made the first wave of anti-Stalinism from within the Communist Parties fashionable. Though the book was later championed in the West by right-wing Cold War warriors, it is a book written by a man who does not renounce Socialism.

Despite her translation of this book and her friendship with Emir Rodríguez Monegal, associated with *Cuadernos* and founding editor in the 1960s of *Mundo nuevo*, the Spanish-language journals financed by the CIA's Congress for Cultural Freedom, there is no evidence that Ilsa sympathised with the US Government's anti-Communism. On the contrary, she had no time for the Spenders and Koestlers who attacked the left alongside their "revelations" of Stalin's crimes. She was made of sterner stuff. The translation of Valentín González's book and her sympathetic introduction confirm indirectly what those who knew her report: that 13 years after the end of the Civil War, Ilsa still believed in the importance and centrality of the working-class in politics.

BBC

As well as earning money throughout the '40s, '50s and '60s from translations, Ilsa worked as an interpreter. On various occasions there is evidence of her working at major Conferences. In 1949, for instance, she interpreted at both the "Free World Labour Conference" in London and the "International Transport Workers' Conference" in Stuttgart. Six years later, she was working for two weeks as an interpreter for an Austrian study group in London. Interpreting was an occasional but regular activity.[48] Interpreting helped her to start broadcasting in English – a career she wanted, but one which never really took off. She pushed quite hard for a number of years in the 1950s, but the BBC archives show, through her letters and the BBC's response, a number of problems.

One drawback was her accent. One of her first broadcasts was an anecdotal piece on interpreting for "Woman's Hour" in 1951 (there is a list of Ilsa's broadcasts below). The producer afterwards questioned her suitability: apparently, when she was nervous, her accent tended to thicken.[49] Probably more decisive in her failure to become an established broadcaster was her unreliability. In 1951 she had a proposal for a talk on Cela's *Viaje a la Alcarria* accepted by the BBC Third Programme. But she was then late in submitting the script due to "flu and neuritis," as she wrote in her effusively apologetic letter.[50] However, this was not something that happened just the once. It was repeated with other scripts; it became a pattern of behaviour.

Ilsa was clearly a person of tremendous nervous energy, who tended to overwork. Nor was her health good. Throughout the '50s she suffered from a constant stream of colds, bronchitis and flu; echoes of the prison bronchitis in the 1920s and her prostration in Paris in 1938. The same nervousness that made her voice thicken and that caused her to speak at people exacerbated these debilitating illnesses. Barea wrote in 1955: "Ilsa is fighting with her rheumatism . . . she could hardly move from November to April".[51] Around this time she began to suffer from diabetes, too. Ilsa was not at all well, but she was unreasonable in expecting other people to make allowances for her failures to deliver. Thus her illness and nervousness became in other people's eyes unreliability, as she failed to meet deadlines.

A third factor militating against a successful broadcasting career was her verbosity. She found it hard to stop talking or to end a letter. We have already noted her long-windedness in her 1939 letter to the BBC seeking work for Arturo. A further example was a letter she wrote to the novelist P. H. Newby, then a programme co-ordinator for the Third Programme, making a number of suggestions and expressing doubts about the programme's title. The points are quite justified in themselves, but long-winded and not tactfully put. It could not have entered her mind that she was intruding on Newby's province. After this programme, she tells Newby: "My accent and certain inflections made me squirm".[52] This second letter, full of apologies, instead of contributing to better relations, compounds the earlier errors of missing the deadline and telling Newby his job, by then over-reacting with self-doubt. In the same letter, she over-reaches with Newby by offering Arturo's story *The Scissors* for broadcast. Newby rejected the story.

Ilsa was too pushy for England, and at the same time revealed too clearly her insecurities about her abilities. Her haughtiness, her bossiness too, are familiar traits of a person affected by nervousness and attempting by will-power to overcome it. The vicious circle is completed by her ill health: rheumatism, diabetes and chronic bronchitis, not helped by smoking.

Nevertheless, during the 1950s, she did a number of broadcasts for both Woman's Hour and the Third Programme. They are varied: on interpreting and translation, on women's changing status in Britain, on Heine and Schnitzler, on being foreign in England, on the continental use of food seasoning, and on pike fishing, about which she was surprisingly an expert and enthusiast. She would fish in Lord Faringdon's lake at Buscot Park, the only recorded leisure activity of Ilsa.

She also made from time to time until 1958 a number of proposals for radio talks, which were not taken up by the BBC and rarely followed up by her. Her last actual broadcast appears to have been about Vienna for the Latin American Service in 1955.

Vienna

Vienna: Legend and Reality was to be the title of her only book in English. Following a TLS article she wrote on Arthur Schnitzler in 1945, George Weidenfeld the publisher, also an Austrian exile, who first met Ilsa in August 1939 at the Monitoring Service, suggested she develop the article into a book on Vienna. She signed a contract with Weidenfeld, which was cancelled by mutual agreement in the mid-50s.[53] Certainly in the mid-50s she was researching, but the book was still ten years away from completion and its eventual publication by Secker & Warburg in 1966.[54]

Vienna is much finer than its 20-year gestation period and the author's problems in broadcasting might lead us to suppose. It is a complex and scholarly overview of her native city's development. She summarised her aim in a letter:

> *(I am) in the very last stages of writing . . . book called "Mirage of Vienna," an attempt at historical portrayal and at the same time evocation of "Old" Vienna, but particularly the Old-New Vienna between 1870 and 1914 which launched the meretricious romantic myth of Viennese gaiety and glamour.*[55]

A more personal motive for the book is expressed in its Preface:

> *In trying to find the roots of both positive and negative Viennese traits, in assessing our common heritage, I could not but uncover some of my own roots . . . In this sense, there is an element of autobiography in the book.*[56]

Vienna is a cultural and social history, not a directly political one, and tantalisingly stops short in 1921. Unlike Arturo Barea, Ilsa did not wish to write about her own life. Yet she embarks on a similar literary journey of self-discovery combined with historical and social investigation, albeit in a very different form. The style she chose was sober and serious, with occasional vivid turns of phrase, these latter often paralleling a sharp insight. She talks of Adler's "hollowed-out liberalism",[57] of another politician's arrival "just as a rattlesnake announces itself",[58] of "the house without eyebrows" by Loos,[59] to mention just three.

The book shows her political formation too, though there is nothing that would lead a reader to believe she had been a revolutionary militant for the two decades of her prime. The politics emerge in her generally materialist approach to the subject matter. For example, she places Metternich in his social and historical position: she has no "great man" view of history.[60]

Her political approach is also evident in the importance she ascribes to the working class in history. The book is generally enriched by the skilful use of her own and her family's memories to illustrate arguments: with regard to the working class, she talks of childhood memory of workers' accent and speech and relates it to their exclusion from the city's architectural heritage, the property of the upper and middle classes.[61] This use of memory provides a telling image of change when she mentions how a decayed palace became workers' tenements in the 1920s.[62]

Ilsa is very conscious too of the strength of popular history. She writes of the importance of commemoration marches in terms of "tenuous pipe-lines of tradition and the annual revival of memory ritualistically repeated".[63] She also examines the formation of the workers' movement in Vienna and why it became social-democratic rather than communist; though the argument that the prevalence of small workshops favoured social democracy (a thorny historical problem) is not convincing.[64]

There are also echoes towards our main subject, Arturo Barea. In talking about the formation of Renaissance Vienna, Ilsa discusses the influence of the century of Spanish rule.[65] (The Spanish dynasty was of course called "the Austrias".) Though with discipline she never steps outside the structure and brief of her book to make direct comparisons, it is clear that when she talks of the "damage" done by the Counter-Reformation, she is continuing a discussion about the nature of Spanish absolutism. Franco too is a shadow discernible in the background of the account of Metternich.[66]

By the most rigorous scholarly standards, *Vienna* might be considered a hotch-potch. Historians should not write about their own family, perhaps; nor overemphasise their own interests at the expense of a more rounded view. The book works, though. It spans different genres effectively and creatively: based on a dialectical view of history, it is more a cultural and social account of a city's development, though one which does not avoid politics. *Vienna* reveals the author as critical, intellectual, highly educated, well-informed, and driven by political and social commitment. One may assume it represented a singular personal triumph too, as with *Vienna* she overcame the disorganisation of her practical and mental life in Britain.

The struggle to breathe

Like Arturo Barea's, Ilse Pollak's life had turned over in the middle. In the second phase of his life, Arturo was able to find his place and a meaning for himself with his writing. It was harder for Ilsa, whose whole adult life up to 1938 had been dedicated to revolutionary politics. Weidenfeld mentioned she was subject to conspiracy theories; and added that the theories may have had a basis in reality.[67] England was an inhospitable place for a clever, bossy foreign woman of her wide culture and left-wing views. She did not fit in easily. She did not, for example, go to the pub with Arturo, who was perfectly happy drinking and chatting at whatever level: it is hard to picture Ilsa in the "Wellington" at Faringdon. She even lost both her names. She changed from Ilse to Ilsa and then inevitably, against her wish, she became known as Mrs Arturo Barea.[68]

As we have chronicled, she was often ill and often incompetent as a free-lance in dealing with employers. These could be interpreted as traits of an undisciplined highly-strung bohemian. The health problems were real, though. We should remember, too, that Ilsa was an outstanding organiser in her work in Spain and at the Monitoring Service. Many of her problems in post-war England can better be understood, I believe, as reactions to an often hostile environment. In this light, *Vienna* is a triumph of achievement and organisation, even though it took her twenty years.

From 1938 until Arturo's death, Ilsa lived in the same places as him (except her advance moves to Evesham in 1939 and Caversham in 1943, and Arturo's 1952 sojourn in Pennsylvania). These places have been documented in Chapter VII.

Though preceding paragraphs suggest she was unhappy, it is a view that needs to be nuanced. There are no recorded arguments between her and Arturo. Most early witnesses describe them as being particularly happy together. Gellhorn saw them in 1937 as two physically unprepossessing outsiders who fitted well together: he was "very silent and dreamy," whilst she was "bossy and Germanic" (!).[69] Weidenfeld said of the 1940s: "they had a strong physical bond".[70] Younger Labour Party colleagues of Ilsa's describe them as a happy couple. Joan Gili, who knew both Ilsa and Arturo well and visited them at Middle Lodge, wrote: "They were very happy there . . . ".[71]

Another 1950s friend, Roland Gant, attested to the closeness of their working relationship:

> Lorca *and later work were helped by and filtered through Ilsa's Central European*

> *intellectualism. Her part in putting him on the (English) literary map and social scene was very important.*[72]

They were complementary personalities in many ways. Though they were, according to most sources, happy together, this should not obscure her frequent patent dissatisfaction and unease with people and life in England. The sometimes grumpy and bad-tempered Arturo was liked for his spontaneous warmth by most people who knew him. Ilsa was more distant, not so easy to get on with. Even so, in everything she did she was patently present, an intense and intelligent figure. She was always respected, but not so often liked. One young Labour Party colleague of Ilsa's in 1950s Faringdon related a telling anecdote:

> *Ilsa was quite capable of rifling through your bag without a "by-your-leave" to scrounge a cigarette, but you would never dream of doing the same to her.*[73]

What was Ilsa's physical appearance like? According to Martha Gellhorn, she was "short and rotund".[74] Lord Weidenfeld confirms she was "small, plump," and adds that she was "ungainly and shapeless, with a shining forehead and a lot of hair".[75] Vladimir Rubinstein describes her as "a little pudding . . . five feet tall".[76] Ilsa was not a conventionally attractive woman. Beauty, though, is subjective. And Arturo Barea tells us of her "gray-green eyes" and how her severe face could dissolve into happiness with her smile and "delightful mouth".[77]

Dress was not important to her. When Weidenfeld met her at the Monitoring Service in August 1939, she was wearing tennis shoes and a floppy sweater. Her copious hair, greying through her years in England, was roughly pulled back behind her head, with chunks often sticking out loose. In Madrid she wore an old raincoat.

Ilsa was active on the Bevanite wing of the lively Faringdon Labour Party in the late 1940s and 1950s.[78] British social democracy was tamer by far than the pre-war Austrian variant, but Ilsa participated fully in the arguments of the day. On occasion she dined at Buscot House, and it is easy to imagine her haranguing right-wing Labour luminaries such as the Minister Susan Lawrence and their Fabian host Lord Faringdon. She would talk non-stop about politics in general, and Spain in particular.

Arturo's funeral was private. His ashes were scattered at Middle Lodge. Poldi's sudden death when she was 35 meant the end of her youth. Now Arturo's sudden death made her old. She wrote to Rodríguez Monegal to thank him for his moving eulogy to Barea:

> *I still can't face Arturo's notes. Despite all my outer strength, I have to be given a little time first. I'll do it soon. But if you cut someone's arms and legs off, you have to learn to walk and work with artificial limbs.*[79]

Late in 1958, Ilsa moved to Lansdowne Terrace in West London and then to Upper Park Road in Hampstead. She seems never to have returned to Faringdon, where she had lived for eleven years. She did not keep up with many people from the past, though she maintained contact with Olive Renier and Margaret Rink. She continued to promote Arturo's work, as she had done since he first began to write. She got *La lección* accepted for the Home Service under the title *Grandmother's Lesson*, and the same story, titled *Big Granny*, published in *Argosy* in 1964. More substantially, she arranged, along with Roland Gant, for the trilogy to be published in paperback for the first time in 1958. She also wrote the prefaces for *Unamuno*, published in a Spanish translation from her English version in Buenos Aires in 1959, and *El centro de la pista*, for which she also selected the stories, published in Madrid in 1960.

In 1958 Ilsa started work as General Editor of Four-Square Books' paperback world classics. In 1962, she moved to the New English Library, still in London, as editor of their Modern Classics series. In 1968, when she retired, she returned to Vienna, which she had left in 1934. Money was not easy. She had sub-let her London flat and had problems with collecting the rent. For long periods she was ill with high temperatures and kidney problems, complications associated with diabetes, yet had to keep working at translations and articles right to the end of her life.[80] Her loyal friends Margaret Weeden and Olive Renier gave her money and assisted her to sort out her affairs in London, respectively.

It was not her first return to Vienna: that had been in 1955, when she visited for two months, but it was her final move. She died there in the first days of January 1972, according to one source while working on her autobiography.[81]

Ilsa Barea's Broadcasts for the BBC

Note: The following lists are not definitive.
All in English unless otherwise stated.

9 September 1941. "Spaniards in Hitler's army," Pacific edition of "Radio Newsreel".

24 June 1951. "A journey in Castile" (On Cela's *Viaje a la Alcarria*).

Late 1951? "Interpreting," Woman's Hour.
8 January 1952. "Techniques of translation," Third Programme.
Starting 12 November 1953. Series of 6 discussions with three others on "The art of translation," Latin American Service. In Spanish.
10 December 1953. "Science of interpreting," Austrian Service. In German.
23 December 1953. "Women's changing status in Britain," Latin American Service. In Spanish.
3 February 1954. "Padre Isla and the *Cartas familiares*."
29 April 1954. "Translation and misinterpretation." On Schnitzler and Heine.
10 December 1954. "Salt on the table," Woman's Hour.
21 December 1954. "Foreigners in England." Discussion with Edward Atiyah and Count Benkendorff.
14 March 1955. "The secret of the pike," Woman's Hour.
22 August 1955. "Vienna," Third Programme.
August or September, 1955. Same "Vienna," Latin American Service. In Spanish.
Aug./Sept. 1955. "The young worker of today – a new type," Third Programme.

Ilsa's Publications in Britain

Ilsa wrote widely in the German-language communist and socialist press in the 1920s and 1930s. She published a book in Vienna in the early 1930s. She edited the quarterly "Sozialistische Tribüne" in Brno (Czechoslovakia) in 1935/6.
Article, *Time and Tide*, Summer 1939 (ref. PR, p. 699).
"The First Flower," *The Spectator* (London), 2 February 1940.
"Viennese Mirage," *TLS*, 1945. On Schnitzler's prose.
SPAIN in the post-war world, Fabian pamphlet 97, 1945 (with Arturo Barea).
"The lure of Scotland Yard," in The Public's Progress (London: Contact Books, 1947), pp. 84–7. On Sherlock Holmes.
Introduction to Valentín González's *Life and Death in Soviet Russia* (1952).
Introduction to Arthur Schnitzler's *Casanova's Homecoming* (1954).
Foreword to her translation of *Cervantes* by S. J. Arbó. 1955.
Article on Vienna for *Harper's Bazaar*, late 1955.
Introduction to *Unamuno* (Buenos Aires, 1959). This introduction was new for the Spanish-language edition.
Introduction to *El centro de la pista* (Madrid, 1960).
Vienna, legend and reality. (London: Secker & Warburg, 1966; New York: Alfred Knopf, 1966). Reprinted in paperback by Pimlico in 1992.
She also wrote at least twelve reviews for the *TLS* between 1949 and 1959 on Schnitzler, Juan Ramón Jiménez, Gerald Brenan and Ramón J. Sender *inter al.*

Ilsa's Translations into English

Books

1943 *The Track*. Barea.
1944 *The Clash*. Barea.
1944 *Lorca*. Barea.
1946 *The Forge*. Barea
1951 *The Broken Root*. Barea.
1952 *Life and death in Soviet Russia*. Valentín González.
1954 *Casanova's Homecoming*. Arthur Schnitzler. Republished in 1998 by both Turtle Point Press and Pushkin Press.
1955 *Cervantes: Adventurer, Idealist and Destiny's Fool*. Sebastián Juan Arbó (Thames and Hudson.)
1955 *Three husbands hoaxed* (*Los tres maridos burlados*). Tirso de Molina (The Rodale Press).
*c.*1956 *Poems* of Hugo von Hoffmanstahl, with Vernon Watkins.
1958 *The triumphant heretic* (*Der siegreche ketzer*). E. Halperin.
1959 *In the darkness of my fear* (*Cuando voy a morir*). Ricardo Fernández de la Reguera Ugarte.
1961 *The horns of fear* (*Los clarines del miedo*). Angel M. de Lera.
1962 *Summer storm* (*Tormenta de verano*). Juan García Hortelano.
1964 *Reach for the ground* (*Cuerpo a tierra*). Ricardo Fernández de la Reguera Ugarte.
1965 *Tàpies 1954–1964*. Alejandro Cirici Pellicer.
1970 *Russia and the Russians*. Valeriy Tarsis.

Ilsa Barea also edited the reprint (undated) of Sender's *The Dark Wedding*, originally translated by Eleanor Clark and published by Grey Walls Press in 1948.

Ilsa also translated into English all Arturo Barea's essays, articles and stories.

Appendix 4
The Córdoba Tape

The Córdoba Tape is a transcript of parts of a radio interview with Arturo Barea on 6, 7 or 8 May 1956 in Córdoba, Argentina. I am grateful to Barea's niece, Leonor, for giving me a copy of the tape.

Presenter: Don Arturo, does your *alias*, *Juan de Castilla*, have anything to do with our Juan Pueblo? [or "Common Man"]

Barea: Well, I've never liked talking under my own name. I took the pseudonym of *The Voice of Madrid* and now *Juan de Castilla*, which I thought of as symbol of the entire people and not the symbol of a city.

Presenter: Perfect, Don Arturo. What stimulated you to write *The Forge*?

Barea: I'd say the reason was personal. The clash of the Spanish Civil War, leaving for France, kicked out on one side and the other, threw me into the search for why we Spaniards were like this, and searching . . . as far as possible, really right back to my birth, and I had to . . . follow from this point the reason why a Spaniard had been thrown about like this, like so many millions.

Presenter: Very good, Don Arturo. This question may seem paradoxical, but perhaps it complements the previous one. Was your vocation as a writer born with *The Forge*?

Barea: No. My vocation as a writer was born when I was 7. I started then to write little verses and stories when I was at school. We had a little paper called *Madrileñitos* and I think that my first, not exactly products, but rather incursions into the field of literature appeared there.

Presenter: Good, Don Arturo, very welcome this memory of childhood. And now a question touching on these poems you wrote. Were they dedicated to some little 7 year-old Madrid girl?

Barea: No, no. They were generally dedicated to the Holy Virgin.

Presenter: Good, perfect, Don Arturo. Can you tell us the reason for your tour of America, and in particular Argentina, which most concerns us?

Barea: Well, the reason is simply that I had already been talking for 16 years to the countries of Latin America and I was fed up with talking to someone whom I didn't know at all. Finally the BBC in London decided to spend a few pounds on sending me to find out about these peoples, so that

I'd talk better on the radio. I don't know if I'll manage it, but at least I'll be talking to someone I know.

Presenter: You've already achieved this and excellently, Don Arturo . . . Can you tell us some of the details of how you joined the British Broadcasting Service?

Barea: Really, it was almost by chance. When the war finished, someone who knew me from Madrid and knew of my radio broadcasts in Madrid suggested I join the BBC's Spanish-language service. I did a talk and the then Head of the service tested my voice and told me, well, it's alright, at least we'll use you for 3 or 4 talks, but I don't think you'll do more. Well, I started in the BBC and went on doing more and more. The person who prophesied my failure is still alive.

Presenter: And you have done hundreds of these 3 or 4 talks.

Barea: Oh yes, some 800 by now.

Presenter: Don Arturo, how do you feel your fatherland when you are so far from it?

Barea: Well, this is a very serious question. I feel the fatherland like an acute pain. Truly like an acute pain to which I have still not become accustomed . . .

. . . I told you earlier, I came to Córdoba with very intense emotions for various combined reasons. Córdoba naturally reminds me of Córdoba in Spain, where I have family, where my sister was born and where several things happened to me that it is not the moment to talk about now.

Notes

Introduction

1 Andrés Trapiello, *Las armas y las letras* (Barcelona: Planeta, 1994), pp. 283–4.
2 Arturo Barea, *The Forging of a Rebel* (London: Granta, 2001), p. 233.
3 Ibid., p. 738.
It is interesting to compare this statement of intent by Barea with what Martha Gellhorn wrote twenty years later:

> "I was always afraid that I would forget the exact sound, smell, words, gestures which were special to this moment and this place . . . The point of these articles is that they are true; they tell what I saw." Introduction to *The Face of War* (London: Hart-Davis, 1959).

The closeness of Gellhorn's and Barea's words has two implications. First, Barea's methods were similar to those of an outstanding journalist in pinpointing detail in order to reveal the reality of a situation; and secondly the impact of what can loosely be called the "school" of left-wing, partisan but realist writer-journalists – Gellhorn, Hemingway, dos Passos, Herbert Matthews and others lesser-known – with whom Barea came into contact when working as a censor during the Civil War, was seminal to his work.
4 FR, p. 234.
5 I was not permitted to consult the Barea Archive held by Ilsa's niece, Uli Rushby-Smith. However, much of this material has entered the public domain with the publication of *Palabras recobradas* in Madrid in April 2000. This collection of texts not previously published in Spain includes several documents not previously published at all, such as letters to and from Barea and his own autobiographical notes. It also includes articles from *La Nación* of Buenos Aires and some essays, which were previously unknown to me.
6 Ramón J. Sender, "The Spanish Autobiography of Arturo Barea," *The New Leader* (USA), 11 January 1947.
7 FR, p. 234.
8 Burnett Bolloten, Letter to Arturo Barea, 10 June 1950 (Hoover Institution).
9 George Orwell, "The Forge," *Horizon* (London, September 1941).
10 Gabriel García Márquez, *Notas de prensa, 1980–1984* (Madrid: Mondadori, 1991), p. 411. "In Castilian," for in this article GGM considered Mercè Rodoreda's *La plaça del diamant* the best post-war Spanish book.

1 Arturo Barea: His Life up to 1939

1 Copy of birth certificate held by Barea's niece, Leonor Rodríguez Barea (LRB). His parents' address was Calle Magdalena, 20.

2 Arturo Barea, *The Forging of a Rebel* (London: Granta, 2001), p. 71. Hereafter cited as FR.
3 Ibid., p. 71. LRB added family reminiscences:
"It's said he was a layabout . . . and when someone came by after his death to be paid a debt, [Arturo's mother] told him: 'this is the address of the debtor, go and look for the money in the cemetery'." Interview with LRB, Madrid, 17 September 1994. Leonor is the oldest daughter of Arturo Barea's sister Concha.
4 Interview with LRB, Madrid, 23 June 1990.
5 FR, p. 93.
6 Ibid., p. 359.
7 The real names of some family members mentioned in the trilogy were supplied by LRB.
8 FR, Chapter One.
9 In the opening days of the Spanish Civil War, Arturo's old school burned before his eyes (*The Clash*, Ch. 8).
10 FR, p. 51.
11 Ibid., p. 51.
12 *La forja de un rebelde*, Part 2, Chapter One, pp. 149–50. This chapter was deleted from later English editions (see Chapter IV, Note 2).
13 *La forja de un rebelde*, Part 2, Chapter Two. Deleted from later English editions.
14 FR, pp. 134–5.
15 Ibid., p. 329.
16 AB, *El centro de la pista* (Madrid: Editorial Cid, 1960), p. 138.
17 FR, p. 322.
18 FR, pp. 201–3.
19 Sir Peter Chalmers-Mitchell, introduction to Arturo Barea, *The Forge* (London: Faber, 1941), p. 9.
20 FR, pp. 227–8.
21 Chalmers-Mitchell, p. 9.
22 "Notas biográficas (1940)," *Palabras Recobradas*, p. 655. This is also mentioned on the Córdoba tape (see Appendix 4). The brilliant 1940 story "Cleptomania" (*Cuentos completos*, p. 94) also gives background to his days in the diamond trade.
23 CP, p. 145.
24 Victor Serge, *Birth of our Power* (London: Writers and Readers, 1977), p. 70.
25 CP, p. 142.
26 CP, p. 142. See too "Notas biográficas (1940)", PR, p. 655.
27 CP, p. 137.
28 Ibid., p. 143.
29 FR, p. 376 ff., and "Historia literaria," PR, p. 659. For further discussion, see Chapter 5.
30 CP, p. 143.
31 Ibid., p. 147.

32 FR, p. 333. See also PR, p. 656.
33 FR, pp. 332–3.
34 Chalmers-Mitchell, p. 10.
35 FR, p. 335.
36 Arturo Barea, introduction to *The Dark Wedding* by Ramón J. Sender (London: Grey Walls Press, 1948), p. 10.
37 Though the English version (FR, p. 532) says "a few months", the later Spanish version (*La forja de un rebelde*, p. 621) says "algunas semanas" (some weeks).
38 FR, pp. 245–7 and frequent subsequent references in *The Track*.
39 FR, p. 316.
40 *La forja de un rebelde*, pp. 366–7 (passage excluded from the English-language edition). Barea also wrote a story "El huerto" (1945), featuring Barea's family in Córdoba (CP, p. 69).
41 LRB. Arturo and Aurelia's children were called Carmen, Adolfina, Arturo and Enrique. *El País* (21 February 1988) reported on a group of Spanish fascists in Paraguay commemorating Carmen Polo (Franco's widow) on occasion of her death. One of the fascists was called Arturo Barea and was reported as a direct descendant of the writer – a sad legacy for an anti-fascist.
42 FR, pp. 474–5; and LRB. Concha had nine children, two of whom died in infancy, between 1922 and 1934.
43 FR, p. 475; and LRB.
44 Arturo Barea, *Struggle for the Spanish Soul* (London: Searchlight, 1941), pp. 34–7.
45 FR, p. 533.
46 Ibid., p. 474.
47 I have followed Barea's dating (FR, pp. 474–5). However, LRB and her daughter, Pilar Rita, showed me copies of the family record in Concha's own hand that Leonor died at the age of 73 on August 26, 1928.
48 FR, pp. 474–5.
49 Ibid., p. 474.
50 Ibid., p. 435.
51 Chalmers-Mitchell, p. 10.
52 Ibid., p. 11.
53 Arturo's meeting with Ilsa is discussed in detail in Chapter VI.
54 FR, p. 489.
55 FR, p. 489; LRB. Aurelia Rimaldos was evidently a snob, who liked to imply she was linked by her surname to the ruling Grimaldis of Monaco.
56 FR, p. 489.
57 Ibid., p. 491.
58 Ibid., p. 572. "light-headed" is Ilsa's curious translation of "libre": "free".
59 Ibid., p. 608.
60 Ibid., p. 622.
61 LRB.
62 After the Civil War (the exact date is not clear), Aurelia emigrated with the

children to South America. She probably went to Chile (LRB), though it may have been Paraguay (see note 41 above). She had become involved in a religious sect, which presumably offered her some way out of the hardships of being a single mother in post-war Spain. Aurelia remains the saddest figure in Barea's story: disliked by his sister, his mother, his nieces ("uncultured and simple," according to his niece Maruja [Letter to the author, Feb. 1995]), his friends and by Arturo himself. The caricature (under the name of Luisa) he presented of her in *The Broken Root* has no redeeming features.

Nigel Townson, in his introduction to *Palabras recobradas* (p. xx), explains that letters in the Barea archive held by Uli Rushby-Smith show that Barea sent money regularly to Aurelia until 1951, when the payments stopped because of his "financial difficulties". LRB remembers a letter from Aurelia in the late 1940s. There is no evidence that Barea ever saw her or his children again after leaving Spain.

63 The general atmosphere of imminent death is best captured in Chapter 12 of *The Clash*. See also the autobiographical story No. X1X "Esperanza" (Hope) in VM, pp. 112–16. This extract is from p. 114:

> "If the Francoists entered Madrid, if they reached this *Telefónica* building, rat-hole of iron and cement, with no way out, right in the path of the invasion, they would shoot her and him."

64 Telephone interview with Martha Gellhorn, 16 August 1990. Gellhorn herself (to her irritation) makes a fleeting appearance in the trilogy, as "the sleek woman with the halo of fair hair, who walked through the dark, fusty office with a swaying movement we knew from the films" (FR, p. 655).

65 Barea quotes from dos Passos' *Journeys between Wars* (London: Constable, 1938) on p. 710 of FR. Dos Passos adds more about the "cadaverous Spaniard and a plump little pleasant-voiced Austrian woman" on p. 367 of his book.

66 Sefton Delmer, *Trail Sinister* (London: Secker & Warburg, 1961), pp. 295–6.

67 Gellhorn called the Florida the "whorehouse hotel". Hemingway punned that it was "full of *hors de combat*" (Gellhorn, 16 August 1990). The atmosphere of press, Russian advisers and prostitutes hob-nobbing there is described in Hemingway's *The Fifth Column* and *For whom the Bell Tolls*. A full account is found in Paul Preston's *We saw Spain Die* (2008).

68 Interview with Martha Gellhorn, 16 August 1990.

69 Francisco Ayala, *Recuerdos y Olvidos* (Madrid: Alianza Tres, 1988), p. 237.

70 FR, p. 719.

71 FR, pp. 726–7.

72 The sources for the year that the Bareas spent in Paris are: the very last chapter of *The Clash* (FR, pp. 726 ff.); Barea's stories "A la deriva" (1943) and "Food Nostalgic" (undated; CC, p. 100); Margaret Weeden's "The Forging of a Rebel" (Canberra 1991); and PR p. 658.

73 The breakthrough in Barea's writing during Summer 1938 in Paris is discussed in Chapter III.

74 FR, p. 749.

II *Valor y Miedo* – Propaganda and Passive Heroism

1 Paloma Tuñon de la Lara in: "La Guerra Civil," *Historia 16* (Madrid 1985), Vol. 17, p. 91. The author lists 12 books in Castilian and 8 in Catalan. She excludes over 20 *novelas rosas* (romantic novels) and "the short novels published by the libertarian *La Novela Ideal* in Barcelona".

A more recent study, *La voz de los náufragos*, by Gemma Mañá et al. (Madrid 1997), names over 20 novels and collections of stories.

2 FR, p. 745; PR, p. 658.

3 FR, pp. 709–26.

4 Ibid., pp. 717–19 and Ayala, *Recuerdos y Olvidos*, p. 278.

Ayala and Barea both portray Kulcsar sympathetically – the former, because of his unhappy sudden death; the latter, after initial dislike, because Kulcsar accepted with dignity that Ilsa had left him and because it was Kulcsar's strings that helped him get an exit visa. In reality, despite his heroic role in the defeated Vienna uprising of February 1934, by the time he reached Spain, Leopold Kulcsar was a Stalinist torturer and interrogator, working for the Comintern within the SIM (Military Intelligence Service). For more on this, see Chapter VI, Note 43.

5 Kulcsar-Wagner's loyalty to the Comintern would not have helped him had he lived. A cadre profile from Comintern archive RTsKhIDNI read as follows:

> 525.
> "Is the husband of Ilse Kulcar (*sic*) and was Press Attaché in the Spanish Embassy in Prague. He is a Trotskyist who has written hostile articles on the Soviet Union. Was formerly a leading personality in the Austrian Party, but was expelled from the KPO because of links to Trotskyists. Was a member of 'Revolutionar-Sozialisten' since 1934."

Signed by Gustav (Szinda), 23 March, 1940. The data, like his name and the belief he was still alive, are wildly inaccurate. If he had still been alive, Poldi's loyalty to Ilsa would have been another nail in his coffin. For Ilsa's entry in the same file, see Appendix III, Note 27. I am indebted to Dr. Barry McLoughlin of Vienna for this information.

6 FR, p. 717; p. 725 for mechanics of *Valor y miedo*'s acceptance.

7 Ibid., p. 707.

8 I have found no details of *Valor y miedo*'s publishers or print-run.

9 "[Arturo Barea] . . . always intended to bring together his stories, at least the ones he thought were good, in one volume, but he put it off from one day to the next. He never did so." Ilsa Barea, *El centro de la pista* (Badajoz: Diputación, 1988), preface, p. 45.

10 FR, p. 736.

11 Ibid., p. 659.

12 Ibid., pp. 662–9.

13 Ibid., pp. 670 & 672.

14 Ibid., p. 675.

15 Ibid., pp. 676–7.

16 Emir Rodríguez Monegal, "Arturo Barea, una voz," BBC Latin American Service transcript, broadcast at Arturo Barea's usual hour on 29 December, 1957. The transcript was sent to the author by Margaret Weeden.
17 María Herrera, introduction to CP, p. 22.
18 Jaume Pont, preface to *Valor y Miedo* (Barcelona: Plaza & Janés, 1984).
19 It is a subjective judgement that the contents of VM are "sketches" rather than stories. The criteria for such an evaluation are that the sketches are short, anecdotal and often unresolved in their plot and theme. The clear exception is "Coñac", one of the subtler studies of VM. This was later published in *Penguin Parade* 7, 1940, under the title "Brandy", I believe the only story from VM to be later published in English: corroboration of the point made earlier in this chapter that Barea rejected VM.
20 The twelve photographs and prints published in the first edition of VM confirm the propaganda intentions of VM. They are entirely within the salt-of-the-earth school of heroic workers and peasants. They are reproduced in: Fernández Gutiérrez and Herrera Rodrigo, *La narrativa de la guerra civil: Arturo Barea* (Barcelona 1988) (hereafter, FG & HR).
21 John dos Passos was liked and respected by Barea (FR, p. 665). When Barea was later being investigated by the SIM, controlled by the Communists, a book dedicated to him by dos Passos was confiscated as suspect, because dos Passos had come out in support of the POUM (FR, p. 700).
22 Questions of the rightness, or otherwise, of Soviet policy in Spain and the USSR's precise relations with the PCE, have, of course, given rise to immense controversy and numerous polemics over the past 70 years. The debate is still alive. It is clear here and in Chapter VI that I am critical of the Popular Front promoted by the PCE and favourable to the POUM and the anarchists. The main and varied historians I have relied on, listed fully in the general bibliography, are Raymond Carr, Fernando Claudín, Burnett Bolloten, Paul Preston and Pierre Broué and Émile Témime.

    Though written from diverse view-points, these and other sources show that patriotism and national chauvinism were essential parts of the Comintern's post-1935 policies and part of the PCE's propaganda and Popular Front policy in Spain.

    For a rebuttal of my evaluation of VM, see Gregorio Torres Nebrera's introduction to his *Las anudadas raíces de Arturo Barea* (Badajoz: Diputación de Badajoz, 2002).
23 VM, p. 17.
24 Ibid., p. 117.
25 For example, Gustave Regler writes in *The Owl of Minerva* (London: Rupert Hart-Davis, 1959):

    "Miaja therefore 'held off the enemy with a strong fist and broke the black tide' – so it was said . . . Franco's Moors were on the verge of perpetrating unthinkable atrocities" (p. 283).

And:

"The Moors slaughtered the lot . . . those animals" (pp. 287–8).

26 VM, pp. 101–3.

27 Ibid., p. 82.

28 Ibid., p. 64.

29 AB, *The Indivisibility of Freedom*, 31 March 1945.

30 José Ortega, "Arturo Barea, novelista español en busca de su identidad," *Symposium*, Winter 1971, pp. 377 ff.

John Devlin, "Arturo Barea and José María Gironella," *Hispania*, XL1, 1958, pp. 143–8.

31 The unnamed priest of "Refugio" is probably the same priest who played an important role in Barea's decision to leave Madrid in 1937, the famous Leocadio Lobo (FR, pp. 702–7). There are a number of priests in the trilogy: the question of Barea's attitude to religion is discussed in Chapter IV.

32 In *The Clash* Barea shows how the Madrid working-class took matters into their hands and decided their destiny at these two crucial historical moments. The sharp contradiction between the honesty of his factual account and his very different ideas about those events is discussed in Chapter VI.

33 VM, p. 9.

34 FR, p. 679.

35 FR, pp. 303–6.

36 José Ortega, *op. cit.*

37 VM, p. 107.

38 Ibid., pp. 114–15.

39 Ibid., pp. 24–8.

40 Ibid., p. 22.

41 Ibid., pp. 18–23.

42 Ibid., pp. 22–3.

43 Like "Servicio de noche," "Los chichones" is also mentioned in *The Clash*. "Los chichones" is explicitly referred to as a radio broadcast:

> "Serafín had a purple bruise on his forehead which never waned and was the butt of countless jokes: every time he jumped because of an explosion, he bumped his head against the upper shelf and every time he wanted to get out of his bunk to help clear up the mess left by a shell in the street, he bumped it too. His fear and his courage both gave him bruises.
>
> I told this story over the wireless . . . " (FR, p. 678)

44 VM, p. 93.

45 FR, p. 303.

46 CP, pp. 73–6.

47 Ibid., p. 75.

48 FR, p. 738.

49 Ortega, *op. cit.*, p. 390.

50 María Herrera, introduction to CP, p. 32.

51 VM, p. 56.
52 Ibid., pp. 45–8.
53 FR, p. 680.
54 VM, p. 68.

– ¿Tú, no habrás oido misa, verdad? Pues, mira: allí hay una 'ermita'.
Cruzaron y entraron juntos en un tabernucho humilde.
– Tú, danos gasolina para la cuesta.
Se bebieron dos vasos de 'matarratas' . . .

55 VM, pp. 96, 49, 50 and 101, respectively.
56 Both Nora and Alborg, *op. cit.*
57 FG & HR, pp. 55–67. For further discussion of this, see Appendix 1.
58 VM, p. 35. As this book went to press, Robert Stradling's *Your Children Will Be Next* was published (Cardiff: University Press, 2008). In an Appendix (pp. 273–8) entitled "Arturo Barea – a Censor Obsessed", Stradling asserts that Barea's "personal obsession with bombing, to the point of paranoia", makes Barea's account of the Vallecas bombing unreliable. His case is that Barea is basically a fiction writer, who exaggerated and/or invented bombing incidents in order to make pro-Communist propaganda. Stradling maintains that Barea sought to create an impression of standing "conscientiously aloof", when in fact he was "an important part of the Republican propaganda machine". This is a polemical misreading, for *The Clash* shows Barea as passionately involved and perfectly aware of his propaganda role. Getting out the news of bombings was a priority for him, in order to denounce British "non-intervention" while Hitler was giving planes and bombs to Franco. As to Barea's fear of bombs and shells, this seems quite a healthy reaction to the threat of sudden death.
59 Ibid., p. 52.
60 Ibid., p. 77.

III Moving beyond "Surface Realism"

1 Arturo Barea, *The Forging of a Rebel*, p. 736.
2 Ibid., p. 736. The Spanish version reads "extranjeros" (foreigners), surely better than "strangers".
3 Ibid., p. 736.
4 See Chapter I, Note 72, for the sources for the year that Arturo and Ilsas lived in Paris.
5 FR, p. 736.
6 Ibid., pp. 737–8.
7 Ibid., p. 738. The Spanish is the more appropriate "forged" (forjado), rather than "hammered".
8 Ibid., p. 738.
9 Córdoba tape. See Appendix 4.
10 Arturo Barea, "Not Spain, but Hemingway," *Horizon* (London, 1941), pp. 350–61.

11 Ibid.

12 Ibid.

Jeffrey Meyers disputes Barea's conclusions in his biography *Hemingway* (pp. 341–2). See also the letter from Barea to the editor of *Horizon*, Cyril Connolly (PR, p. 673).

13 Arturo Barea, "New writing in Franco Spain," *London Forum* (Winter 1946), p. 67; also in PR, p. 80.

14 Arturo Barea, "A quarter century of Spanish writing," *Books Abroad* (Spring, 1953), Vol. XXVII, p. 123; also in PR, p. 135.

15 Ibid.

16 Ibid.

17 Ilsa Barea, preface to *El centro de la pista*, p. 45.

18 *The Times*, 23 March 1946.

19 Mario Benedetti, "El testimonio de Arturo Barea," *Número* (Montevideo 1951), Vol. III, pp. 374–81.

20 Emir Rodríguez Monegal, "Mask of Realism," *Times Literary Supplement*, 2 May 1952. Rodríguez Monegal was later a good friend of both Arturo and Ilsa. He composed Arturo's radio eulogy on his death and worked with Ilsa to translate *Unamuno*. In 1956, Barea stayed at Rodríguez Monegal's home in Montevideo.

21 Francisco Ynduráin, "Resentimiento español. Arturo Barea," *Arbor* (Madrid, enero 1953), Vol. XXIV, pp. 73–9.

22 Eugenio de Nora, *La novela española contemporánea* (Madrid: Gredos, 1970), Vol. III, p. 62.

23 José Marra-López, *Narrativa española fuera de España (1939–1961)* (Madrid: Guadarrama, 1963), p. 292.

24 Emir Rodríguez Monegal, *Tres testigos españoles de la guerra civil* (Caracas: Revista Nacional de Cultura, 1967), p. 13.

25 Rafael Conte, *Narraciones de la España desterrada* (Barcelona: Edhasa, 1970), p. 37.

26 José Ortega, "Arturo Barea, novelista español en busca de su identidad," *Symposium* (New York, winter 1971), p. 387.

27 Ibid., pp. 387–8.

28 Segundo Serrano Poncela, "La novela española contemporánea," *La Torre,* 2 (Puerto Rico, 1953), p. 108.

29 There are many of these autobiographical novels. The most famous are Ramón Sender's *Crónica del Alba*, José María Gironella's *Los cipreses creen en Dios*, Carmen Laforet's *Nada* (about which Barea wrote in "New writing in Franco Spain" in *New Forum*, London 1946) or the work of Max Aub.

A later generation is still more at home with the autobiographical novel, or novelised autobiography. There are numerous examples, from Juan Goytisolo's *Señas de identidad* to much of Francisco Umbral's or Jorge Semprún's work.

30 FR, pp. 233–5. This introduction to the English edition serves as Barea's most

articulate and condensed "Credo". It was published for the first time in Spanish in PR, p. 17.

31 Victor Serge, *Carnets*, quoted in Richard Greeman's appendix to Serge's *Birth of our Power* (London: Writers and Readers, 1977), p. 283.
32 Victor Serge's trilogy is: *Conquered City* (London, 1976), *Birth of our power* (London, 1977) and *Year One of the Russian Revolution* (London, 1978). They were originally published in French in the early 1930s.
33 Victor Serge, *op. cit.* in note 31, p. 284. In a letter to Cyril Connolly (PR, pp. 674–5), Barea wrote: "The theory that true artists should not adopt a definite position is bizarre" (*Es peregrina la teoría de que el verdadero artista no debe tener* parti pris).
34 Jay Mcinerney, "Fitzgerald revisited", *New York Review of Books*, 15 August, 1991, p. 26.
35 FR, Chapter 2, pp. 20–8.
36 McInerney, p. 26.
37 Letter to the author from Joan Gili, 6 March 1990.

IV The Child's Eye: *The Forge*

1 Santos Sanz Villanueva, *Historia de la novela social española* (Barcelona: Ariel, 1988).
2 In the Spanish-language version of the trilogy, each of the three volumes has two parts of ten chapters. This was also the case in the (now rare) Faber & Faber 1940s editions in English.

However, in all later English editions, including the Granta edition used in this book, *The Forge* has 8 and 9 chapters in its two parts and *The Track* has 9 and 8 chapters, respectively. *The Clash* has always been the same length in both Spanish and English. Thus, there are now six fewer chapters in English.

The unexplained cuts in the later English editions remove the chapters "The School", "Theatre Royal" and "The Church" from the first part of *The Forge* and combine some of the material of these three chapters into a new chapter, "School and Church". In the second part of *The Forge*, the chapter originally between Chapters 11 and 12 has been removed. This is a brilliant chapter recreating old Madrid, which deals with Arturo's first job in Don Arsenio's haberdashery.

It is a pity that Granta failed to restore the missing chapters in the most recent edition of the trilogy.

3 FR, p. 7.
4 The strength and skill of the child's-eye view is demonstrated negatively by the rare occasions when Barea departs from it, for example:

> "Old Madrid, the Madrid of my childhood, is a great surge of clouds or of waves . . . " (FR, p. 91)

This sentence is part of a long intrusion in the author's own voice, where he attempts to evoke his lost youth in a pseudo-poetic style, which breaks the flow of the child's eye and voice.

5 FR, p. 8.
6 Mario Camus' 1990 film of *La forja de un rebelde* (Televisión española) falls to some degree into a sentimental view of life in the slums. Part of its failure to show the reality of slum poverty may well be due to the loss of the narrative voice in the passage from book to film.
7 FR, p. 8.
8 Ibid., p. 8.
9 Ibid., p. 8.
10 Ibid., p. 9.
11 Ibid., p. 13.
12 Ibid., p. 25.
13 Mario Benedetti, p. 375.
14 Ibid., p. 375.
15 Ibid., p. 376.
16 FR, p. 55.
17 Ibid., p. 682.
18 FG & HR, p. 103.
19 Arturo Barea, introduction to: Camilo José Cela, *The Hive* (London: Gollancz, 1953), pp. 14–15.
20 Ibid., p. 15.
21 *La forja de un rebelde*, p. 27. Passage not included in later English-language editions.
22 Ibid., p. 28.
23 Juan Luis Alborg, p. 230.
24 FR, p. 39.
25 Henry Miller, *Big Sur and the Oranges of Hieronymous Bosch* (New York: New Directions, 1957), p. 101.
26 *La forja de un rebelde*, pp. 109, 113.
27 AB, introduction to *The Hive*, p. 13.
28 FR, p. 34.
29 Ibid., p. 35.
30 These three references to "marica" occur on pages 35, 55 (his sister Concha) and 77 (translated here as "pansy") of FR. Chapters I and VI discuss Barea's attitudes to women and sex, formed by these experiences and reactions. For this chapter's purpose, it suffices to note how his rage at taunts of *marica* is closely linked to his sensitivity about being a *señorito* who hides in his aunt's skirts.
31 FR, p. 71.
32 Ibid., p. 68.
33 Ibid., p. 117.
34 Ibid., p. 473.
35 Ibid., p. 473.

36 John Devlin, pp. 161–8.
37 FR, p. 172.
38 *Valor y Miedo*, p. 97.
39 VM, p. 97.
40 FR, p. 170.
41 Ibid., p. 140.
42 *La forja de un rebelde*, p. 172.
43 FR, p. 140.
44 Ibid., p. 145.
45 Ibid., p. 147.
46 Ibid., p. 177.
47 Ibid., p. 200.
48 Ibid., p. 222.
49 Alborg, p. 238.
50 Ibid., p. 230.
51 Ibid., p. 229.
52 FR, p. 234.
53 Hugh Thomas, "Spain Before the Falange," *The Nation*, 3 May 1975, pp. 535–6.

V Anti-imperialism in Morocco: *The Track*

1 Helen Grant, introduction to the 1973 edition of *The Forging of a Rebel* (London: Davis-Poynter, 1973), p. 9.
2 Ibid., p. 10.
3 FR, p. 239.
4 Ibid., p. 237.
5 Ibid., pp. 275–5.
6 Ibid., p. 428.
7 Ibid., p. 301–7.
8 Ibid., p. 261.
9 AB, *Struggle for the Spanish Soul*, Chapter VII.
10 FR, p. 379.
11 Ibid., pp. 303–5. In Ceuta today there is still a statue of Millán Astray.
12 Ibid., p. 304.
13 Ibid., pp. 332, 333 & 336.
14 Ibid., p. 375.
15 Ibid., p. 381.
16 Marra-López, p. 322.
17 See Raymond Carr, *Spain 1808–1975* (Oxford University Press, 1982).
18 AB, *Unamuno*, p. 53.
19 Marra-López, p. 323.
20 Arturo Barea, "A quarter century of Spanish writing," p. 119. PR, p. 138.
21 FR, pp. 327–8.
22 Gerald Brenan, "An Honest Man," *New York Review of Books*, 6 March 1975, p. 3.

23 For these occasions, see FR, p. 656 ff (*The Clash*, Chapter 16) and p. 731 *inter al.*; and letter from Barea to W. Stirling (WAC, 23 June 1944).
24 Barea wrote later: "I read *Imán* while my own experiences of the disastrous Moroccan campaign were only too fresh in my mind, and it seemed to me that Sender had expressed all the misery, degradation, muddle, and resentment of any soldier who is an unwilling part of an ugly war machine." Introduction to Ramón J. Sender, *The Dark Wedding* (London: Grey Walls, 1948), p. 11. See also *Palabras recobradas*, p. 104.
25 Though Barea's anti-intellectualism was modified in his later work, when he himself became an "intellectual" as a literary critic (see Chapter VIII), it is a recurring note in the trilogy (see FG & HR, p. 73 ff). The term "double refusal to submit" comes from Mario Benedetti, p. 376, and is discussed in Chapter III.
26 FR, p. 349.
27 Ibid., p. 350.
28 Ibid., pp. 350–1.
29 Francisco Ynduráin; J. L. Aranguren, "La evolución espiritual de los intelectuales españoles en la emigración," *Cuadernos Hispanoamericanos* (febrero 1953), Nº. 38, p. 152; Alborg, p. 227; *inter al.*
30 FR, p. 351.
31 Ibid., p. 401. In "A quarter century of Spanish writing" (pp. 122–3), Barea praised Valle-Inclán. "He had always been the 'absolute' artist dedicated to the cult of beauty . . . [but in the late '20s] Valle-Inclán, until then an aloof rebel, made a frontal attack on the Spanish monarchy, and a vast public responded to it with avid enthusiasm."
32 Ibid., p. 353.
33 Ibid., p. 354.
34 John Devlin, *op. cit.*
35 Ramón J. Sender, *Imán* (Barcelona: Destino, 1979), p. 194.
36 FR, p. 315.
37 Ibid., p. 347.
38 Ibid., p. 666.
39 Ibid., p. 234.
40 VM, pp. 36–49.
41 FR, pp. 68–9.
42 Ibid., p. 317 ff.
43 Ibid., p. 304.
44 Ibid., p. 303.
45 AB, *Struggle for the Spanish Soul*, p. 62.
46 Ibid., p. 62. PR contains a previously unpublished profile of Franco (PR, pp. 543–8).
47 FR, p. 290.
48 Ibid., p. 366.
49 Gerald Brenan, *The Literature of the Spanish People*, quoted in Barea's introduction to *The Hive*, p. 13.

Barea discussed the question of the poor's twin hungers for food and knowledge most fully in the opening chapter of *Lorca* (see Chapter VIII). He also refers to the question in his introduction to *The Dark Wedding* and in "A quarter century".

50 FR, p. 360.

51 Córcoles also appears in Barea's outstanding story, "Una paella en Marruecos," first published in *Cuentos completos*. In this story Barea combines a classic picaresque story of hunger and corruption with a powerful battle scene.

52 If Barea's relatively positive attitude to Primo de Rivera appears surprising, it should be remembered that the policy of Barea's union, the UGT, was favourable to Primo de Rivera; and that many people saw him as the man who managed to halt the Moroccan War (not unlike de Gaulle and Algeria 30 years later).

53 Chapter Two of *Struggle for the Spanish Soul* delves further into the character of Franco, "product of the Spanish Foreign Legion".

54 Several more corruption scandals are reported in *Struggle for the Spanish Soul*, pp. 92–4.

55 John Miller, *op. cit*., p. 58.

56 FR, p. 395.

57 *La forja de un rebelde*, pp. 356–8.

58 José Ortega, "Arturo Barea, novelista español en busca de su identidad," *Symposium*, Winter 1971.

59 FR, pp. 234–5.

60 Ibid., p. 281.

61 Gerald Brenan cast doubt on another aspect of Barea's veracity. He alleged Barea got the geography of Morocco wrong. " . . . there are some episodes [in *The Track*] that he describes in the first person but which I suspect he did not witness." ("An honest man").

62 FR, p. 235.

VI *The Clash*: The Flame of Revolution

1 FR, p. 682.

2 Marra-López, p. 329.

3 FG & HR, p. 143.

4 Letter from Burnett Bolloten to Arturo Barea, 10 June 1950 (*Bolloten collection*, Box 5, Folder 10, Hoover Institution, Stanford University). Translation by author.

5 Ralph Bates, 19 July 1947.

6 FR, pp. 480 & 521. PR, pp. 656–7.

7 PR, p. 675. Letter from Barea to Cyril Connolly.

8 FR, p. 245.

9 Ibid., pp. 557–73.

10 Ibid., pp. 532 and 717 *inter al*. Serafín's bar also appears in one of the best stories of *Valor y Miedo*, Chapter XIV, "Los chichones". Many incidents from

Valor y miedo overlap with *The Clash* or could have been included in it.

11 Ibid., pp. 543–4.

12 Ibid., p. 544.

13 Arturo Barea, "The indivisibility of freedom," *Socialist Vanguard*, London, 1945.

14 In "Notas biográficas" (PR, p. 655), Barea says he was a Socialist Party member in the First World War. However, he mentions in *The Forge* only that he was a member of the UGT. Whichever version is true, it is definite that he was more a union militant than a party one, both in the second decade of the century and in the 1930s.

15 Speech at Caxton Hall, London, 31 March 1945. Published as "The Indivisibility of Freedom".

16 FR, p. 474.

17 Ibid., p. 481. Antonio was possibly Barea's old friend Antonio Calzada, referred to in *The Track* (FR, p. 395).

18 Ibid., pp. 548–9. Barea's laments against disunity and factional interest are clearly heartfelt. However, he never assigns responsibilities for who was causing disunity, which ultimately makes the laments empty and abstract.

19 Ibid., pp. 545–63 (*The Clash*, Chapter 9).

20 Ibid., p. 566.

21 Ibid., pp. 569–70.

22 Helen Graham, *Socialism and War*, p. 6.

23 FR, pp. 590–1.

24 Ibid., p. 591.

25 Ibid., p. 591.

26 FR, *The Clash*, Chapter 14.

27 Ilsa's story is covered in Appendix 3.

28 Letter from Ilsa Barea to Burnett Bolloten, 20 June 1950.

29 FR, p. 573.

30 Ibid., p. 574.

31 Ibid., p. 616.

32 Ibid., p. 617.

33 Ibid., pp. 616–17. Paul Preston's *We saw Spain Die* (London: Constable Robinson, 2008) tells the story of the foreign correspondents and the censorship in detail.

34 Ibid., p. 690.

35 Ibid., pp. 693–4.

36 See Chapter II of Soledad Fox's *Constancia de la Mora in War and Exile* (Brighton & Portland: Sussex Academic Press, 2007). The description of de la Mora's sectarian loyalty to the PCE is all the more striking because Fox is broadly sympathetic to her.

37 Ibid., p. 695; "hedged-in administrators" is an odd translation of "administradores untuosos" (smalmy administrators).

38 Ibid., p. 721.

39 Ibid., pp. 718–19.

40 Ibid., p. 700.

41 In FR, p. 707, Barea cites Ilsa as the main intellectual influence on his keeping quiet about the PCE. Later, in Britain, it was for both of them a question of pride not to join the rush to attack the Communists. Barea did portray the PCE negatively in *The Broken Root*, but even so did not touch on the PCE's record in the Civil War.

His comment in a late (1952) article may be taken to apply to himself too: "[Sender] . . . suffered the great disillusionment with communism that inevitably comes to a humanist and individualist" ("A quarter-century of Spanish writing", p. 125).

42 In retrospect it may seem strange that so many people who had suffered from the PCE's rise to influence and control kept quiet. In the context of the war it is understandable and common. The Bolshevik leaders condemned in the Moscow show trials during this period thought within the same framework as Ilsa Barea: that any public dissent could only damage the cause they had fought for all their adult lives. If Ilsa had been the Trotskyist she was accused of or a POUMist, she would have had an alternative course to fight for within the Republican ranks. She was not. She was a disillusioned but loyal ex-Communist.

It is not unjust to add that, like many, Ilsa may have been psychologically inhibited from denouncing Stalinist persecution by her sense of guilt. She had previously, like Arturo Barea, collaborated with the persecution of the POUM and the anarchists in the sense that she allowed through the censorship false articles attacking them. She may well have reflected a few months later, when she herself came into the firing-line, that these articles had discredited the Republican side more than any hypothetical denunciation by her might have done. Yet she would have been silenced by her own collusion in that persecution.

43 Hugh Thomas summarises well the disingenuous omissions by Barea that imply that his silence was bought by divorce and exit visas:

> "We are made [in *The Clash*] to feel a little sorry for Poldi, who 'looked very ill and was suffering pain; he confessed to a serious stomach complaint rendered worse by his way of living, the late nights, the irregular food, the black coffee . . . ' But these late nights were caused by his endless interrogations and even tortures of alleged Trotskyists. 'My historic mission,' Poldi said to Katia Landau, 'is to find the proofs that, among twenty trotskyists, eighteen are the agents of Hitler and Franco.'" (Hugh Thomas, "Spain before the Falange," *The Nation*, 3 May 1975).

44 FR, p. 718.

45 Rubiera continued to fight against the PSOE right and PCE for a more revolutionary course. In a speech in August 1937, for instance, he polemicised against the PCE: "there are many in Spain interested in palliating the impulse of the revolution". Burnett Bolloten, *op. cit.*, p. 840.

46 Rodney Gallop, "Civil War", *Times Literary Supplement*, 23 March 1946.
47 Carlos Baker, *Ernest Hemingway* (London: Pelican, 1969), p. 413.
48 Helen Grant, introduction to *The Forging of a Rebel* (London: Davis-Poynter, 1972).
49 Ralph Bates.
50 Barea refers on the Córdoba tape to his feeling of being "thrown about" by events. See Appendix 4.
51 *The Clash*, Chapter 9: FR, pp. 545–63.
52 FR, p. 549.
53 Ibid., p. 551.
54 Ibid., p. 554.
55 Ibid., p. 555.
56 Ibid., p. 563.
57 Ramón J. Sender, *Seven Red Sundays* (London: Penguin 1938); Victor Serge, *Year One of the Russian Revolution*, *Birth of our Power*, *Conquered City* (London, 1974–1977).
Malraux's *L'espoir* also uses the technique of brief quickly changing scenes and characters to express the disruption of revolutionary Madrid.
58 Ibid., pp. 51–2.
59 Ibid., p. 53.
60 FR, pp. 35, 55 and 77. See also Chapter IV, Note 30.
61 Ibid., p. 228.
62 All mentioned in *The Forging of a Rebel.*
63 Ibid., p. 478.
64 Ibid., pp. 608–9.

VII Barea in England: 1939–1957

1 FR, p. 750.
2 About 80 of Barea's radio scripts (from between 1941 and 1947) are kept in the Written Archives Centre (WAC) of the BBC at Caversham, near Reading.
3 AB, "Final," broadcast on BBC Latin American service, 14 May 1945 (WAC).
4 AB, "Vacaciones," 30 March 1947 (WAC).
5 These letters to Ilsa are published in *Palabras recobradas*, pp. 679–700. "Señora Smith", broadcast 18 March 1946 (WAC), contains details of their life in Puckeridge before Ilsa went to Evesham.
6 AB, "Final", 14 May 1945 (WAC).
7 Ilsa Barea, Letter to the BBC, 25 July 1939 (WAC).
8 AB, Letter, 14 July 1940 (WAC).
9 Margaret Weeden, "The Arturo Barea Story," *En Australia y Nueva Zelanda*, October 1991, magazine published by the Spanish Embassy, Canberra.
Margaret Weeden's view of the dependence of Arturo on Ilsa during this period is supported by the insight of Gerald Brenan, who met them a little later: "Ilsa, calm and mature, the perfect wife and mother figure, had kept him going" (Gerald Brenan, "An Honest Man," *The New York Review of Books*, 6 March 1975).

10 Margaret Rink is the Margaret Weeden already quoted, who was a close friend of Arturo and Ilsa from 1939.
11 Margaret Weeden, "The Arturo Barea Story".
12 Ibid.
13 María Herrera, "El joven rebelde que quiso ser payaso," *Quimera*, January 2005.
14 *Cuentos completos*, pp. 100–3.
15 Ibid., p. 101.
16 Letter to the author from Lesley Bennett, 20 January 2008.
17 Interview with Lord Weidenfeld, 24 September 1990.
18 For more on Ilsa's parents, see Appendix 3.
For further information on Fladbury, see Olive Renier, *Before the Bonfire* (London: Drinkwater, 1984), pp. 100–1. "Arturo spoke French and English equally badly and lapsed into Spanish when pressed. 'Leche', he would yell . . ."
19 Joan Lynam, Letter, 29 June 1940 (WAC).
20 Peter Stuckey, Letter, 12 July 1940 (WAC).
21 Margaret Weeden, Letter to the author, 1 November 1992.
22 AB, Letter, 23 May 1941 (WAC).
23 AB, Letter, 20 December 1940 (WAC).
24 Interview with Leonor Rodríguez Barea, 23 June 1990.
25 AB, *The Broken Root,* p. 56. Page 31 of *The Broken Root* suggests something of Barea's anguish and guilt about those he left behind in Spain.
26 Sir Peter Chalmers-Mitchell (born 1866) was British consul at Málaga at the outbreak of the Civil War and a strong supporter of the Spanish Republic. He attempted unsuccessfully to save Arthur Koestler from arrest, a story told in *My house at Malaga*.
27 Tosco Fyvel, preface to Barea's *Struggle for the Spanish Soul*, p. 5.
28 FR, pp. 742, 743, 747 *inter al.*
29 Ralph Bates, "Arturo Barea," *The Nation*, July 15 1947.
30 Arturo Barea, Letter, 21 January 1955 (WAC).
31 Letter from W. Galbraith, 21 January 1955 (WAC).
32 Joan Lynam, Letter, 29 June 1940 (WAC). See Appendix 4 for Barea's comments on how he was first hired.
33 Ilsa Barea, Letter, 25 July 1939 (WAC).
34 Hannen Swaffer, "Foreign Office Mystery," *Daily Herald*, 3 June 1941.
35 Gerald Mansell, *Let truth be told* (London: Weidenfeld & Nicholson, 1982), pp. 166–7.
36 Ibid., p. 167.
37 According to Mansell, p. 168, the BBC official who actually said the immortal words "We do not employ reds" was H. Duckworth Barker.
38 AB, "Los seis elefantes blancos," 28 October 1940 (WAC).
39 Margaret Weeden, "The Arturo Barea Story".
40 According to Nigel Townson, who had access to the Barea Archive held by Uli Rushby-Smith, Barea wrote and broadcast at least 856 scripts (PR, Introduction, p. xxii). Seventy are published in *Palabras recobradas*.

41 H. Lyon Young, internal BBC memo, 26 April 1946 (WAC).
42 Ilsa Barea, preface to *El centro de la pista* (Madrid: Cid, 1960).
43 Letter to the author from Margaret Weeden, 29 October 1992.
44 Letter from J. Camacho to W. Stirling, 10 October 1944 (WAC).
45 Letter from Ilsa Barea to J. B. Clark, Director of External Broadcasting, BBC, 1 January 1958 (WAC).
46 Letter from Arturo Barea to J. B. Clark, 21 May 1955, in reply to a letter of congratulation on having done 750 talks (WAC).
47 Letter from C. V. Salmon, 2 August 1940 (WAC).
48 Letter from P. H. Newby, 26 June 1953 (WAC).
49 "The Scissors" was published in *Horizon* in 1941 and appears as "Las tijeras" in *El centro de la pista*.
50 AB, Letter, 4 October 1943 (WAC).
51 Gerald Brenan, "An Honest Man," p. 4.
52 The opening chapters of *The Broken Root* provide background to the Majorca.
53 Letter to the author from Maruja Wallich, February 1995. The view of the youngest daughter of Barea's sister Concha is that Barea never adjusted to life in England and that Ilsa made his life a misery in later years and strangled his literary talent.
54 Letter to the author from Joan Gili, 6 March 1990.
55 See Barea's essay "Ortega and Madariaga" and my comments on it in Chapter VIII.
56 This social patriotism comes out in several broadcasts: 10 November 1940, 13 May 1945, 3 June 1945 *inter al.* (WAC).
57 AB, "The indivisibility of Freedom," in *Freedom for Spain* (London: Socialist Vanguard, 1945), p. 12.
58 Ibid., p. 12.
59 Ibid., p. 13.
60 Ibid., p. 14.
61 Ibid., p. 15.
62 AB, *The Broken Root*, p. 29.
63 Ibid., p. 30.
64 Interview with Gladys Langham, Margaret Carter and Bill Carter, 14 November 1989.
65 Ibid.
66 Letter to the author from Olive Renier, 6 August 1992.
67 Ibid.
68 Interview with Gladys Langham, Margaret Carter and Bill Carter, 14 November, 1989.
69 Ibid.
70 Letter to the author from Roland Gant, 14 June 1990.
71 AB, "Señora Smith," 17 March 1946 (WAC).
72 "Fortunately, he had not lost his old love for books, and the inexhaustible English literature became his refuge and his best teacher of the language. Even

if he could never get rid of his accent or pronounce some of the more abstruse sounds, he had no difficulty in talking with people after the first couple of years." *The Broken Root*, p. 28.

73 Letter from Roland Gant, 14 June 1990; interview with Lord Weidenfeld, 24 September 1990.

74 Lord Weidenfeld.

75 Interview with Gladys Langham, Margaret Carter and Bill Carter, 14 November 1989; and with Olive Renier, 6 July 1992.

76 Letter from the Duque de Primo de Rivera, Spanish Ambassador in London, 6 June 1956 (4850–3, Archive of the Ministerio de Asuntos Exteriores, Madrid).

77 Press release from Pennsylvania State College, February 1952 (University Archives).

78 Letter from Ramón J. Sender to Barea on 1 December 1951 (PR, pp. 713–14).

79 Letter to the author from Helen Shepard, 18 March 2002.

80 Letter to the author from Professor Gerald Moser, 12 October 1990.

81 Ginger Opczenski, "Americans' Activity Astounds Spaniard," *The Daily Collegian*, 28 February 1952. I am grateful to Professor Moser for sending me this extract from the Penn. State campus newspaper.

82 Ibid.; Barea also discusses traffic in a letter to Ilsa Barea, February 1952 (PR, pp. 701–2).

83 Letter from unnamed official of the British Embassy, Buenos Aires, 15 May 1956 (WAC).

84 Sarcastic hostile leaflets were printed publicising lectures by "Mister Arthur Barea ('Beria')". An article was written on the same theme ("The ex non-combatant, ex-Madrid native and ex-Spaniard . . . " etc.) in the *Nuevo Correo*, Buenos Aires, 28 April 1956 (R5048-11, Archive of the Ministry of Foreign Affairs, Madrid).

85 Article in *El País*, Montevideo, 28 May 1956, by General Larre Borges. Luis Monferrer adds certain details to Barea's week in Montevideo:

"On 22 May 1956, he reached Montevideo, where he stayed at the home of the critic and journalist Emir Rodríguez Monegal. The Uruguayan press heaped praise on him. The Spanish Republican Centre declared him 'Guest of Honour'. At the British Embassy he received journalists and made hostile statements against the Franco regime." (Luis Monferrer, *La colaboración de Arturo Barea en la BBC*, GEXEL, volume 1, p. 165).

Monferrer also lists some of Barea's lectures: on Lorca, on "English personalism and Spanish individualism," and on "For whom does the contemporary writer write?" on the 24, 25 and 26 May, respectively.

86 Letter from Spanish Ambassador in Chile, 22 May 1956 (Archive of the Ministry of Foreign Affairs).

87 See Appendix 4. Twenty of these articles are reprinted in *Palabras Recobradas*. They are mainly commentaries on British and world affairs.

88 Emir Rodríguez Monegal, "Arturo Barea, una voz."

89 Letter to the author from Joan Gili, 6 March 1990.
90 Letter to the author from Olive Renier, 6 August 1992.
91 This is the opinion of Maruja Wallich (Letter to the author, February 1995) and Bill Carter (Interview, 14 November 1989).
92 Letter to the author from Professor Ian Michael, 10 January 1990.
93 Letter to the author from Lesley Bennett, 20 January 2008.
94 Ibid.
95 Letter to the author from Olive Renier, 6 August 1992. The memorial is a rugged slab of granite in the annex to Faringdon churchyard, beside the tomb of Ilsa's parents.

VIII Hunger to Read: Criticism and Stories

1 Barea devotes an entire article to this question: "El lector español y sus autores" (PR, pp. 91–101), which is really a sociological essay on the literary education of the working-class. Several other articles touch on the theme. He talks movingly about Blasco Ibáñez and the priests' response in FR, pp. 85–6.
2 Arturo Barea, "Not Spain, but Hemingway," *Horizon*, May 1941, pp. 350–61.
3 AB, "A Quarter Century of Spanish Writing," *Books Abroad* (1953).
4 Ibid.
5 Ibid.
6 AB, "The Spanish Labyrinth," *Horizon*, September 1943, pp. 203–9.
7 There is an exchange of letters between Barea and Connolly in *Palabras recobradas* (pp. 673–5 and 707). The first of these is particularly interesting for Barea's views on Ernest Hemingway.
8 AB, "New writing in Franco Spain," *London Forum*, Winter 1946, p. 61.
9 Ibid., pp. 62–3. Barea based himself on Gustavo Gili's *Bosquejo de una política del libro*, a book published privately within Spain (1944), to explain the Spanish censorship.
10 Letter from Arturo Barea to Programme Organiser, BBC Third Programme, 2 February 1947 (WAC). Starkie was Head of the British Institute in Madrid from 1940–1954. His politics were right-wing; his literary choice, affected by his politics.
11 Ibid.
12 Ibid.
13 AB, "New writing in Franco Spain," p. 68.
14 Manuel Aznar Soler, "El Partido Comunista de España y la literatura del exilio republicano (1939–1953)" in *El Exilio Literario Español de 1939* (Barcelona: Gexel, 1998, Volume 2). Aznar reproduces Semprún's 1950 article on *Nada* in its totality.
15 AB, "New writing in Franco Spain," p. 69.
16 Ibid., p. 70.
17 Ibid., p. 71.
18 Ibid., p. 71.
19 AB, "Realism in the Modern Spanish Novel," *Focus Two* (1946) (PR, p. 66).

20 AB, "A Quarter Century of Spanish Writing," *Books Abroad*, Spring 1953, p. 128.
21 AB, introduction to Camilo J. Cela, *The Hive* (London: Gollancz, 1953), pp. 8 & 13.
22 Ibid., p. 8.
23 Ibid., p. 16.
24 AB, "A Quarter Century of Spanish Writing."
25 Ibid., p. 119.
26 Ibid., p. 120.
27 Ibid., p. 126; and AB, introduction to: Ramón J. Sender, *The Dark Wedding* (London: Grey Walls, 1948), p. 15.
28 AB in *The Dark Wedding*, pp. 14–15.
29 Ibid. p. 15.
30 Marra-López, p. 339.
31 AB, "Las raíces del lenguaje político de García Lorca," PR, p. 49.
32 AB, "El lector español y sus autores," PR, p. 100. See also FR, p. 754.
33 On 17 November 1944, Barea gave a lecture on Lorca in the *Instituto Español*, London (WAC). This was later published in the *Bulletin of Hispanic Studies* and in PR, pp. 48–60.
34 Ramón Sender, "The Spanish Autobiography of Arturo Barea."
35 *Lorca*, p. 12.
36 Ibid., p. 13.
37 Ibid., p. 11.
38 Ibid., p. 19.
39 AB, "An Andalusian Poet," *TLS*, 6 May 1948.
40 *Lorca*, p. 30.
41 Ibid., p. 35.
42 Ibid., p. 50.
43 Ibid., p. 52.
44 For more on Barea's personal sexual history, see Chapter VI. Indirect evidence of Barea's views is also contained in the discussion on women between Antolin and Eusebio in the second chapter of *The Broken Root*.
45 *Lorca*, p. 56.
46 Ibid., p. 60.
47 Ibid., p. 60.
48 Rafael Martínez Nadal, introduction to F. García Lorca, *Poems* (London: Dolphin, 1939), p. xxvii. On page 55 of *Lorca*, Barea cites this essay. I am grateful to Mr. Martínez Nadal for sending me a copy of his introduction.
49 Ynduráin, p. 76.
50 Anon, "In permanent opposition," *TLS*, 5 December 1952.
51 Ilsa Barea, preface to *Unamuno* (Buenos Aires: Sur, 1959).
52 *Unamuno*, p. 58.
53 AB, "Ortega and Madariaga," *University Observer*, Chicago 1948, p. 36.
54 In her introduction to *El centro de la pista*, Ilsa implied there were other stories

she had not collected, but I did not find any. Erroneously I thought that most of the stories of *El Centro de la pista* had not previously been published. Debate's publication of *Cuentos completos* in 2001 showed that nearly all HAD been previously published, in British magazines or in Argentina, Austria and Scandinavia. *Cuentos completos* also includes 14 stories not included in *Valor y Miedo* or *El Centro de la pista*, from Uli Rushby-Smith's archive on Barea.

55 These nine are: *El cono* (1942), *El testamento* (1942), *El centro de la pista* (1945), *El huerto* (1945), *Agua bajo el puente* (1947), *Madrid entre ayer y hoy* (1948), *Física aplicada* (1948), *La rifa* (1954) and *La lección* (1957).

56 AB, "Big Granny," *Argosy*, November 1964, pp. 12–19.

57 She was the same pagan grandmother, Inés, whose intervention had saved the child Arturo from the Jesuits, celebrated in Barea's very last story (September, 1957), as she had been at the start of his writing in *The Forge* (see Chapter IV).

58 AB, *Argosy*, p. 14.

59 Ilsa Barea, Introduction to *El centro de la pista* (Badajoz: Diputación, 1988), p. 44.

60 AB, *Argosy*, p. 19.

61 AB, *El centro de la pista*, pp. 113 and 117.

62 Ibid., p. 121.

IX Exile without Resentment

1 Francisco Ynduráin, "Resentimiento español," p. 73.

2 Marra-López develops his arguments in *Narrativa española fuera de España* (Madrid: Guadarrama 1963), pp. 51–130 and pp. 289–340 (the chapter on Barea).

3 Marra-López, p. 90.

4 The two exceptions are *Mr. One* and *Bajo la piel,* both in *El centro de la pista.*

5 Marra-López, p. 65. The essay quoted is by Francisco Ayala, in *La estructura narrativa* (Barcelona: Crítica, 1984), pp. 181–204.

6 Marra-López, p. 123 ff.

7 Ibid., p. 128.

8 *The Broken Root*, p. 231.

9 Arturo and Ilsa's 1950s neighbours, the Vine family, went twice to Spain in the 1950s to visit his family. "We knew that Arturo could never return to Spain so we went for him . . . When we came back we had to tell Arturo everything about our visit, and bring him back things from Spain." Lesley Bennett, Letter to the author, 20 January 2008.

10 FR, p. 787.

11 Only *Unamuno*, three stories in *El centro de la pista* and two essays of criticism were written in the 7½ years of Barea's life after completion of *The Broken Root*.

12 Joan Gili, in *The Times* obituary of Barea (27 December 1957) and Mario Benedetti, *op. cit.*, p. 374, refer to another novel.

13 When Barea went to South America in 1956, the BBC made sure he was

briefed in Spanish, as they feared his English was inadequate to understand the terms of the trip (WAC, 10 March 1956).

14 Margaret Weeden, "The Spaniard who came to England" (Australian Broadcasting Commission, 1958).

15 "A Spaniard in Hertfordshire," *The Spectator*, August 1939. *Cuentos Completos*, p. 89.

16 David Vine's daughter, Lesley, wrote: "On Sundays Arturo and my father would go for a drink in the pub at Buscot, on Saturdays they'd go to the Bell in Faringdon. They both enjoyed pub culture." (Letter to the author from Lesley Bennett, 20 January 2008).

17 It is not known who the Bareas' sponsor was. It may have been the economist Sir Norman Angell, for whom Ilsa Barea wrote articles when she was in Paris; possibly a contact from Ilsa's Vienna days, such as Hugh Gaitskell; or one of the journalists, like Sefton Delmer, whom Barea knew in Madrid.

18 José Luis Abellán, "El éxodo republicano," *Historia 16* (noviembre 1977), p. 26.

19 *The Broken Root*, pp. 12–14 and 27–9.

20 Interviews with Gladys Langham, Margaret Carter and Bill Carter (14 November 1989) and with Olive Renier (6 July 1992).

21 As well as the sources in the previous note, LRB, Roland Gant and Margaret Weeden supplied me with information on Barea's visits to the Majorca. Luis Monferrer (GEXEL, Vol. 1, pp. 159–60) is the source for Barea's presence at the *Hogar español* and articles for *Españoles*.

22 His lecture in Oxford was to the undergraduate Spanish Club in the 1950s (Letter to the author from Professor Ian Michael, 10 January 1990).

23 Letter from AB, 2 February 1947 (WAC).

24 Olive Renier, *Before the Bonfire* (London 1984), p. 100; and letter to the author from Bill Carter, February 1990.

25 FR, pp. 349–54.

26 *Lorca*, p. 12.

27 FR, p. 354.

28 Ibid., p. 683. Barea's view of these intellectuals is mild when compared with George Orwell's. In a review of *The Clash*, he complained bitterly of "the 'Anti-Fascist Writers' who held their congress in Madrid and ate banquets against a background of starvation." (*The Observer*, 24 March 1946); reprinted in *Orwell in Spain* (London: Penguin, 2001), p. 372.

29 John dos Passos, *U.S.A.* (London: Penguin, 1976).

30 See Chapters III and VIII.

31 *Lorca*, p. 64. Barea expanded on the theme of Lorca's "exile" in New York in his 1944 lecture to the *Instituto español* (PR, 48–60).

32 *Lorca*, p. 68.

33 In the United States, *The Broken Root* was better received. The *New Yorker*, the *Herald Tribune* and Ramón Sender in the *New York Times* all praised the book in reviews. John dos Passos wrote in a 1951 letter to his publisher that *The*

Broken Root, in its portrait of "the dark Spain of today", was as good as *The Forging of a Rebel* (Nigel Townson, introduction, PR, p. xxix). However, dos Passos was vehemently anti-Communist by this time and probably over-responded to the negative portrait of the Communists in Barea's novel.

34 Marra-López, p. 332.

35 Alborg, *op. cit.*, tomo II, p. 242.

36 Ynduráin, p. 77. Ironically, Ynduráin (writing under Francoism in the 1950s) criticised Barea for being ignorant about conditions in Spain, not because he exaggerated how bad the black market was, but because he understated the situation and held up as a scandal what everyone knew about! Ynduráin is surely right, however, in criticising as completely unrealistic Barea's writing that a corpse would be left unburied in a flat for four days in mid-summer because of the vengeance of the Church.

37 FG & HR, p. 151.

38 Barea's niece Leonor, who arrived at Faringdon in August 1947, told me that Barea was always questioning her about conditions in Madrid. In her view, criticism of Barea's accuracy is unfounded (LRB, 17 September 1994).

It should also be noted that the first chapter of *Struggle for the Spanish Soul*, written several years previously, contains many details on conditions within Spain, which Barea had gleaned from the radio. There is, therefore, no reason why *The Broken Root* should be wrong in its factual details.

39 Marra-López, p. 336.

40 *The Broken Root*, p. 7.

41 Ibid., p. 9.

42 Ibid., p. 162.

43 Ibid., p. 194.

44 Ibid., p. 210.

45 Ibid., p. 6.

46 Ibid., p. 291.

47 Ibid., p. 320.

48 Ynduráin, p. 78.

49 Anthony Powell, *Times Literary Supplement*, 11 May 1951.

50 LRB, 23 June 1990.

51 According to LRB, the original for Antolin was Manolo, a waiter at the *Majorca* on Brewer Street (LRB, 17 September 1994).

52 José Ortega, *op. cit.*, p. 388.

53 *The Broken Root*, p. 29.

54 Ynduráin, p. 77.

55 Ángel Ruiz Ayúcar, *Arriba*, 21 January 1958.

56 J.M. Castellet "En la muerte de Arturo Barea, novelista español," *Papeles de Son Armadans*, January 1958, p. 104.

57 Ibid., p. 105.

58 Ibid., p. 105.

59 Ibid., p. 103.

60 Arturo Barea, "Final" (WAC).

Conclusion

1 Jean-Pierre Ressot, *Historia de la Literature española, Siglo XX* (Barcelona: Ariel, 1995), Tomo VI.

Appendix I Publishing History

1 FR, pp. 375–6.
2 Ibid., p. 391.
3 "Historia Literaria," PR, p. 659.
4 FR, pp. 660 and 722–3.
5 Ibid., p. 749 and CC, p. 199.
6 FR, p. 782 and *Cuentos Completos*, which contains the known dates and places of publication of Barea's stories.
7 The title page of *Struggle for the Spanish Soul* reports the enemy action. Bernard Crick's introduction to George Orwell's *The Lion and the Unicorn* supplies further information about the "Searchlight" publishing project.
8 These figures of sales for the first year of publication, like all the Faber sales figures, are from a letter to the author from Constance Cruikshank, archivist at Faber & Faber (6 June 1990).
9 Faber and Faber's files concerning T.S. Eliot will not be released until Valerie Eliot's biography of T.S. Eliot is completed. Faber's current archivist, Robert Brown, confirmed in February 2008 that a file of correspondence between Faber and Barea does exist. However, it is still not possible to examine it or know what it contains.
10 Letter to the author from Margaret Weeden, 1 November 1992.
11 Nigel Townson, Introduction to *La forja de un rebelde* (Madrid: Debate, 2000), p. ix.
12 *The Daily Collegian*, State College, Pennsylvania, 28 February 1952; "Obituary of Arturo Barea," *The Times*, 28 December 1957.

As well as in English and Spanish, *The Forging of a Rebel* was published in Italian (by Garzanti, Milan), Dutch, Swedish, Finnish, French (by Gallimard), Danish (translated by Ilsa Barea's sister Lotte), Czech and Norwegian. Source: covers of Buenos Aires first editions. Later it was published in German.

13 *Index Traslationum*, UNESCO. Barea's niece, Leonor Rodríguez Barea, drew my attention to this.
14 See Appendix 2.
15 Lord (Gavin) Faringdon was a Labour peer, who in 1938 provided accommodation in the grounds of Buscot Park for one of the colonies of Basque refugee children. The Bareas went to live in one of the lodges in June 1947. Lord Faringdon was involved in Spanish solidarity activities during the Civil War and after (Interview with Gladys Langham, ex-secretary Faringdon Labour Party, 14 November 1989). See Adrian Bell, *Only for Three Months* (Norwich: Mousehold Press, 1996) on Basque children.
16 Nicolás Rita (Interview, 23 June 1990) told me that when he was working on

the railways in Madrid in the 1950s, *La forja de un rebelde* was one of the illegal books that passed from hand to hand. It also circulated in university circles. Mario Camus, later director of the TVE films of *La forja de un rebelde*, explained: "In the university, around 1953/54, I was lent a copy of *The Forging of a Rebel*. For my generation, it was an important book, it was the first on the Civil War" (Talk at Badajoz, Conference to commemorate 50 years since Barea's death, 15 November 2007).

17 Eugenio de Nora wrote: "Barea's style is made ugly by certain infelicities, which make the translation better" *La novela española contemporanea* (Madrid: Gredos, 1982), Vol. II, pp. 15–16.

18 Articles cited by José Luis Aranguren, Francisco Ynduráin and José Luis Alborg, *inter al.*

19 FG & HR, pp. 55–67.

20 Ynduráin, *op. cit.*

21 For example, Ángel Ruiz Ayúcar (*Arriba*, 21 January 1958).

22 *La forja de un rebelde*, p. 14, quoted in Marra-López, p. 292.

23 Marra-López, p. 292.

24 Ibid., p. 332.

25 Letters to the author from Olive Renier (6 April 1992) and Margaret Weeden (1 November 1992, 14 October 1993 and 12 July 1997).

26 Ilsa Barea, prefacio to *Unamuno* (Buenos Aires: Sur, 1959).

27 José Luis Giménez-Frontín, *La Vanguardia*, 8 May 1986.

28 Rafael Martínez Nadal, "Tres viñetas. Tercera. Ilsa-Arturo Barea", in *El exilio literario español de 1939* (Barcelona: GEXEL 1998), Volume II, pp. 650–1.

29 Ibid.

30 Letter to the author from Margaret Weeden, 14 October 1993.

31 Letter to the author from Margaret Weeden, 12 July 1997.

32 "When he died he was at work on another book" (*The Times*, 28 December 1957).

33 "His Brothers' Keepers". Mario Benedetti, p. 374.

34 The three late stories are: *Bajo la piel*, *La rifa* and *La lección*.

35 Ilsa Barea, *Unamuno* (Buenos Aires), preface.

Ironically, the essay in this series on Barea's beloved Lorca was written by Barea's political opponent and BBC colleague, the South African pro-Franco poet Roy Campbell. Ynduráin (*op. cit.*) saw Campbell's book as a successful rebuttal of Barea's own book on Lorca.

36 Ilsa Barea, introduction to *El centro de la pista*, p. 45.

37 "TVE presents *La forja de un rebelde*, the most ambitious production in its history. This nine-hour series has cost over 2,000 million pesetas to make." (*El País*, 30 March 1990).

Barea's niece, Leonor, considered that the TVE production showed Arturo as too much the passive observer. It neither caught the happy side she remembered, nor showed him as a participant in events (Interview with LRB, 23 June 1990).

38 Giménez-Frontín.

39 In addition, the Badajoz City Council has named a street "Calle Arturo Barea".

Appendix 2 Chronological Table of Barea's Books and Articles

Notes to Appendix 2 are presented on page 175.

Appendix 3 Ilse Pollak/Ilsa Barea (1902–1972)

1 Margaret Weeden, "Ilsa Barea. Some notes on her life." (Unpublished: October, 1992). Ilse had a brother Willy, two or three years younger than her, and a sister Lotte five years younger. Both married Danes. Willy later emigrated to Australia. Lotte was with Ilsa during the last days of her life.
2 Letter from the Duque de Primo de Rivera, Spanish Ambassador in London, 6 June 1956 (4850-3, Archive of the Ministry of Foreign Affairs, Madrid).
3 Ilsa Barea, *Vienna* (London: Pimlico, 1992), p. 86.
4 Margaret Weeden, "Ilsa Barea, Some Notes . . . "
5 "In memoriam," a broadcast by Barea on October 10, 1948, is a moving tribute to Ilsa's mother (PR, pp. 243–6). Barea's letters from Puckeridge in August and September 1939 describe the background to Ilsa's parents' arrival in England (PR, pp. 679–700).
6 FR, p. 603. Letter to the author from Margaret Weeden, September 7, 1992.
7 Patrick Seale & Maureen McConville, *Philby, the Long Road to Moscow* (London: Penguin, 1978), p. 83.
Margaret Weeden believed Ilsa said that the imprisonment in Hungary was for three months in 1920 (not four months in 1925) and that she shared a cell with a murderess who taught her tatting ("Ilsa Barea . . . ", *op. cit.*).
8 Seale & McConville, p. 85; and interview with Lord Weidenfeld, 24 September 1990.
9 FR, pp. 714–17.
10 Seale & McConville, p. 86; Letter to the author from Stephen Spender, 24 January 1990.
11 Ilsa Barea, *Vienna*, p. 89.
12 FR, pp. 696–7.
13 Letter to the author from Isabel de Madariaga, 8 March 1992: "She [Ilsa] was the very typical Middle European party-member, proud of her friends among senior Russian generals in the Civil War." (Professor de Madariaga added that she did not like Ilsa or Arturo).
Also: interview with Gladys Langham, Margaret Carter and Bill Carter, 14 November 1989.
14 Letter to the author from Olive Renier, 6 August 1992.
15 FR, p. 604.
16 Ibid., p. 602.
17 Ibid., p. 605.
18 Francisco Ayala, *Recuerdos y Olvidos* (Madrid: Alianza Tres, 1988).
19 She was known as "Ilsa de la Telefónica" to distinguish her from another Ilsa.

The journalists sending out their dispatches had to bring them first to her in Room 402. Sefton Delmer, Ernest Hemingway (see his biography by Carlos Baker, p. 374), Martha Gellhorn and Arturo Barea all mention her dynamism, capacity for work and influence.

20 Telephone interview with Martha Gellhorn, 16 August 1990.

21 Interview with Peter Heller, 6 July 1992.

22 Interview with Olive Renier, 6 July 1992.

23 Sefton Delmer, *Trail Sinister* (London: Secker and Warburg, 1961).

24 Martha Gellhorn, 16 August 1990.

25 Ibid.

26 Ibid.

27 Ilsa's cadre profile in the Comintern Archives reads:
"KULCAR Ilse.
Husband of Kulcar Leopold. Was expelled from KPO because of links to Trotskyists. Member of the SPOE in Spain and worked in the Press Censorship in Madrid. She was an open Trotskyist with links to Gestapo agents and spy-elements, including contact to German Schwarzen Front via Grunow alias Bar. Spent some time in the USSR, was expelled from there. Carried out spying activities in Spain." Gustav, 23/3/40. (RTsKLIDNI, 545/6/73:69). I am indebted to Dr. Barry McLoughlin for supplying me with this material, translated from the German.
Nearly every fact in this profile is nonsense, but the note demonstrates chillingly the extreme danger of being arrested in Spain as a Trotskyist. Her husband Leopold was referred to in similar terms, even though he was clearly a witch-hunter of "Trotskyists". See Chapter II, Note 5.
Compare too with Note 28, following, to demonstrate the nightmarish atmosphere of not being able to trust anyone.

28 Ilsa's contacts with Kulcsar in Barcelona led to the most serious allegations by Katia Landau, also an Austrian and wife of the murdered pro-POUMist, Kurt Landau (Katia Landau, "Stalinism in Spain", *Revolutionary History*, Volume 1, No. 2, London, Summer 1988). In December 1938, Katia was under illegal arrest in a Communist "*xeca*" (secret prison) during the witch-hunt of POUM members and their foreign sympathisers. She was interrogated by Leopold Kulcsar, whom she paints as a ruthless psychopath. She wrote: "We saw her [Ilsa] twice in the Paseo San Juan [*xeca*], assisting in the interrogations."

Víctor Alba picked up the story and claimed in his autobiography, *Sisyphe i el seu temps* (Barcelona: Laertes, 1999), p. 243: "Katia [Landau] said that the boss of the woman's *xeca* . . . was a certain Ilse Kolosar (*sic*), married to an Austrian, Leopold, who gave the orders." As Ilsa spent only five weeks in Barcelona, she could not have been boss of a secret women's prison there. The basis for Katia's story may have been Ilsa's visit to Poldi when he was interrogating an Austrian woman who recognised Ilsa (FR, p. 718).

Katia Landau also accuses Ilsa of being involved in the murders of Kurt Landau and Marc Rhein. It is possible that Ilsa was operating as a Stalinist agent in Spain, but it seems very unlikely, given all the other evidence on her activities, including being victim of a slander campaign spread by Stalinists. I tend to think Katia Landau was right about Leopold Kulcsar and jumped to conclusions about Ilse.

Katia gives yet another (a third) date for when Ilsa left the Austrian CP. She says that both Ilsa and Kulcsar were expelled in 1927 "under suspicion of being police informers".

29 FR, p. 726.
30 Ibid., p. 733.
31 Renier and Rubinstein, *Assigned to Listen* (London: BBC, 1987), p. 20.
32 Letter from Ilsa Barea, 16 May 1951 (WAC); Margaret Weeden, "Ilsa Barea . . . ".
33 Margaret Weeden, "Ilsa Barea . . . ".
34 There are several letters from Ilsa in the seven Arturo Barea files at the BBC's Written Archives Centre, as well as in the one file under her own name.
35 Letter from Ilsa Barea, 25 July 1939 (WAC).
36 Ilsa often dictated these translations to Margaret Weeden when they got home after a 4 to midnight shift at the Monitoring Service (Margaret Weeden, "Ilsa Barea . . . "; Letter to the author, 12 July 1997).
37 Interview with Olive Renier, 6 July 1992.

Rafael Martínez Nadal called Ilsa, Olive Renier and Margaret Weeden "The Holy Trinity", because of the closeness of their collaboration on Arturo Barea's work (Letter to the author from Martínez Nadal, 14 June 1993). For discussion of Martínez Nadal's wrong view of the trilogy's composition and dismissive approach to Arturo Barea, see Appendix 1.

38 AB, *The Forge* (London: Faber, 1941), p. 18.
39 For example, "Caramba" (FR, p. 390). Margaret Weeden wrote: "Chalmers-Mitchell was a sweetie, but he could not cope with the street-children's Spanish, which was why Ilse had to do her own translation." (Letter to the author, 12 July 1997).
40 FR, p. 93.
41 *The Forge* (London: Faber, 1941), p. 131.
42 *La forja de un rebelde*, p. 407.
43 FR, p. 358.
44 Ibid., pp. 288–9.
45 *La forja de un rebelde*, p. 318.
46 *Unamuno* (Buenos Aires: Sur, 1959), p. 8.
47 Ilsa Barea, preface, *El centro de la pista* (Badajoz: Diputación, 1988), pp. 43–4.
48 Ilsa Barea file at the WAC, BBC; PEN Club correspondence (University of Tulsa).
49 Letter from Ilsa Barea, 11 February 1954 (WAC).
50 Letter from Ilsa Barea, 2 June 1951 (WAC).
51 Letter from AB to Emir Rodríguez Monegal, 7 November 1955 (Monegal collection, Princeton).
52 Letter from Ilsa Barea to P.H. Newby, 26 June 1951 (WAC).

53 Interview with Lord Weidenfeld, 24 September 1990.
54 Letters from Ilsa Barea to Anna Kallin, 11 February and 14 February 1955 (WAC); Letter from AB to Rodríguez Monegal, 7 November 1955.
55 Letter to Anna Kallin, 11 February 1955 (WAC).
56 *Vienna*, p. 14.
57 Ibid., p. 252.
58 Ibid., p. 287.
59 Ibid., p. 258.
60 Ibid., p. 189.
61 Ibid., p. 109.
62 Ibid., p. 201.
63 Ibid., p. 334.
64 Ibid., p. 44 ff.
65 Ibid., p. 52.
66 Ibid., p. 189.
67 Interview with Lord Weidenfeld, 24 September 1990.
68 Letter from Ilsa Barea, 15 May 1951 (WAC).
69 Martha Gellhorn, 16 August 1990.
70 Lord Weidenfeld, 24 September 1990. Weidenfeld's insight is confirmed by the publication (in *Palabras recobradas*) of nine letters written by Arturo to Ilsa in August and September 1939. Ilsa's almost daily letters from Evesham to Arturo at the same time do not survive, but there is no way Arturo could have written such emotionally and sexually intimate letters if his feelings had not been reciprocated.
71 Letter to the author from Joan Gili, 6 March 1990.
72 Letter to the author from Roland Gant, 7 March 1990.
73 Interview with Margaret Carter, 14 November 1989.
74 Martha Gellhorn, 16 August 1990.
75 Lord Weidenfeld, 24 September 1990.
76 Vladimir Rubinstein, 6 July 1992.
77 FR, pp. 610 & 605.
78 Letter to the author from Bill Carter, February 1990.
79 Letter from Ilsa Barea to Emir Rodríguez Monegal, 9 January 1958 (Monegal Collection, Princeton).
80 Letter from Ilsa Barea to Olive Renier, 18 August 1971.
81 The title page of the Pimlico (1992) edition of *Vienna* comments that she died while working on her autobiography.

Glossary of Spanish Words

barrio	neighbourhood
una beata	exceptionally devout woman
buhardilla	garret
cacique	rural boss
calle	street
cédula	identity card
charla	talk
chupatintas	pen-pusher
Comité obrero	Workers' committee
costumbrista	recording former customs and habits
un duro	a five-peseta piece
escuela pía	school run by the Escolapian order
estampa	sketch
estraperlista	dealer in contraband
Junta de Defensa	Defence Council
kabila	Moroccan village
machista	male chauvinist
madrileño	inhabitant of Madrid
marica	sissy/pansy
miliciano	militia-man
la patria	fatherland
pueblo	village
señorito	young gentleman/ toff
Telefónica	Telephone Company building
Tercio	The Foreign Legion
tertulias	café discussion groups
¡Viva la muerte!	Long live Death!
vivencia	lived experience
Voz incógnita de Madrid	Unknown voice of Madrid
xeca (Catalan)	Secret prison run by PSUC &/or Comintern agents.

Bibliography

The Bibliography is divided into five sections. Where quotations are given in the text from books or articles listed here in Spanish, the translation is by the author.

1 Biographical articles about Arturo Barea.
2 Critical articles about Arturo Barea.
3 Books containing in-depth studies of Arturo Barea.
4 General background books and articles.
5 Works of fiction.

1 Biographical articles about Barea

Barea, Ilsa, Introduction to: *Unamuno* (Buenos Aires: Editorial Sur, 1959).

Chalmers-Mitchell, Sir Peter, Introduction to: *The Forge* (London: Faber & Faber, 1941).

Eaude, Michael, "Arturo Barea, Exile without resentment," *London Magazine*, London, April/May 1994.

——, "An exile without resentment," *Lookout*, September 1997, Málaga, pp. 62–4.

Fernández, Uría, "Un hombre sencillo," *El Periódico Extremadura*, Mérida, 7 July 2000. Based on interview with Leonor Rodríguez Barea.

Gant, Roland, "Vida y obra de Arturo Barea," *El Mundo*, Madrid, 19 March 2001. Transcript of a radio broadcast of 1959.

Grant, Helen, Introduction to: *The Forging of a Rebel* (London: Davis-Poynter, 1972).

Martínez Nadal, Rafael, "Tres viñetas," in: *El exilio literario español de 1939*, Volume II (Barcelona: GEXEL, 1998).

Monferrer, Luis, "La colaboración de Arturo Barea, 'Juan de Castilla', en la BBC," in: *El exilio literario español de 1939*, Volume 1 (Barcelona: GEXEL, 1998).

Opoczenski, Ginger, "Americans' Activity astonishes Spaniard," *The Daily Collegian*, Pennsylvania State College, 28 February 1952.

Renier, Olive, *Before the Bonfire* (London: Drinkwater, 1984), pp. 100–1.

Townson, Nigel, Introduction to: *Palabras recobradas* (Madrid: Debate, 2000).

——, Introduction to: *La forja de un rebelde* (Madrid: Debate, 2000).

Weeden, Margaret, "Arturo Barea: the Spaniard who came to England," script for *Australian Broadcasting Commission*, Canberra, 27 April 1958.

——, "Arturo Barea: an appreciation," *Meanjin Review*, Vol. XV111, April 1959.

——, "The Arturo Barea story: the forging of a rebel," *En Australia y en Nueva Zelanda*, Vol. 1V, No. 9 (Canberra: Spanish Embassy, October 1991).

——, "Ilsa Barea. Some notes on her life." (Unpublished, October 1992).

2 Critical articles about Barea

Altisent, Marta E, "Autobiografía, testimonio y propaganda en la ficción de Arturo Barea," in: *Las literaturas del exilio literario español de 1939*, Volume 2 (Barcelona: GEXEL, 2000).

Anon., "In permanent opposition," review of *Unamuno*, *TLS*, London, 5 December 1952.

——, "Arturo Barea," obituary in *The Manchester Guardian*, 28 December 1957.

Bates, Ralph, "Arturo Barea," *The Nation*, New York, 19 July 1947.

Benedetti, Mario, "El testimonio de Arturo Barea," *Número*, III, Montevideo 1951, pp. 374–81.

Black, John, review of "*The Forging of a Rebel*" in *The Guardian*, 5 January 1973.

Brenan, Gerald, "An honest man," *New York Review of Books*, New York, March 1975, pp. 3–4. Review of *The Forging of a Rebel.*

Carr, Raymond, "Escaping a vanished past," *Times Literary Supplement*, 18 January 2002. Article plagued with inaccuracies.

Castellet, José María, "En la muerte de Arturo Barea, novelista español," *Papeles de Son Armadans* (Madrid, 1958), Vol. VIII, No. XXII, pp. 101–6.

Conte, Rafael, "Arturo Barea: al otro lado del espejo," *ABC*, Madrid, 13 May 2000.

Devlin, John, "Arturo Barea and José María Gironella – Two interpreters of the Spanish labyrinth," *Hispania*, XLI (1958), pp. 143–8.

Domingo, José, "La obra autobiográfica de Arturo Barea" in: *De la postguerra a nuestros dias* (Barcelona: Nueva Colección Labor, 1973).

Eaude, Michael, "El exilio fecundo," *El Mundo*, Madrid, 6 November 1993.

——, "Una mirada impasible," *Quimera*, September 1997, Barcelona, pp. 58–62.

——, "Triunfo en la medianoche del siglo: Arturo Barea," in: *Las literaturas del exilio literario español de 1939*, Volume 2 (Barcelona: GEXEL, 2000).

——, "Triunfo en la medianoche del siglo," review of *Palabras recobradas*, *Lateral*, February 2001.

Fernández, Uría, "Los otros escritos de Barea," *El Periódico Extremadura*, Mérida, 12 May 2000.

Gallop, Rodney, "Varied lives," review of *The Forge*, *TLS*, London, 12 July 1941.

——, review of *Struggle for the Spanish Soul*, *TLS*, London, 9 August 1941.

——, "Divided House," review of *The track*, *TLS*, London, 14 August 1943.

——, "Poet of the Spanish People," review of *Lorca*, *TLS*, London, 8 April 1944.

——, "Civil War," review of *The Clash*, *TLS*, London, 23 March 1946.

Gant, Roland, review of *The Forging of a Rebel*, *The Daily Telegraph*, 25 January 1973.

García-Posada, Miguel, "Barea: Notario Poético de la Verdad," *El País*, Madrid, 20 May 2000.

Gili, Joan, "The eye of realism," obituary of Arturo Barea in *The Times*, London, 28 December 1957.

Giménez-Frontín, José Luis, "Arturo Barea, una asignatura pendiente," *La Vanguardia*, Barcelona, 8 May 1986.

Herrera Rodrigo, María, Introduction to: *El centro de la pista* (Badajoz: Diputación, 1988).

——, "El joven rebelde que quiso ser payaso: Arturo Barea en *El centro de la pista*," *Quimera*, January 2005.

Howe, Irving, "The forging of a rebel," *Partisan Review*, Summer 1947.

Jackson, Gabriel, "Homenaje a Arturo Barea," *El País*, 19 April 2001.

Mañá, Gemma et al., "*Valor y miedo*, de Arturo Barea," in: *La voz de los náufragos,* pp. 243–50 (Madrid: Ediciones de la Torre, 1997).

Ortega, José, "Arturo Barea, novelista español en busca de su identidad," *Symposium*, Syracuse, Winter 1971, pp. 377–91.

Orwell, George, "The Forge," review in *Time and Tide* (London, July 1941).

——, "The Forge," review in *Horizon* (London, September 1941), pp. 214–17.

——, "Voice of Madrid," review of *The Clash* in *The Observer*, 24 March 1946.

Pecellín, Manuel, "Arturo Barea Ogazón," in *Literatura en Extremadura II* (Salamanca: Universitas, 1981).

Pont, Jaume, Introduction to *Valor y Miedo* (Barcelona: Plaza y Janés, 1986).

Powell, Anthony, "Broken root," *TLS*, London, 11 May 1951.

Rodríguez, Emma, "Arturo Barea, la recuperación de un rebelde," *El Mundo*, Madrid, 10 May 2000.

Rodríguez Monegal, Emir, "The forging of a rebel," *TLS*, London, 2 May 1952. Review of first Spanish-language edition.

——, "Arturo Barea, una voz," 29 December 1957. Eulogy broadcast the week after Barea's death at Juan de Castilla's normal time.

Rodríguez Richart, J., "*Valor y miedo* y *La forja de un rebelde*, de Arturo Barea," *Anthropos*, No. 148 (Barcelona, September 1993), pp. 72–6.

Ruiz Ayúcar, Angel, "Arturo Barea, o la forja de un hombre," *Arriba*, Madrid, 18 August 1957.

——, untitled, *Arriba*, Madrid, 21 January 1958.

Sanz Villanueva, Santos, "Ocasión para un rescate," *El Mundo*, Madrid, 10 May 2000.

Sender, Ramón J., "The Spanish Autobiography of Arturo Barea," *New Leader* (USA), 11 January 1947, p. 12.

——, Review of *The Broken Root*, *New York Times Book Review*, 11 March 1951, p. 4.

Suñén, Luis, "Arturo Barea," *Camp de l'Arpa*, Barcelona, March 1979.

Thomas, Hugh, "Spain Before the Falange," *The Nation*, 3 May 1975, pp. 535–6. Review of *The Forging of a Rebel.*

de Torre, G., "Arturo Barea, La forja de un rebelde," *Sur*, 205 (Buenos Aires, 1951), pp. 60–5.

Trapiello, Andrés, "Crónica de un hombre modesto," *El País*, 13 September 1997. In an unfortunate article, Trapiello tells us Barea was a telephone company employee, and that his second wife was "an Englishwoman called Olga".

——, "Un relatar modesto," *El País*, 12 May 2001.

Valls, María Antonia, "El rostro de Arturo Barea," *Telepaís*, No. 79, Madrid, 13 April 1990.

de Villena, Luis Antonio, Prólogo a *La forja* (Madrid: Bibliotex, 2001).

Woodhouse, Christopher, "Spanish facts," review of *The Forging of a Rebel*, *TLS*, 30 March 1973.
Ynduráin, Francisco, "Resentimiento español. Arturo Barea," *Arbor*, XXIV, Madrid, January 1953, No. 85.

3 Books containing in-depth studies of Arturo Barea

Alborg, Juan Luis, *Hora actual de la novela española* (Madrid: Taurus, 1968), tomo II.
Conte, Rafael, *Narraciones de la España desterrada* (Barcelona: Edhasa, 1970).
Devlin, John, *Spanish Anticlericalism* (New York: Las Américas, 1966).
Eaude, Michael, *Triunfo en la Medianoche del Siglo* (Mérida: Editora Regional de Extremadura, 2001). Earlier Spanish version of this book.
Fernández Gutiérrez, José María and Herrera Rodrigo, María, *La narrativa de la guerra civil: Arturo Barea* (Barcelona: PPU, 1988).
GEXEL (Grup d'Estudis de l'Exili Literari, Departament de Filologia Espanyola, Universitat Autònoma de Barcelona), *El Exilio Literario Español de 1939*, 2 volumes (Barcelona: GEXEL, 1998).
Marra-López, José R., *Narrativa española fuera de España (1939–1961)* (Madrid: Guadarrama, 1963).
Miller, John C., *Los testimonios literarios de la guerra español-marroquí: Arturo Barea, José Díaz Fernández, Ernesto Giménez Caballero, Ramón Sender* (unpublished thesis: Ann Arbor, 1978).
Monferrer, Luis, *La producción intelectual de los exiliados españoles en Gran Bretaña (1936–1975)* (unpublished thesis: Universidad Central de Barcelona, 1991).
de Nora, Eugenio, *La novela española contemporánea* (Madrid: Gredos, 1970), volumes II and III.
Rodríguez Monegal, Emir, *Tres testigos españoles de la guerra civil* (Caracas: Editorial Arte, 1971).
Stradling, Robert, *Your Children Will be Next. Bombing and Propaganda in the Spanish Civil War 1936–1939* (Cardiff: University of Wales Press, 2008). Accuses Barea of manipulating propaganda in favour of the Communist Party, in particular of lying about Madrid being bombed.
Torres Nebrera, Gregorio, *Las anudadas raíces de Arturo Barea* (Badajoz: Diputación, 2002).

4 General background books and articles

There are, of course, a phenomenal number of books about the period during which Barea lived, especially the Civil War. I have restricted this list to: (a) books/articles with at least one reference to Barea, (b) key background books, such as the ones by Fraser or Abella, and (c) books which I have directly referred to in the text, e.g. Ackroyd or Crick.

Abella, Rafael, *La vida cotidiana durante la guerra civil* (Barcelona: Planeta, 1975).

Abellán, José Luis, "El éxodo republicano," *Historia 16*, Año II (Madrid, November 1977), No. 19.

Ackroyd, Peter, *Dickens* (London: Sinclair-Stevenson, 1990).

Alba, Víctor, *Sisyphe i el seu temps* (Barcelona: Laertes, 1999). Contains a calumny against Ilsa Barea on p. 243.

Aranguren, José Luis, "La evolución espiritual de los intelectuales españoles en la emigración," *Cuadernos Hispanoamericanos* (febrero 1953), No. 38.

Ayala, Francisco, *La estructura narrativa* (Barcelona: Crítica, 1984). Discusses problems of exiled writers after 1939.

——, *Memorias y recuerdos* (Madrid: Alianza Tres, 1988). Contains a portrait of Leopold Kulcsar.

Aznar Soler, Manuel, "El Partido Comunista de España y la literatura del exilio republicano (1939–1953)" in: *El Exilio Literario Español de 1939,* Volume 2 (Barcelona: Gexel, 1998).

Baker, Carlos, *Ernest Hemingway* (London: Collins, 1969). Comments on Ilsa and Barea as censors.

Barea, Ilsa, *Vienna, legend and reality* (London: Pimlico, 1992). Originally 1966.

Bell, Adrian, *Only for Three Months* (Norwich: Mousehold Press, 1996).

Bertrand de Muñoz, Maryse, "La figura del personaje 'republicano' en la novela de los exiliados", in: *El exilio literario español de 1939*, Volume II (Barcelona: Gexel, 1998).

Bolloten, Burnett, *La Guerra Civil española* (Madrid: Alianza, 1989).

Brenan, Gerald, *The Spanish Labyrinth* (Cambridge: Cambridge University Press, 1943).

——, *The Literature of the Spanish people* (Cambridge: Cambridge University Press, 1951).

Broué, Pierre and Témime, Emile, *The Revolution and the Civil War in Spain* (London: Faber & Faber, 1972).

Caro Baroja, Julio, in: Baroja, Pío, *La busca* (Madrid: Salvat, 1969), prólogo, pp. 7–13.

Carr, E. H., *The Comintern and the Spanish Civil War* (London: Macmillan, 1984).

Carr, Raymond, *España 1808–1975* (Barcelona: Ariel, 1982).

——, *The Spanish Tragedy* (London: Weidenfeld, 1993).

Claudín, Fernando, *From Comintern to Cominform* (Oxford: Oxford University Press, 1975).

Crick, Bernard, *George Orwell: a Life* (London: Penguin, 1982). Pages 52 & 402 mention Barea.

Delmer, Sefton, *Trail Sinister* (London: Secker & Warburg, 1961). Includes description of Barea as censor.

Dos Passos, John, *Journeys between Wars* (London: Constable, 1938). Description of Ilsa and Arturo, p. 367.

Ehrenburg, Ilya, *Eve of War 1933–1941* (London: Macgibbon & Kee, 1963).

Esteban J. and Santorja G., *Los novelistas sociales españoles (1928–1936)* (Barcelona: Anthropos, 1988).

Fox, Soledad, *Constancia de la Mora in War and Exile* (Brighton & Portland: Sussex Academic Press, 2007).

Franklin, Sidney, *Bullfighter from Brooklyn* (London: Hutchinson, 1952). Comments on censors in war-time Madrid, p. 220.

Fraser, Ronald, *The Blood of Spain* (London: Allen Lane, 1979).

García Márquez, Gabriel, *Notas de prensa 1980–1984* (Madrid: Mondadori, 1991).

Garosci, Aldo, *Los intelectuales y la Guerra de España* (Madrid: Júcar, 1981).

Gathorne-Hardy, Jonathan, *The Interior Castle, a Life of Gerald Brenan* (London: Sinclair-Stevenson, 1992). Comments on Barea's and Brenan's visits to each other in 1943.

Gellhorn, Martha, *The Face of War* (London: Hart-Davis, 1959). Contains her introduction of aims, very similar to Barea's.

González, Valentín and Gorkín, Julián, *Life and death in Soviet Russia* (London: Heinemann, 1952). Translated into English by Ilsa Barea.

Graham, Helen, *Socialism and War* (Cambridge: Cambridge University Press, 1991). Background on the PSOE, Barea's party.

Hemingway, Ernest, *By-line* (London: Penguin, 1969). Contains some of Hemingway's dispatches from Madrid.

Knightley, Phillip, *The First Casualty* (London: Pan, 1989).

Landau, Katia, "Stalinism in Spain," *Revolutionary History*, Vol. 1, No. 2, Summer 1988. Accuses Ilsa of being a Stalinist agent.

Lee, Laurie, *A Moment of War* (London: Penguin, 1992). Chapter 7 contains an account of a radio broadcast from Madrid.

Lukács, Georg, *Studies in European Realism* (London: Merlin Press, 1972).

de Madariaga, Salvador, *Spain* (London: Jonathan Cape, 1942).

Mañá, Gemma et al., *La voz de los náufragos (La narrativa republicana entre 1936 y 1939)* (Madrid: Ediciones de la Torre, 1997).

Mansell, Gerard, *Let Truth be Told* (London: Weidenfeld & Nicholson, 1982). Describes conflicts over broadcasts to Spain during WW2.

Martínez Nadal, Rafael, *Antonio Torres y la política española del "Foreign Office"* (Madrid: Casariego, 1989).

McInerney, Jay, "Fitzgerald revisited," *New York Review of Books*, 15 August 1991, pp. 23–8. Explains the "double vision" of the writer.

Meyers, Jeffrey, *Hemingway* (London: Paladin, 1987). Contains a rebuttal of Barea's critique of *For whom the Bell Tolls*.

Orwell, George, *The Lion and the Unicorn* (London: Penguin, 1986). Bernard Crick's introduction explains the *Searchlight* publishing project.

Payne, Stanley, *Falange* (Madrid: Sarpe, 1985).

ed. Preston, Paul, *Revolution and War in Spain* (London: Methuen, 1984).

Preston, Paul, *Las tres Españas del 36* (Barcelona: Plaza y Janés, 1999). The chapter on Millán Astray uses Barea's writing as source material.

——, *We saw Spain Die: Foreign Correspondents in the Spanish Civil War* (London: Constable Robinson, 2008). Includes descriptions of Barea and Ilsa in the *Telefónica*.

Regler, Gustav, *The Owl of Minerva* (London: Rupert Hart-Davis, 1959).
Renier, Olive and Rubinstein, Vladimir, *Assigned to listen* (London: BBC, 1986). Includes references to Arturo and Ilsa Barea at Wood Norton.
Ressot, Jean-Pierre, *Historia de la Literatura española, Siglo XX* (Barcelona: Ariel, 1995), Volume VI.
Sanz Villanueva, Santos, *Historia de la novela social española* (Barcelona: Ariel, 1988).
ed. Schneider, Marshall, J. & Stern, Irwin, *Modern Spanish and Portuguese Literatures* (New York: Continuum, 1988).
Seale, Patrick and McConville, Maureen, *Philby, The Long Road to Moscow* (London: Penguin, 1978). Refers to Ilse Pollak's role in the Vienna events of February 1934.
Serrano Poncela, Segundo, "La novela española contemporánea," *La Torre*, 2, Puerto Rico 1953, pp. 105–28.
ed. Socialist Platform, *The Spanish Civil War: the view from the left* (London: Revolutionary History, 1992).
Spiel, Hilde, *Vienna's Golden Autumn* (London: Weidenfeld & Nicholson, 1987).
Thomas, Gareth, *The Novel of the Spanish Civil War* (Cambridge: Cambridge University Press, 1990).
Thomas, Hugh, *The Spanish Civil War* (London: Penguin, 1965).
Trapiello, Andrés, *Las armas y las letras. Literatura y guerra civil (1936–1939)* (Barcelona: Planeta, 1994).
Tuñon de Lara, Manuel, *La España del Siglo XX* (Barcelona: Laia, 1978). Three volumes.
Tuñon de Lara, Paloma, "La novela durante la guerra civil," *Historia 16* (Madrid 1986), No. 17.
Williams, Philip, *Hugh Gaitskell* (Oxford: Oxford University Press, 1982). Mentions Gaitskell's friendship with Ilse Pollak in Vienna.

5 Works of fiction

This list is restricted to works of fiction referred to in the text.

Aub, Max, *Campo cerrado* (Madrid: Alfaguara, 1978).
——, *Campo abierto* (Madrid: Alfaguara, 1978).
Baroja, Pío, *El mundo es ansí* (Madrid: Espasa Calpe, 1973).
——, *La busca* (Madrid: Salvat, 1969).
Cela, Camilo J., *La familia de Pascual Duarte* (Barcelona: Destino, 1969).
——, *La colmena* (Barcelona: Destino, 1986).
——, *The Hive* (London: Gollancz, 1953).
Díaz Fernández, José, *El blocao* (Madrid: Cenit, 1935).
Dickens, Charles, *David Copperfield* (London: Penguin, 1985).
Dos Passos, John, *U.S.A.* (London: Penguin, 1976).
Gironella, José María, *Los cipreses creen en Díos* (Barcelona: Planeta, 1976).
Goytisolo, Juan, *Marks of Identity* (London: Serpent's tail, 1988).
Guïraldes, Ricardo, *Don Segundo Sombra* (London: Penguin, 1959).

Hemingway, Ernest, *For whom the Bell Tolls* (London: Penguin, 1966). Originally published 1940.

——, *The Fifth Column* (London: Penguin, 1968).

Istrati, Panait, *Los cardos de Baragán* (Barcelona: Ediciones 29, *c.*1980).

Jackson, Angela, *Warm Earth* (Cambridge: Pegasus, 2007). Chapter 3 portrays Barea in the censorship.

Laforet, Carmen, *Nada* (London: Harvill, 2007). Originally published in Spanish, 1945.

Malraux, André, *Man's Hope* (London: Penguin, 1969). Translation to English of *L'espoir* (1937).

Miller, Henry, *Big Sur and the Oranges of Hieronymous Bosch* (New York: New Directions, 1957).

Remarque, Erich Maria, *All Quiet on the Western Front* (London: Pan, 1974).

Salazar Chapela, Esteban, *Perico en Londres* (Buenos Aires: Losada, 1947). Mentions Barea.

Sender, Ramón J., *Imán* (Barcelona: Destino, 1983). Originally published 1930.

——, *Crónica del alba* (Barcelona: Destino, 1987). Nine novels in 3 volumes.

——, *Siete domingos rojos* (Barcelona: Destino, 1985).

——, *The Dark Wedding* (London: Grey Walls, 1948). Translation of *Epitalamio del prieto Trinidad.*

——, *Réquiem por un campesino español* (Barcelona: Destino, 1984).

Serge, Victor, *Birth of Our Power* (London: Writers and Readers, 1977).

——, *Conquered City* (London: Victor Gollancz, 1976).

——, *Year One of the Russian Revolution* (London: Writers and Readers, 1978).

de Unamuno, Miguel, *Paz en la guerra* (Madrid: Espasa Calpe, 1968).

Index

Arturo Barea is referred to as AB; Ilsa Barea, as IB